❀ Kaleidoscope

Kaleidoscope

'THE WAY OF WOMAN'
AND OTHER ESSAYS

BY HELEN M. LUKE

EDITED BY ROB BAKER

PARABOLA BOOKS

1992

KALEIDOSCOPE:
"THE WAY OF WOMAN" AND OTHER ESSAYS
BY HELEN M. LUKE

A Parabola Book/June 1992

"The Bridge of Humility" originally appeared in PARABOLA Magazine (XVI:4). "The Perennial Feminine" and "Demeter and Kore" originally appeared in PARABOLA (V:4) and later were included in *Woman: Earth and Spirit — The Feminine in Symbol and Myth* (New York: Crossroad, 1981) and are reprinted here with the permission of Crossroad. "The Sense of Humor" appeared in PARABOLA (XII:4), as did "Pride" (X:4) and "The Stranger Within" (XV:4).

The sections on Eowyn, Orual, and Dindrane were originally published as an Apple Farm pamphlet entitled "The Way of Woman: Ancient and Modern." The material on the novels of Charles Williams is adapted from a longer study in another Apple Farm pamphlet entitled "Through Defeat to Joy." The chapter on Brunhilde is adapted from another pamphlet, as is the chapter entitled "Levels." All other chapters in "The Way of Discrimination" section (except "The Secret and the Open," which has not been previously published) are from *The Voice Within* (New York, Crossroad: 1984), as are the stories "The Hunter and the Hunted" and "Salmon-Fisher Boy." That collection is now out of print, as is *The Inner Story* (New York: Crossroad, 1982), in which "The Inner Story," "The Story of Jacob," "The Story of the Exodus," "The Story of Saul" and "The Little Prince" first appeared.

All these selections have been re-edited for the current volume and are printed by permission of Helen M. Luke, as is the new additional material for this volume. Quotations from the novels of Charles Williams are reprinted by permission of their current U.S. publisher, Wm. B. Eerdmans Publishing Co. Excerpts from C.S. Lewis' *Till We Have Faces*, © 1956 by C.S. Lewis and renewed 1984 by Arthur Owen Barfield, are reprinted by permission of Harcourt Brace Jovanovich, Inc.

Parabola Books is a publishing division of The Society for the Study of Myth and Tradition, a not-for-profit organization devoted to the dissemination and exploration of materials related to myth, symbol, ritual, and art of the great religious traditions. The Society also publishes PARABOLA, *The Magazine of Myth and Tradition.*

ISBN 0-930407-24-5

PARABOLA BOOKS
656 Broadway
New York, NY 10012

Manufactured in the United States of America

Contents

Introduction

A KALEIDOSCOPE CAN fascinate for hours: each turn of the end of the tube causes new arrangements in the tiny shards of colored glass refracted in the mirror-lens, so that relationships between the fragments shift, change, realign themselves, and no two patterns are ever quite the same. Individuation — the attempt by each individual to see and understand his or her unique, inner self more clearly — implies a like process that is at once exploratory, revelatory, never-ending, and distinctly (to use one of Helen M. Luke's favorite terms) numinous.

Images of light and color — and an attempt to find meaning in their symbolic resonance — have always been essential to Helen Luke. In her unpublished autobiography, she recalls the earliest dream of her childhood, in which she was swept along the arc of a rainbow. Late in life the dream recurred, but with a difference:

> I glimpsed a rainbow river of life, in which I was not swept away afraid and unknowing, but which flowed within, flowed without, and which seemed to 'resound' with beauty. I woke with this strange word in my mind — sound and vision in one image.

Helen Luke was born in England in 1904. Two of her great-grandfathers had been missionaries in India, one Anglican, one Scotch Presbyterian. Her father and mother were both born in India, and her father, after education in England, returned to India and became an officer in the Bombay police. Her mother returned to England for her confinement, and Helen was born there. Her father died in India, after a brief illness, when Helen was eight months old.

Luke's early life followed the usual English pattern of boarding school and college (at Oxford University, where she studied Italian and French languages and literature, particularly Dante and Molière). She then married and has two sons. During World War II, she was introduced to the writings of C.G. Jung; she eventually trained as a therapist with one of Jung's students in London and also for a time in Zurich, where she was granted an interview with Jung him-

1

self. In her forties, she divorced and moved to Los Angeles, where she began a therapy practice with a friend she had met in Zurich.

After 12 years, her two sons having grown up and returned to study in England, Luke moved to the Midwest where she hoped, with three close friends, to found a small lay community, in association with the Anglo-Catholic Church, to offer counselling in Jung's way of dream and image. It was a time of great turmoil in the churches during the early '60s, and it became clear that the new venture must be absolutely free from any dependence on institutional structures. Finally, the four friends bought an old farm house in Three Rivers, Michigan, with forty acres mainly of apple orchards, and the Apple Farm Community was officially chartered as a non-profit charitable foundation. It has been generously supported ever since the beginning in 1963 by friends and members who have moved to live in or near Three Rivers and by the guests who come for short visits at intervals for rest and counselling.

In Los Angeles, Luke and her partner had begun to study myths, stories, and the inner world of images in small groups, and this kind of discussion group—which in no way resembled the encounter groups of the same period and later— was continued with her colleagues and with the guests who came to Apple Farm. The sharing of ideas was much like that between the English writer Charles Williams and certain of his friends and associates who constituted a "company," which A.M. Hadfield has described as follows:

> There was no pledge or initiation, no standard asked by others. . . . In all matters the compulsion is interior . . . it is a spirit which will work within everything we do, and will reject nothing of our ordinary life. . . . It is the birth and life of love, of Christ, here and now.

One guest at Apple Farm described it after her first visit as a place where "one meets individuals breathing free air and finding their own way."

After a time, as the numbers grew, the Farm began to print small pamphlets, in which Luke had been requested to write down the substance of the group meetings. She had no thought of publication, but after some years others sought publishers for her work, and her other calling in life came to light—the writing of her responses to great stories and to the values of the spirit and of the heart. So at that point in life when the active and the contemplative, the secret and the open, the various paths towards individuation had come together, Luke was able to share the results of a lifetime of learning, living, and testing the experiences of the inner and outer worlds.

Such a process leads to real *knowing,* based on a proper discrimination: a rigorous but open examination of all aspects of truth. She is not concerned with politics, party lines, or any other type of rigid dogmatism (including hard-line Christianity or hard-line Jungianism: Luke has always been a bit of a iconoclast in these areas as in every other area of her thinking). Such discrimination demands that one risk and dare to be true to the ever-changing dictates of one's own heart, one's real conscience.

So, in a sense, Luke's path has always been the way of woman, the way of discrimination, and the way of story, all at once, with a careful balance of thinking and feeling, of honest objectivity and deeply-examined subjectivity, of the inner and the outer. Her writings are a kaleidoscope of that ever-shifting, extremely individual inner journey.

She also makes a great pot of tea. "The secret," she smiles, with the grace and delight of a true storyteller, "is to make sure the water is really boiling, and always to bring the pot to the kettle, not the kettle to the pot."

***

These essays span Helen M. Luke's full writing career, from 1962 to the present. They have been selected, by myself and D.M. Dooling, the founding editor of Parabola, the summer before Mrs. Dooling's death in October, 1991; they are drawn from various Apple Farm pamphlets, as well as articles written by Luke for Parabola Magazine. Selections are also included from two books, *The Voice Within* and *The Inner Story,* originally published by Crossroad Publishing Company but no longer in print. "The Perennial Feminine" and "Demeter and Kore" appeared together under the former title as an article in Parabola (Vol. V, No. 4) and were subsequently included in *Woman: Earth and Spirit — The Feminine in Symbol and Myth* (New York: Crossroad, 1981). Two other books by Luke are also available from Parabola Books: *Old Age: Journey into Simplicity* (1987) and her study of Dante's *Divine Comedy,* entitled *Dark Wood to White Rose* (1989), first published by Dove Publications of Pecos, New Mexico.

The collection ends with two short pieces focusing on Christmas, the holiday that for many symbolizes a time of renewal: both an end and a beginning. "Christmas 1962" was Helen Luke's first published article, written for "Benedicite," the newsletter of St. Gregory's, an Episcopal Benedictine priory in Three Rivers, Michigan. The second is the most recent of her Christmas talks, which are given annually to the friends and associates who gather during the holiday season at Apple Farm. The two Christmas musings bring into focus much of what Luke's writings is about: hard questions of who we are and might be, even (or perhaps especially) at a moment of celebration: the necessity of acknowledging our darkness as well as our light, and of never forgetting either side of our nature, be it spider or fly.

Various mythological and Jungian terms have been defined on their first appearance in this collection, but for easier reference they have also been included in a glossary at the back of this collection.

—*Rob Baker*

Acknowledgements

I FIRST WISH to express, however inadequately, my deep gratitude to Rob Baker, co-editor of PARABOLA, who has overseen this book with so much skill and devotion. I cannot thank him enough for his response to my writings, for his understanding and patient courtesy, and for his creation of its form. To the late Dorothea Dooling I owe a profound debt for her contribution of warm encouragement in the last months of her life, which she expressed in her final letter to me, and that encouragement has been continued by her daughter, Ellen Dooling Draper, co-editor of the magazine; to her I owe a special "thank you" for her suggestion of the title of this book. I want to add here a word of thanks to all the men and women of PARABOLA who have encouraged me through the years, particularly Joseph Kulin, PARABOLA's Executive Publisher, for his splendid work. And finally I would like to add my abiding thanks to the former editor, Lorraine Kisley, who first introduced me to that wonderful magazine and remains a true friend.

As for the essays themselves, they would not have been written at all if they had not been inspired by the responses, support, and love given by my friends and colleagues, by both the workers and the guests of Apple Farm Community, of which Rob Baker has written in his Introduction. The names are beyond counting, including, as they do, not only those who live nearby, but many from all over the country and also from England, Scotland, Ireland, Canada, and Australia. These come when they can to visit and to contribute to our small groups; often in talks with me, they have shared so much of themselves. I cannot possibly name them all and must hope that each one will realize his or her unique gift to me and my deeply felt thanks.

—*Helen M. Luke*
March, 1992

The Bridge of Humility

WHAT IS THAT forever elusive yet longed for thing, humility? It is the one quality that, if one could ever think of oneself as possessing it, would in that instant be lost. Perhaps the very longing for it — for the safety of it — is proof that it is not there. What greater pride could there be than the ego's boast, "I have found humility!"

The word comes from *humus*, the soil. It is the quality of the soil, the passive earth, the "dirt" in American parlance, from which all things grow. The feminine soil — if only one could be just that — passive, quiet, receiving the seed, waiting for the sun to shine, for the rain to fall from Heaven — quite without responsibility for anything. What a rest that would be from all foolish striving. Would one not simply be humble then, identified with the *humus*, the soil of life? But humility, alas! is not *humus* — it is not a quality of nature but of man.

Even the simplest woman cannot remain simply "herself," pure female, if she is not to lose that most vital of all her qualities — her humanity. She cannot abdicate from the responsibility of consciousness, however rudimentary, and it is a responsibility which demands that she, no less than man, her brother, must never "cease from exploration" (T.S. Eliot, "Little Gidding") until she finds within her own being the sower of the seed, the creator of the light, as well as the passive earth; and all the time both man and woman are inevitably held in never-ending tension between hubris ("I am the sun") and inertia ("I am the helpless victim") which can so easily be disguised behind the self-satisfied masks of good works or of resignation.

Only humility can release us from this tension. Could it be defined as the final realization that all creation is feminine to God in the "heavens" of the Spirit? The sun as well as the soil? As long as one yearns to be only the one or only the other, there is no creation, no marriage of human and divine, no child and no humility.

For instance, as I lay still and relaxed, and suddenly these thoughts and images began dropping into my mind, I felt a spurious peace. I was *humus*, the soil. But the real peace lies beyond thought and image, and it can only come—as I have learned over many years— after I have fought the inertia of my feminine passivity—after I have obeyed the demand from the core of my being and made the often agonizing effort to put into words the emerging thoughts. Why? Says my spurious humility—why do you have to do this? You'll probably only wreck their spontaneity with your clumsy expression and you only do it so as to get approval. And anyway, there is nothing important about preserving them.

For another the imperative may be to paint or build or to form the passive image in any one of a thousand ways. For me and for many women, it is the discipline of the word. The point is that one must make incarnate in some form or other both the active sun and the passive earth of being. And one day instead of leaping from one to the other, the two together will become "feminine to God," in humility.

As I lay writing these things, the facile dozing of old age took over for brief minutes and, as ever, I was aware of seemingly incoherent images of all sorts just over the edge of consciousness, and I felt again the fear of fragmentation. And then came the image of that most fascinating of toys—the kaleidoscope, and I saw all those tiny bits of colored glass jumbled together meaninglessly until I looked through the glass at the end of the tube and saw them in beautiful mandala patterns through the process of "reflection." "Reflection"—a bending again—a looking anew from a different angle. The word kaleidoscope is made up of *kalos*, beautiful; and *eidos*, form; and *scope*, outlook or view. Our view for most of the time of all the little colored chips of life is meaningless, has no form, but if we could only "reflect" thus, re-bend them, then we should see the beautiful form in them with the eye of the Godhead in whom they are whole, and we should recognize at once the great mandala pattern in which the ego's hubris and inertia disappear.

Meanwhile, the reflecting, the re-bending in search of the beautiful form must be worked at consciously little by little, again and again, without pride in achievement, without despair in failure. Indeed, then, out of our sight the seed may sprout, the flower may be drawn upwards to the light of the sun, and the roots may reach down into the soil to the waters under the earth; and then at last water, sun, soil, seed and flower and the fruit of human consciousness itself—all become the *humus* of God; and so humility can be born.

In his novel *The Place of the Lion* (Grand Rapids, Michigan: William B. Eerdmans Publishing Co., 1965), Charles Williams wrote:

> No mind was so good that it did not need another mind to counter and equal it, and to save it from conceit and blindness and bigotry and folly. Only in such a balance could humility be found, humility which was a lucid speed to welcome lucidity whenever and wherever it presented itself. How much he owed to Quentin! How much—not pride but delight urged the admission—Quentin owed to him! Balance—and movement in balance, as an eagle sails up on the wind—this was the truth of life, and beauty in life.

The Way
of
Woman

C h a p t e r   O n e

The Perennial Feminine

THE WOMEN'S MOVEMENTS of this century have brought many splendid changes and have given to the lives of millions of women a freedom rarely dreamed of 100 years ago. But, as always, such rapid changes bring with them great dangers which can become the roots of evils which remain unrecognized and are therefore projected onto convenient "enemies" such as man. It is therefore vital, if the new freedoms are to become real in our lives, that individual women recognize the necessity of connecting the theories expounded and the emotions aroused in her with the symbolic life of her feminine psyche. Without this inner work, however things may appear on the surface, the new freedoms may turn to dark and destructive conflicts in her soul.

Where, however, is a woman to look for nourishment for her inner imagery as her new personality struggles for birth? The changes in the way of Eve have come with staggering swiftness, but it seems to me that only recently has the realization broken through that a deeper awareness of the nature of these changes is now essential. If we are to stop the wreckage caused by the disorientation of women, by their loss of identity under the stresses of the new way, then the numinous meaning of the great challenge they face must break through from the unconscious; for no amount of rational analysis can bring healing. Only so can the images of the masculine and feminine, which have become more and more dangerously mixed in our society, be discriminated once more, so that they may come to a new synthesis in both woman and man.

It is important that we attempt to arrive at some degree of clarity about various attitudes and assumptions which are currently prevalent when people talk about woman. Those who assert that the only difference between men and women is biological, and that in every other way they are equal and have the same inborn potentialities, have disastrously missed the point. Equality of value between indi-

13

viduals is an eternal truth, beyond all comparisons, whereas "superior" and "inferior" are relative terms defining abilities or degrees of
consciousness. Equality of opportunity for women has indeed to be
fought for, but equality of value can never be understood until we
have learned to discriminate and accept *difference*. The biological
difference between man and woman is never a "nothing but"; it is a
fundamental difference, and it does not stop with the body but
implies an equally fundamental difference of *psychic* nature. No
matter how consciously we may develop the contrasexual principle
within us, no matter how strong our intuition of the ultimate union
between the masculine and feminine elements in each individual, as
long as we remain in our bodies here in space and time, we are
predominantly either male or female, and we forget this at our peril.
Disaster awaits a woman who imitates man, but even a woman who
aims at becoming half man, half woman, and imagines she is thereby
achieving archetypal "androgyny" will certainly be inferior on both
counts. A woman is born to be essentially and wholly a woman and
the more deeply and consciously she is able to know and live the
spirit, the Logos, within her the more surely she will realize this
truth. One of the most frightening characteristics of our present
Zeitgeist is the urge to destroy difference, to reduce everything to a
horrible sameness in the cause of "equality."

Whether a woman is efficient or brilliant in some sphere hitherto
deemed masculine, or whether she remains in a traditionally feminine role, modern woman must discriminate and relate to the image
of the masculine spirit within her, while at the same time maintaining her roots in her basic feminine nature—that which receives,
nourishes, and gives birth on all levels of being through her awareness of the earth and her ability to bring up the water of life from
under the earth. All her true creativeness in every aspect of her life,
private or public, springs from this.

As we look back on the extremely rapid emergence of women in
this century into the masculine world of thought and action, it is not
surprising that woman has fallen into increased contempt for her
own values. It has surely been a necessary phase, but its effects have
been devastating not only on woman herself but also on the men
around her. For the animus—the unconscious masculinity in a
woman—when it takes possession of her femininity, has a terrifying
power, charged as it is with the numinosity of the unconscious—and

most men in their turn, when faced with this power in their women, either retreat into an inferior passive femininity, seeking to propitiate the power of the animus, or else react with brutal aggressive masculinity. Small wonder that women thus possessed, having lost their true roots in nature, are constantly beset by the anxious feeling of being useless, however outwardly successful. The dreams of modern women are full of this basic insecurity.

It is time for woman to turn from this hidden contempt for the feminine values so that she may cease to identify creativity solely with the productions of thought and with achievements in the outer world. It is exceedingly hard for us to realize, in the climate of Western society, that the woman who quietly *responds* with intense interest and love to people, to ideas, and to things, is as deeply and truly creative as one who always seeks to lead, to act, to achieve. The feminine qualities of receptivity, of nurturing in silence and secrecy are (whether in man or woman) as essential to creation as their masculine opposites and in no way inferior.

But these are all rational thoughts *about* the situation. What of the images without which, as I said at the outset, no change is possible? How is a woman, when she feels the immense fascination of the power of the spirit stirring in her, to welcome it and yet remain true to her womanhood, or how is she to rediscover her femininity if she has lost it? How is a man to realize the values of the heart without losing the bright sword of his spirit in the fogs of emotion? There are no intellectual answers. Only the images by which we live can bring transformation. The future hangs on this quest for the heart of love by both sexes.

Each of us has a well of images within, which are the saving reality and from which may be born the individual myth carrying the meaning of a life. That new images are now emerging in the tales and poetry of our time is now beyond doubt. But any truly valid "new myth" cannot be rationally invented. It must be born out of the crucible of our own struggles and suffering as we affirm our new freedom without rejecting the perennial truth of the feminine way.

Chapter Two

Demeter and Kore

THE ANCIENT MYTH of Demeter and Kore is a seedbed of feminine experience for women of all times and places, and I shall now try to explore some of its unchanging wisdom. The story, taken from the Homeric Hymn to Demeter, is as follows.

Demeter's lovely daughter, Persephone, was playing with her companions in the meadows and, wandering off by herself, she saw a flower, a narcissus with one hundred blossoms, which Zeus himself with help of Gaia, goddess of Earth, had caused to grow as a snare for her. Fascinated by this flower, with its intoxicating scent, she reached to pick it. At that moment the earth opened, and the Lord of the Dead himself appeared from the depths with his immortal horses and, seizing her in spite of her cries, carried her off to the underworld, unseen and unheard by any except the goddess Hecate who, as she was thinking "delicate thoughts," heard the cry from her cave. Otherwise only Helios the Sun himself witnessed the act. Persephone cried out to Zeus to save her, but he took no notice at all, for he himself had planned the whole thing.

The mountains and the depths of the sea, however, carried the sound of her voice, and "her lady mother heard her." For nine days the sorrowing mother, the great goddess Demeter, wandered over the earth carrying burning torches and stopping neither to eat nor to wash, but no one anywhere could give her news of her lost daughter.

But on the tenth day the goddess Hecate came, bearing a torch, and told the seeking mother that her daughter had been ravished away, but that she had only heard and not seen who the ravisher might be. Then together the two goddesses went to Helios, the Sun, as he drove his chariot across the heavens, and Demeter entreated him to tell her what he had seen. He answered that Zeus himself had given Kore to his brother Hades as his wife, and he urged her to cease lamenting as this was a good marriage for her daughter.

But her grief only increased the more and she wandered unknown, and disfigured by sorrow, among the cities of men, until she came one day to Eleusis and there she sat by the wayside beside the Maiden's Well where the women came to draw water. She bore the form of an old woman past childbearing, and she sat in the shade of an olive tree. Then came the four daughters of the King of Eleusis to draw water, and when they saw her, they questioned her, and she told them that she was far from her home in Crete and was seeking work—to nurse a child perhaps. Then the princesses led her to their father and mother, for they needed a nurse for a late-born son. With her dark robe and her head veiled she came into the house of the king, and her great height and the light which came from her struck awe into them all. At first she sat sad and speechless, but the ribald jokes of an old woman cheered her. When they offered her wine, she refused it saying she was not permitted to drink it and asking for meal and water mixed. Then she took the child from his mother and held him "on her fragrant heart," and he grew daily stronger and more beautiful on food that was more than mortal. Each night she took the child and laid him in the fire like a brand while his parents slept. But one night the child's mother came in the night and saw what was being done to her child; she cried out in terror and anger and snatched him from the goddess, thus depriving him of immortality. The goddess revealed her identity, upbraiding the mother for her "witlessness" in destroying the child's chance of immortality, and she ordered that a great temple be built for her there in Eleusis. When this was done she sat within the temple and mourned for her daughter.

Now she brought a terrible year on mankind, for she withheld growth from the earth, and no seed came up, and all the fruits of the earth were withering, so that mankind would surely have perished, and the gods would have been left without worshipers. So now Zeus in his heaven sent Iris to Demeter and begged and implored her to return among the gods and restore fertility to the earth, but she was deaf to all his pleading, even when each and all of the gods had come one by one to persuade her. And then at last Zeus sent Hermes to his brother Hades to tell him he must release Kore to her mother Demeter so that she might no longer withhold the seed from the earth.

Hades then turned to the still grieving Persephone and said that she might go, but offered her a pomegranate seed to eat as she departed. And she, though she had eaten nothing in the underworld, now, in her joy, took it and ate it, thus ensuring that she must return. Only if she had not eaten could she stay always with her mother. Henceforth she must return always to the underworld for one-third of the year. Then Hecate came again and kissed Kore many times and from that day was her "queenly comrade." And then Spring burst forth on the earth, but for one-third of each year the trees were bare and the land lay fallow. And as Demeter caused the grain to grow rich and fat again, she taught the meaning of it to all the rulers in Eleusis and gave instructions as to her rites and the mysteries which should be celebrated there.

In his essay on the Kore (the primordial maiden) Jung has said:

> Demeter and Kore, mother and daughter, extend the feminine con-sciousness upwards and downwards—and widen out the narrowly conscious mind bound in space and time, giving it intimations of a greater and more comprehensive personality which has a share in the eternal course of things. . . . It seems clear enough that the man's anima found projection in the Demeter cult. . . . For a man, anima experiences are of immense and abiding significance. But the Demeter-Kore myth is far too feminine to have been merely the result of an anima projection. . . . Demeter-Kore exists on the plane of mother-daughter experience which is alien to man and shuts him out.

There is an immense difference between the mother-son and the mother-daughter experience. On the archetypal level the son carries for the mother the image of her inner quest, but the daughter is the extension of her very self, carrying her back into the past and her own youth and forward to the promise of her own rebirth into a new personality, into the awareness of the Self. In the natural pattern of development the boy will feel his separateness from his mother by reason of his masculinity much sooner than the girl and will begin his striving for achievement. Everywhere, however, before the twen-tieth century, the growing girl remained at home contained in the orbit of her mother until the time came for her to become a mother herself and so reverse her role. Thus she would grow naturally from the passive state of being protected into the vital passivity of opening herself to receive the seed, the transition point being marked actu-ally or symbolically by the violent breaking of her virginity.

Margaret Mead has written that education has made women restless and questing, even in the face of child-bearing. For better, for worse, she has been made so. It can lead a woman either to disaster or to her great opportunity, and if she is to succeed in bridging the gap it is vital that, in one way or another, she pass through the Demeter-Kore experience in her inner life.

In ancient Greece the Eleusinian mysteries of Demeter bear witness to this overwhelming need of woman in her already growing separation from the natural pattern of the primitive feminine—the need for the Goddess to teach her the *meaning* of the deep transformation of her being from daughter to mother to daughter again. How much greater is that need today, when so often the woman lives almost like a man in the outer world and must find the whole meaning of her motherhood inwardly instead of physically, and when so many of those who do bear children are simply playing at "mothers and babies," never having allowed themselves to experience consciously the violent end of their daughter identification. There is strong evidence that the man initiated into the mysteries also "became" the *Goddess*, not the *God*. He too, in the flowering of Athenian civilization and the growing split between the conscious and unconscious, and between reason and the ancient goddesses of the earth and moon, must go through a profound experience of his anima and rediscover the meaning of the feminine within, must free his infantile emotions from possession by the mother, and then find her again as mature and objective feeling, mother and maiden in one.

Persephone is playing with her companions in the eternal Spring, completely contained in her carefree belief that nothing can change this happy state of youth and beauty. Underneath, however, the urge to consciousness is stirring, and "the maiden not to be named" strays away from her fellows, and, intoxicated by the scent of a narcissus, she stoops to pick it and in so doing opens the door through which the Lord of the Underworld rushes up to seize her. We may notice here that Gaia, Mother Earth, is clearly distinguished from Demeter in this myth. She is Zeus's fellow conspirator as it were! Kerenyi says, "From the Earth Mother's point of view, neither seduction nor death is the least bit tragic or even dramatic."

It is through the father that the daughter first becomes conscious of her self. When there is no adequate father-image in a girl's life, the identity of daughter and mother can assume a tremendous intensity, or else when the father-image is very negative and frightening, the daughter may unconsciously take on the mother's problem in a peculiarly deep way, sometimes carrying it all her life, long after the mother's death, and so remaining crippled in her effort to face her own fate in freedom. Normally the girl begins to detach from the mother, and to become conscious of her own potential motherhood through love of the father. Thus she is ready for the intoxicating moment of finding the narcissus—seeing *herself* as a person (as Narcissus saw his own face in the water), and the inevitable rape will follow. Dionysos was admiring himself in a mirror when he was set upon by the Titans and torn to pieces, the dismemberment which led to his rebirth. He is a male counterpart of Persephone.

The moment of breakthrough for a woman is always symbolically a "rape"—a necessity—something which takes hold with over-mastering power and brooks no resistance. The arranged marriages of the primitive were often accompanied by a ritual stealing of the woman. The carrying of the woman over the threshold has survived through the centuries, becoming finally a joke, its connection with myth being lost. Any breakthrough of new consciousness, though it may have been maturing for months or years out of sight, comes through a building up of tensions which reaches a breaking point. If the man or woman stands firm with courage, the breakdown becomes a breakthrough into a surge of new life. If he or she cannot stand it and settles for an evasion, then there is instead a regression into neurosis.

The Lord of the Underworld is he who arises, bursting forth from the unconscious with all the tremendous power of instinct. He comes "with his immortal horses" and sweeps the maiden (the anima in a man) from the surface life of her childish paradise into the depths, into the kingdom of the dead—for a woman's total giving of her heart, of herself, in her experience of her instincts is a kind of death. This statement in no way equates this total giving with the outward experience of intercourse with a man. This is a normal part of it and by far the easiest way, but the instincts may be experienced just as fully, and sometimes perhaps even more profoundly, by a woman whose fate does not bring her the fruition of intercourse on the physical plane. An immature man may experience his instincts in a compartment, so to speak, without deep-seated damage—but not so a woman. If she does so she pays a very great price. It was not merely a man-made piece of injustice that condemned a woman's adultery as so much more shameful than a man's. The horrible cruelty of conventional prejudices should not blind us to the archetypal truths from which these distorted collective judgments spring. The woman who gives herself on the instinctual level without the love of her heart betrays the very essence of her being as woman. A prostitute, so called, whose warmth of *heart* flows out to the man in her every encounter is a far more moral person than the respectable wife who fulfills her "duty" with hidden hatred in her heart.

Persephone cries out in fear and protest as the cord of her tie to her mother, to her unconscious youthfulness, is violently cut, and nearby, Hecate, the goddess of the moon, hears her in her dark cave, though she does not see the abduction. There are three goddesses in the myth, Demeter, Persephone, and Hecate, and they are three aspects of woman. Hecate is the goddess of the dark moon, of the mediumistic intuition in woman, of that which *hears* in the dark but does not see or understand. In this myth she appears as beneficent, linked positively to the others, but she also has her negative side. Disconnected from the other aspects of woman or from a man's undeveloped feeling, she becomes the goddess of ghosts and witches and of the spells with which the unconscious binds us, or those near to us, from below. Mother Earth and the sea, the mother of all, also carry the sound of the daughter's voice, and Demeter, the mother, hears and knows that the daughter is lost, but she does not know how. For nine days she wanders over the earth in fear and sorrow, searching for her daughter but not *understanding*. She is wholly identified with her grief, swallowed by it, even her body forgotten so that she does not eat or wash. It is the beginning of the unspeakably painful struggle of a woman to separate from her possessive emotions, the struggle which alone can give birth to love. As Demeter sank into her grief, so every time we are shocked out of some happy identification with another, which we have fondly imagined to be an unbreakable state, we are beset by the temptation to this surrender, to this despairing search for that which has been lost, demanding that it be restored to us exactly as it was, without any effort to discover the meaning of the experience. If we imagine we have succeeded in restoring the status quo, then the whole story will begin again and repeat itself endlessly and pointlessly until we can follow the goddess to the next step—the dawning of her attempt to *understand*. This cut, this loss, must be experienced by every woman both as daughter and as mother or, especially in later years, as *both* at the same time, for in every relationship between two women the mother and the daughter archetypes are constellated; each may mother the other, each may depend on the other and ask to be mothered—the balance weighted now one way, now the other.

At this point let us look at the specific experience of the loss of the daughter in older women. It is the loss of the young and carefree part of oneself, the opportunity for the discoveries of meaning which are the task of the second half of life: it is the change from the life of outer projection to the detachment, the turning inward, which leads to the "immediate experience of being outside time" in Jung's words. In the language of this myth Death rises up and takes away the woman's belief in everlasting spring. The great majority of women today, having no contact at all with the Demeter mystery, have extreme difficulty in giving up this unconscious clinging to youth, their partial identification with man's anima image, the unraped Persephone eternally picking flowers in blissful unconsciousness of the dark world below her. To such women the menopause brings long, drawn-out disturbances of the body and the psyche as the conflict grows more acute and remains unresolved.

Karl Kerenyi has written, "To enter into the figure of Demeter means to be pursued, to be robbed, to be raped" (as Persephone), "to rage and grieve, to fail to understand" (as Demeter), "and then to get everything back and be born again" (as Demeter and Persephone—the twofold single reality of Demeter-Kore). There can be no short cuts in this experience. All through her nine-day search (the symbolic nine of pregnancy), in her unconscious abandonment to grief the goddess had nevertheless carried burning torches in her hand, symbols perhaps of that small fire of attention which must be kept burning through the darkness of our journey when all meaning seems to have left us. On the tenth day Hecate, the hitherto dormant intuition, came, also bearing a torch, and told Demeter that her daughter had been ravished away, though she does not know who the ravisher may be. Demeter's moon nature brings the first rift in the isolation her absorbing personal grief has created. The stricken mother begins to intuit, to hear for the first time a voice which leads her to reflect upon that which has brought about her loss. She emerges enough from her self-concern to seek the aid of conscious reason. Together the two goddesses approach and question Helios, the sun, and he tells Demeter what has happened—that Zeus himself has arranged this marriage for her daughter and that this should be accepted as a good, a happy fate. But although her conscious mind has seen and understood, she cannot accept this reasonable answer. "She fails to understand" with her essential being and continues "to rage and to grieve."

Strangely enough, a woman is certainly right to reject this all too easy rational solution. "Let us be sensible," we say. "Our loss is good for us." Our grief was nothing but a childish reaction, and so on. Nevertheless the sun's calm reasoning has affected us. We must go on living. We must emerge from this totally self-centered, self-pitying, sorrow and be awake to other people. We must work, we must relate, but we must not deny our grief. And so Demeter comes to the well of the maidens at Eleusis—the place where the woman consciously draws the water up from the depths and listens to the wisdom of the unconscious. There sitting under an olive tree she meets the king's daughters and offers to work as nurse to a child or at any menial task. No longer obsessed with *her* child, she can look again on the beautiful daughters of others and respond.

She goes to the palace. There she takes a lowly seat and her royal hosts offer her a cup of wine. But this she refuses and asks for a mixed drink of meal and water. It is not yet time for the wine of new life, the wine of full communion. We may remember here the words of Christ before his Passion: "I will not drink henceforth of the fruit of the vine until that day when I drink it new with you in my Father's Kingdom."(Matthew 26:29) There is a time when all seeking of release from tension must be refused, and the drink must be plain and tasteless.

The goddess remains deeply sad in her bearing, and there follows the delightful image of the first smile appearing on her face as she listens to the crude jokes of Iamba, the serving woman. Her load is not lightened by some lofty thought, but by a most earthy kind of humor. The ancients were not cursed with the puritanical split between earth and the holy.

This then is the next step, after a loss, after any emotional blow, even after a seemingly trivial incident involving hurt feelings. We must return to the well of feminine wisdom. We can always work and we can always serve and we can recover our sense of humor, if we will descend far enough from our goddess-like superiority. Demeter here appears as woman past child-bearing—she has lost her own child, she can never bear another in the flesh. Even the partial acceptance of this means that she can now give of her wisdom to the children of others. Demeter, being a goddess, has the power to bestow immortality, and she feeds the child of the King and Queen with inner wisdom, and at night she thrusts him like a brand into the fire which burns but does not consume.

What is the meaning of this incident for us? It can perhaps be seen from two opposite angles. The fear and the protest of the human mother is on the one hand a warning of how fatal to a child's inner life is the overprotective possessiveness of mother love which tries to prevent all suffering and danger from touching the beloved son. But from another angle, on another level, the human mother's instinct is surely right. This is a human baby and must grow up into a human being, subject to death. If he is to reach immortality, he must reach it on the hard road of human experience and the battle for consciousness—not be given immunity and deprived of the suffering and dignity of manhood by a goddess. She is right, as a mother's instinct so often is, even if for the wrong reasons. It may be noted that the goddess here descends to something like a temper tantrum, throwing the child heartlessly onto the floor and reviling the mother for her witlessness and for her lack of vision.

It could be that the goddess' behavior at this point gives us a glimpse into another danger of the way. After a violent awakening to loss, inner or outer, when already we have been greatly matured by this, and when we have, perhaps with great courage, decided to do our best to serve and to work, it is often a great temptation to seek assuagement for our anger and grief in the satisfaction of passing on to others who are still in a very unconscious state our hard-won wisdom, and then to get very angry when this priceless gift is refused.

In a woman, it would not be so much a matter of preaching ideas, but of being quite sure she can save someone else from having to go through the same agony. To feed the infant the food of divine wisdom is well, but to thrust him into the fire of premature transformation is to deprive him of his choice as a human being. Many women do this when they unconsciously lay on their sons the burden of their

own unlived inner quest, thrusting them inexorably into the priesthood or similar "spiritual" vocation at an early age. Of this particular child we are told that all his life long the food of the goddess made
him wiser than other men, but thanks to his mother, he remained a
man, retained his human fate and his human dignity.

As is the way with myth, this in no way invalidates the other
meaning — the danger of overprotection. There are very few mothers
who do not react as this one did when they see the Great Mother, life
itself, thrusting their child — their outer or their inner child — into
the fire. Only when she herself will accept the Demeter experience is
she strong enough to consent to this. This is why the woman's
experience of the dark side is so often expressed in myth by the
descent of the child — daughter or, more often, son — into hell. It is a
more terrible experience for the feminine psyche than her own
descent. The woman does not hang on the cross. She stands at its foot
and watches the torment of her son. This is an image expressing the
truth that immortality can only be realized through the sacrifice of
the most precious thing of all — and that for a woman is her child,
whether of the flesh or of the spirit. Christ was the Word Incarnate
and his life's work was mocked and spurned and came to igno-
minious failure. Mary was the mother incarnate and her sacrifice was
quite simply the complete acceptance of that which happened to her
son, which meant the death of every shred of possessiveness. Every
archetypal story tells of the experience in its pure form. It is the
theme upon which the endless variations in the individual psyche are
built.

Demeter's effort to transmit immortality to the unconscious child
may also be seen as an attempt at a short cut, if we think of the child
for a moment as her own new consciousness. After a partial awakening it is easy to imagine that we have already arrived, or that the
"baptism of fire" can now take place immediately through some kind
of miracle or through self-imposed, dramatic purging — that we
won't need to suffer it through in actual experience over the years.
Demeter has a long road to travel before she comes to the Holy
Marriage of the mysteries and the birth of *the* divine child. Paradoxically it is the failure of this attempt to play the goddess and use her
powers on the human child that recalls her to her true goddess
nature. She remembers who she is, reveals herself, and immediately

begins to prepare for the passing on of her vision, her essence, on an altogether different level — the symbolic level of the mysteries.

Demeter's center of gravity has changed, and she orders a temple to be built for her in Eleusis. It seems totally illogical that at *this* point she orders the temple to be built, for there is still a long road to be traveled before the opposites can be reconciled, before that which is to be worshiped and experienced at Eleusis is understood by Demeter herself. But myth, particularly feminine myth, is not logical. Its truth is of another order. Demeter has emerged from her wholly personal grief; she consciously knows that she is living a great mystery and that no matter how long her suffering may last, the end of it is certain. The *heirosgamos*, the Holy Marriage, which is the unity of all opposites, is an established possibility — she *remembers* her true nature. It is a moment of recognition, a kind of remembering of that which somewhere at bottom we have always known. The current problems are not solved, the conflicts remain, but such a person's suffering, as long as he or she does not evade it, will no longer lead to neurosis but to new life. The individual intuitively glimpses who he is.

So the goddess remembers herself and builds her temple, within which she now encloses herself, and in which she sits down again in a grief more terrible than before. It is not regression; it is her cave of introversion. Whereas at first she had simply surrendered to her sorrow, she now enters consciously into it. She is in a ritual, holy place, contained. She does not yet know the solution, but she herself must accept the dark, and inner death, if her daughter is ever to return to the light of day. And as the Goddess withdrew, so the earth dried up and withered, the sap of growth departed, and the land lay dying. The wasteland around the Fisher King in the Grail legend carries the same meaning — when it is time for a transformation of the whole personality, the birth of a totally new attitude, everything dries up inwardly and outwardly and life becomes more and more sterile until the *conscious* mind is forced to recognize the gravity of the situation, is compelled to accept the validity of the unconscious.

The gods now become frantic at what is happening on earth — pretty soon there will be no more men to worship the mighty gods of reason! As always happens they get busy bribing Demeter to emerge from her temple and her sorrow — urging her to settle for a pleasant life of peace and honor on Olympus and to forget about her daughter down below, who can be left to keep the dark powers happy and prevent them from bothering the upper gods. So do reason and the fear of the dark speak to us. "Even if my greatest value does stay buried forever, it is foolish and arrogant of me to make so much fuss about it. I must conquer my misery, stop thinking about it, make the best of things as they are. Surely the great god Zeus must know best, and he is offering me ease and a position of great importance." But Demeter does not for a moment yield to good sense arguments. There can be no half-way solution, no stopping at the state of separation of the opposites. She is deaf to all the entreaties and appeals of every god in turn. She uses the invincible weapon of the woman who, when something utterly irrational and against all conscious values rises up from the root of her being, simply sits still and refuses to budge. No man can resist this, but unfortunately a woman too often uses this tool when she is moved not by a real intuition from her roots, but by her overpowering emotional possessiveness or an opinion of her animus.

The gods give in to Demeter, of course, and at last the conscious and the unconscious, the masculine and the feminine begin to pull together. It seems at first simply a capitulation of consciousness to the regressive longing of the mother. Zeus sends Hermes to tell Hades he must give Persephone back and restore the status quo, for Zeus himself cannot produce the solution which reconciles the opposites. Only when Hades the Lord of Death, Zeus's dark brother, will cooperate can the answer come. It is he who gives Persephone the seed of the pomegranate to eat—and she, who has hitherto rejected all food—refused to assimilate the experience—now in the moment when she is full of joy at the thought of not having to accept it, takes the pomegranate seed involuntarily, but voluntarily swallows it. In spite of her protests, she really has no intention of regressing to identification with her mother again. This is an image of how the saving thing can happen in the unconscious before the conscious mind can grasp at all what is going on. There are many dreams in which the dreamer tries to return to an old thing or situation but finds, for example, the doors barred or the telephone broken. The ego still yearns for the status quo but further down the price has been paid, and we *can't* go back. Hence the great value of dreams in making us aware of these movements below. Even Demeter in her conscious planning, still half yearns for her daughter to return as before, but her questioning is quite perfunctory. As soon as she knows the seed has been eaten, there is no more said on the subject—all is joy. Persephone has eaten the food of Hades, has taken the seed of the dark into herself and can now give birth to her own new personality. So also can her mother. They have both passed through death to the renewal of a new spring—the inward renewal which age need never lose—and have accepted the equal necessity of winter and life in the darkness of the underworld.

The two become Demeter-Kore instead of Demeter and Kore. Now, to complete the unity, Hecate joins the others; she too is united to Persephone, becoming from that day her "queenly comrade," mother, maiden, and sibyl—the threefold nature of woman made whole. The images unite; they no longer merge or fight or possess each other, and the woman who knows this experience becomes "one in herself."

THE MYSTERIES

Demeter, united to her daughter, taught the rulers of Eleusis her rites and her mysteries, and these mysteries were for a thousand years a center of the inner religious life of antiquity. It is a measure of the power and depth of experience of the initiates that in all this time the secrets were never revealed by any one of the vast numbers involved. The merest hints leaked out, so that we can only know that certain symbols played a part, but very little is known about the rituals which led to the final revelation.

It is certain that the rites were not a mystery-drama, not an acting out of the story of the two goddesses, though each element of the myth was *symbolically* experienced. The initiates gathered in Athens on the first day—anyone could be a candidate if he or she spoke Greek and was not guilty of the shedding of blood—and went through a purification ritual of bathing in the sea. Probably these initiates had already been through the lesser mysteries of Persephone at Agrai in which water and darkness played a major part, and each candidate experienced the passive suffering of the raped Persephone in the underworld through a conscious act of surrender. After the bathing there was a procession to Eleusis of the purified, bearing torches. Various symbolic actions were performed along the way, and on arrival outside Eleusis there was a time of fasting. The journey and the fasting were the symbols of Demeter's nine days of wandering and grief; Eleusis itself was the place of the *finding*.

It is probable that the rites proper began with a dance. Euripides wrote that on the night of the dance round the "fountain in the square of beautiful dances—the stormy heaven of Zeus begins to dance also, the moon and the fifty daughters of Nereus, the goddesses of the sea and the ever flowing rivers, all dance in honor of the golden-crowned maiden and her holy mother." Already the individual is lifted out of his small, rational, personal ego, and the whole universe is dancing with him.

There was also, it is thought, a communion drink—meal and water, probably, as drunk by Demeter in the king's hall—and the rites moved on through we know not what pattern to the climax of a ritual marriage by violence—not, as one might expect, that of Hades with Persephone, but the marriage of Demeter and Zeus. These are the mysteries of Demeter (not of Persephone, except insofar as she is an aspect of Demeter), of the Great Mother, whose experience of loss and finding led her to the *hierosgamos*, the union of the earth with the creator God, which means the birth of the divine child who is the "whole."

After the sacred marriage, a great light shone and the cry of the hierophant rang out "The great goddess has borne a sacred child—Brimo has borne Brimos." The goddess has acquired a new name which means "the strong one," "the power to arouse terror." Without terror, without experience of the terrible face of God, there can be no divine birth. It must be remembered that Persephone also, in her dark, negative aspect, is Medusa, the Gorgon's head, which she herself sends forth from the underworld—"a monstrosity," says Kerenyi, "the nocturnal aspect of what by day is the most desirable of all things." Only the birth of the child who bears the name Brimo can resolve the intolerable tension of these opposites: the child who is Demeter, Persephone, Hecate, Zeus, and Hades in one living image. The child is a boy, but also a girl, the androgynous fruit of the holy marriage. It is known that a single child initiate played a part in the mysteries, and that this could be either a boy or a girl, as the omens should decide.

The marriage and the birth, however, were not the final revelation. The most profound vision of all, the actual experience of immortality came in deep silence, when a mown ear of corn (or wheat, as it would be called in the New World) was held up and *seen* by the initiate. Nor can words ever accompany such an experience. The ancients said that at this point the idea of immortality "lost everything confusing and became a satisfying vision."

The mown ear of corn is a perfect symbol of immortality, of eternal rebirth. It is the fruit of life, the harvest, which feeds and nourishes, it is the seed which must sink into the earth and disappear in order to give birth again. It is mown down in the moment of its ripeness, as Persephone was mown down and torn from her mother, as every achievement in our lives outer or inner must be mown down in order to give birth to the new. It is the mother who nourishes, it is the seed of the father, and it is the child born of them both, in one image. The elevated Host in the Mass is the same symbol, the same silent epiphany, "showing forth" of immortality, with a tremendous added dimension. Bread is that which has been produced by man from the raw grain. *Consciousness* is added to the purely natural symbol, for Christ has consciously lived the myth. His initiates too must experience the mowing down, the burial and the rising again in a conscious realization of the Christ within. "Unless a grain of wheat fall into the ground and die, it remaineth alone, but if it die, it bringeth forth much fruit." That which must die is not the evil and the ugly, but the thing of greatest beauty and meaning, the maiden of stainless innocence, so that we may finally know that over which death has no power.

There is evidence that the final act at Eleusis was the setting up of two vessels which were tipped over, so that the water flowed towards the east and the west, the directions of birth and death. Thus the ritual began and ended with water, symbol of the unconscious beginnings of all life and of the wise spirit of the conscious end—the living water "springing up into eternal life."

It should be stressed that the rites at Eleusis were neither an allegory nor a miracle but a mystery. An allegory exists in the realm of ordinary knowledge; it is a metaphor, a story, reflecting, for example, the cycle of the seasons or speaking of the living on of man in his descendants—facts which we all know of but which have, for the most part, little power to affect or change our personalities. As Kerenyi says, "There is a vast difference between knowing *of* something and knowing it and being it." Of the difference between miracle and mystery, he writes that a miracle causes people to talk endlessly about it, whereas the true mysteries are kept silent so that they may transform us from within through the symbols which in Jung's words "alone can reconcile the warring opposites, conveying to man in a single image, that which is thought *and* feeling and beyond them both."

The Homeric hymn ends with the words "awful mysteries which no one may in any way transgress or pry into or utter, for deep awe of the gods checks the voice. Happy is he among men upon earth who has seen these mysteries; but he who is uninitiate and who has no part in them never has lot [or share] of like good things once he is dead, down in the darkness and gloom." The ancient hymn thus asserts the three essentials of all the mystery rituals of all the religions. First, the rites must not be transgressed, altered in any way; second, they must be accepted without analysis and without question; third, they must not be spoken of, must be kept absolutely secret.

It is immediately obvious that modern man, even in the Roman Church which has been the guardian of the Christian mysteries for so long, is busy breaking all these essentials of a ritual mystery. We are changing it, we pry into everything, and we speak about it all incessantly. The element of awe is being deliberately banished. All this is not something which can or should be avoided. The growth of consciousness inevitably and rightly means that we pry into, we question everything with our hungry minds, and to try to stop this would be futile obscurantism. But it is equally futile and an arrogant folly to imagine that having banished the mystery from our outer cults, we can now dispense with it altogether. Then indeed, we shall end up in the "darkness and gloom," denying reality to the psyche itself and its truths. Without vision, without mystery, all of our fine intellectual understanding and its great values turn to dust.

The hymn refers to the fate of the initiate after death. In this context Kerenyi writes, "The 'eidola' in the realm of the dead . . . are the images with which the deceased individual, through his uniqueness, has enriched the world." Only to the extent that a man has lived his unique individual meaning does he attain to immortality. Persephone was called "the eternally unique" because she had united the two worlds, the dark and the light.

Surely the meaning of the dogma *extra ecclesiam nulla salus*, is that there is no salvation without experience of the mystery. It became a cruel and bigoted statement when it was interpreted in the literal outer sense (a kind of interpretation from which all the great dogmas of the Church have suffered immeasurably), and it gave sanction to such horrors as the Inquisition. The ecumenical movement today is tackling this distortion on its own level with arguments of reason and good sense, but it misses the essential point, which is that man should recognize and experience the level of his being where this dogma is eternally and *individually* true. Outside the "Church," outside the mystery, there is no salvation.

When the outer cult loses its *mana* — its spiritual force or power — for a man, then the mystery falls into the unconscious and must there be rediscovered by the individual journeying alone in the dark places to the experience of the symbols within. When images of power and beauty rise up in dreams or fantasies, they make an immediate impact. We are in awe before them. Sometimes there comes a specific dream of initiation which may alter the whole course of a man's life. Such images are not something thought up or pried into, they cannot be altered, and instinctively we sense that they must not be spoken of except to another "initiate." When one does expose them wrongly, one can *feel* the power go out of them. Although their details are individual, unique, they link a man to the whole experience of mankind, and their impact can be immensely increased through a knowledge of the content and meaning of ancient myth, of the eternal themes which have embodied through the ages the truths of the human psyche. Our individual images may invoke perhaps, the dance of the primitive, the flood, Demeter-Kore, Isis-Osiris, the Buddha's Flower sermon, the Zen Master's koan, or, for us in the West most powerfully of all, the birth and death of Christ, the bread and wine of the Mass. The analyzing mind which has destroyed mystery is thus linked again to the immediacy of the inner experience, and the redeeming symbol is reborn.

The quotes from C.G. Jung and Karl Kerenyi throughout this chapter are from their book, Introduction to a Science of Mythology, *translated by R.E.C. Hull (London: Routledge and Kegan Paul, 1951).*

Chapter Three

Eowyn

In J.R.R. Tolkien's *The Lord of the Rings*, the character of Eowyn, niece-daughter of Theoden, King of the Mark, has a profound relevance to some aspects of the feminist movement in our time. In the story she is the slayer of the deadly King of the nine black Ringwraiths and her life is very different from the usual pattern of the feminine in most ancient myths and legends — for example the way of a Penelope, whose patient waiting and indomitable love nourish the man as he goes forth to wield his sword. It will be remembered that in this twentieth century myth, no *man* could have killed the dark king, however strong or brave he might be; even Gandalf, the great wizard, was able to do no more than repulse him temporarily. Only through the woman with a sword could his power be brought to an end.

The Ringwraith's weapon was fear and despair; man and beast fled before him as panic seized them and all hope died in their hearts. On the field of Pelennor only Theoden the King, who had passed through darkness to a great awakening in his old age, stood fast when the dark king, riding on a winged beast, descended upon him. But Theoden's horse, Snowmane, terrorstricken, reared and fell upon him.

But first let us go back and trace the story of Eowyn before she took to herself the disguise of Dernhelm the young warrior, one of Theoden's knights. We first see her standing behind the throne of her uncle-father, Theoden, as he sits, old and demoralized, with Wormtongue at his feet — Wormtongue the cunning, the plausible, who has gradually undermined the old king's personality, whispering lies into his ear about his weakness and the hopelessness of any resistance to the evils of time. Wormtongue is the mouth-piece of Saruman, the corrupted wizard, who has betrayed the inner wisdom, seeking personal power and dominion. Eowyn has grown up in this atmosphere, has watched the gradual decay in the old man she loves.

There is no mother, no feminine warmth at this court, and she, as a woman, has no influence in the counsels of the king, no outlet for her generosity of spirit. She must even endure the secret knowledge that the contemptible Wormtongue is lusting after her and means to possess her at the last. She has indeed a brother, Eomer, whom she loves and trusts; he is young and brave and intelligent, but is in disgrace with the king, suspected of treason almost, through the scheming of Wormtongue.

It is very clear what this kind of situation has done to one of her nature, reared as she was on the tales of chivalry and courage of her family's past. The heroic lives only in her fantasy; in outer life she must watch betrayal and decay, and she has encased herself in armor outwardly and inwardly. No natural warmth of passion has yet touched her; the springs of her womanhood are frozen, and she longs to be a man, to fight, to conquer or to die in battle wielding a sword in place of that which Theoden has given into the keeping of Wormtongue. She has become the shield maiden of Rohan, beautiful but cold — cold as a woman that is, but not cold — indeed consumed with frustration and passion in the regions of her burning spirit.

As we read, we must surely feel how all this mirrors the predicament of many women in this century. Born into a family in which, perhaps, the father has succumbed to the softness of his anima while the mother, as mother, is simply absent, since she is buried in a mass of animus opinions, the daughter is brought up without a clear image of either masculine or feminine, while all around her the decay in the collective attitudes dominating consciousness presses in upon her. The betrayals of Saruman and the whisperings of Wormtongue have achieved unprecedented power in our society. The old virtues of honor and justice and the values of eros, of individual relatedness, are in grave danger. The Nazgul (human beings who had given their whole life to serving the Dark Lord and who have become like wraiths) are indeed abroad in the land, mounted not as before, on ordinary horses (instinct still in normal form though turned to dark purposes), but on the monstrously evil and archaic winged beasts. This horror may be recognized, perhaps, in the utter senselessness of so much violence and lust in our society and in the spread of the present terrorist attitude to life in the abuse of children.

What has been the effect of all this on women of great potential warmth and nobility? Like Eowyn they grow up either determined to enter the battle on the masculine level, fighting with all they have for a cause or an idea, or, at the opposite pole, succumb to the lust of Wormtongue and an indiscriminate instinctual sexuality which, cut off from relationship, ends by destroying eros itself. Nevertheless there are not a few who come, as did Eowyn, through suffering and courage, to find their wholeness as women.

We may indeed hope that the shocks of recent years will be to our time like the shock of Gandalf's staff breaking the spell over Theoden, restoring to him his sword, sending him forth on his last great ride to his death and the rising of a new king, a new conscious ruler. If so, then indeed, as in the War of the Ring—the war which was to substitute love and the value of the individual for the ruling demon of power—the moment is upon us when victory will hang upon the readiness of women to confront the most powerful of all the dark forces ranged against us—that which no man can conquer with his sword, that which is vulnerable only to the newly found sword of the feminine spirit.

The Nazgul King is the image of the despair which can undermine even the best and the bravest among us; it is a despair born of the emptiness, the isolation and lack of communication and consequent loss of meaning which is overwhelming our culture. It is a bisexual image: the mind of man turned demonic in its intellectual pride, emptied of human compassion, rides in the air on the mindless beast into which the instinctive feminine regresses when human beings reject the values of the heart. The inevitable outcome of this unholy union is the despair which breeds first indifference and ultimately active cruelty and violence in all its forms.

Let us watch the phases of Eowyn's journey. In the moment of Theoden's awakening, she has looked upon Aragorn, the carrier of the new consciousness of the Self, the king of the future. For the first time she experiences romantic love; but like so many women of her type who have grown afraid of their femininity and are shut off from it, she projects her animus onto a man whom she unconsciously knows to be unattainable. He carries for her her inner image of a heroic figure who personifies her fantasies of great deeds, who compensates for the pitiful failure of the father. Her love for Theoden has been deeply wounded—has gradually turned to pity and unconscious contempt. In Aragorn she sees her ideals in human form, but, as he so clearly perceives, she remains cold; she does not see him as a person. She longs to join him not as a woman but as a companion warrior on his quest—to follow him in *his* way, not hers. He refuses her with great compassion as he rides away on the Paths of the Dead, and she is left with a frozen heart but a fierce determination not to be left behind when Theoden rides to war.

Theoden also refuses her his permission to go with the Riders. He refuses without understanding, with the usual hackneyed masculine lecture on woman's place being in the home. But Eowyn, like all awakened women since this century began, knows that if she accepts this platitude any longer and refuses to stand by her certainty that she has the courage and the ability to "wield a sword," then her creative spirit will wither and die, and despair will finally destroy her. It is absolutely essential for Eowyn at this point that she defy the father's authority—as it became essential for modern woman to rebel and to disobey and to enter the arena of the male-dominated world. And at first, like Eowyn, in order to free themselves, they have been compelled to disguise themselves as men—and many have come to imagine that there really is no difference any more. They forget they are disguised and so identify with the emerging spirit.

It is, however, precisely at this point in the story, that Eowyn's repressed and despised femininity begins to assert itself from her unconscious. It is the crucial moment for every woman who is driven by the creative spirit into the Logos world. Will she imitate man, in which case her spirit will turn sterile and demonic; or will she, in the midst of her intoxicating freedom, be true to her basic nature? If she chooses the latter then indeed she may come at infinite cost to confront and destroy that fell wraith, riding on the beast of cruelty and greed, who yields to no power but that of the true woman who has dared to grasp the sword of the spirit.

We see then Eowyn, disguised as Dernhelm, young and slender, sitting on her horse, whose name is Windfola, as the men of Rohan gather and prepare to set forth on their great ride to the battle with the Dark Lord. Sitting there she hears Theoden saying farewell to Merry, the hobbit, and forbidding him to go with them. "You are too small, though stout of heart. You could do nothing but get in the way. You must stay here with the women and children." She sees in despair, the misery, so like her own, in Merry's eyes, and as the companies depart she rides up to him and offers to take him up behind her on her horse, which can easily carry them both.

It would be hard indeed to conceive of any young man, going forth
to his first battle to prove his courage and his manhood, who would
consider for a moment such a thing. Yet Eowyn, intoxicated as she
must have been by the coming fulfillment of her day dreams, suddenly sees Merry as a person and is filled with compassion. It is a
truly feminine reaction. No matter how it may restrict and encum-
ber her new freedom, she cannot leave him behind. She is only
disguised as a man. Symbolically seen, she takes with her on her
journey the childlike earth-wisdom in the person of the small hobbit.
We are reminded of the Kabiri, the little earth men who accompany
the goddesses of the ancient world. Her heroic fantasy world is
suddenly "earthed," we may say, by the strong infusion of "hobbit
sense."

As the host of Rohan sweep into battle, Merry notices that Dernhelm keeps as close as he can to the king. All fly before the sword of
Theoden, but be it noted that Eowyn has not yet drawn her sword,
though all fight around her. She does not in fact draw it until she
hears the voice of the Nazgul as she stands over the body of her uncle-
father to protect it from the foul beast. She had spoken of fighting
like a man with men, but in the heat of the battle the inherent
strength of her womanhood instinctively takes over. She cannot kill
for any cause, however great, simply to conquer. She can only kill to
save a person whom she loves.

The woman's way of redemption through all the ages is the giving
of her life's blood for another. But it is no longer so simple for the
Eowyn of our time. She is equally willing to die for another, but first
she must draw the sword of her spirit—the sword of her conscious
discrimination, of her intelligence and her imagination. With this
sword she destroys first the devouring monster of greed and then
with all her feminine strength she strikes into the head (he has no
heart) of that ghost-like horror of the masculine spirit turned demonic, which would destroy not only her personally, but also all
warmth of human kindness and therefore all hope in our civilization.

We may learn much from the few lines describing Eowyn as she
struck this blow. First, when the winged beast plunged its claws into
the body of Snowmane, her father's horse, and was about to devour
both dead horse and king, she raised her voice in defiance. "Begone
foul dwimmerlaik, lord of carrion! Leave the dead in peace!" A
major cause of our despair lies surely in the fact that as traditional

moral codes and rigid standards of behavior inevitably and rightly crumble and die, men have fallen disastrously into contempt for the human and divine values on which those codes, however outdated in form, were originally based. The heroic figure of Theoden King on his white horse of chivalry must indeed die, but if his body were to be torn to pieces and devoured by the shadow king and his beast, no transformation of his heroism could take place. Instead of a new birth of the dead hero on a deeper level of awareness, which alone can save us in the era which is dawning, the old attitudes are simply replaced, eaten up, by empty despair.

One of the basic qualities of the feminine psyche is its capacity for total devotion. A mother in defense of her child will stop at nothing; a woman's love once truly given to a person is the most tenacious thing in nature, and no collective or moral standards of any kind have power to alter this devotion. A mature woman whose love is purged of possessiveness will risk everything to save a person—any person—from destruction. (The negative side of this is, of course, a woman possessed by a shadow-animus combination who gives *blind* devotion to a cause or a person.) Eowyn on the field of Pelennor is an archetypal picture of a modern woman who can no longer, as in past centuries, simply offer passively to give her blood. How the Nazgul would laugh! No, she must actively use her sword, but in that moment she has no thought of causes or of her own wish to be as like a man as possible. The hand which wields the sword of her spirit is wholly a woman's hand. Faced with the threat of the worst that despair can do to mind and body she laughs in face of the horror. "Do what you will—but I will hinder it, if I may." She will defend the integrity of personal devotion, of the human heart, to the death and beyond. And now she reveals herself with pride and joy as a woman indeed. "Thou fool. No living man may hinder me," he cries, and she answers:

> But no living man am I! You look upon a woman. Eowyn I am, Eomund's daughter. You stand between me and my lord and kin. Begone, if you be not deathless! For living or dark undead, I will smite you, if you touch him.

Tolkien further tells us: "Her eyes grey as the sea were hard and fell, and yet tears were on her cheek."

So many women have forgotten how to weep that they have lost the meaning of tears. "Women must weep": this is not a badge of weakness; it is an essential strength. (Weak tears of self-pity are of course quite another thing.) Eowyn's cheeks are wet at the moment of her greatest masculine act.

The king of despair now raised his great black mace to destroy Eowyn. It is worth noting that the Nazgul does not fight with a discriminating sword, but with an annihilating club. He shattered her frail shield and broke her arm, but Merry the small earthbound hobbit, whose strength had been rejected by the heroic Theoden but recognized by Eowyn, saw with love and wonder the slender woman standing there in her beauty and courage, her sword gleaming in her hand, and he rose from his own grovelling terror to help her in her need. Plunging his own sword into the Nazgul's leg, he enabled the woman with her last strength to drive her sword into the head under the crown, and the King of Despair in that age of the world dissolved into nothingness before Merry's eyes, while Eowyn herself lay as one dead. It was then that the old king regained consciousness for a moment. He saw only Merry, and he passed away in peace and honor instead of in horror, speaking gently words of good hope for those who would create a new world after him, for Eomer and Eowyn whom he loved but could not understand. The old era would be transformed, not destroyed.

At exactly the same time that this meeting took place between the woman and the king of the Nazgul, another battle with the great enemy, despair, was going on in the citadel of Gondor. The steward of Gondor, Denethor, long threatened by this enemy, became completely and crazily possessed by it when he heard of the fear of the Nazgul that was running through the city, and he carried his wounded son Faramir, into the burial places of the kings and there tried to set fire to himself and his son. Faramir was saved by Gandalf, the wise man, but Gandalf would have arrived too late had it not been for two simple people. First, once again, a hobbit was the essential link, and secondly the simple soldier, Beregond, who with great moral courage retained his sense of *personal* values in the midst of disintegration.

The synchronicity of this with the victory of Eowyn and Merry is obvious; and almost immediately afterwards comes the final victory in this battle, with the arrival of Aragorn, sailing up the river after his ordeal on the Paths of the Dead. Without any one of these men of integrity and true feeling, there could have been no going on to the final defeat of the Dark Lord, and the destruction of the Ring of Power by Frodo could not have succeeded. It is, however, abundantly clear that, after the sword of Eowyn had brought about the dissolution of the Nazgul king, the armies of Gondor were freed from the terrible contagion of despair which would have frustrated all the attempts of Gandalf and Aragorn to lead them to the last battle at the gates of Mordor. No man in that last battle had any illusion about the likelihood, the almost certainty, of defeat and death; but that is a very different thing from despair. Indeed the capacity to face defeat and death is the proof of the victory of faith over despair, as Winston Churchill wrote.

This, then, I believe, is the great challenge to modern woman. Unless she can find the courage and the vision, the individual freedom of spirit, to plunge her sword into the head of the despair which threatens humanity, then hope wanes and darkness thickens upon us. It is no longer enough for woman to act instinctively as a link to the wisdom in the unconscious for man. We have drifted so far away from this wisdom into sterility that an instinctive return means the all-too familiar fall into violence and sensuality. What an image it is—the black terror of the Ringwraith riding an obscenely horrible beast! Therefore the woman must not simply "know" the spirit (instinctively and unconsciously as in the past), but—to quote Charles Williams' telling phrase—must "know she knows," and so she consciously takes up the sword to slay both beast and wraith so that the shadow may pass and man may remember in his heart as well as his head the undying spark over which defeat and death have no power. And she must do this as woman, not at all in imitation of man. If she falls into this imitation, then her sword thrusts become mere pinpricks which succeed only in wounding the masculinity of the men around her.

In an individual's life, what does this mean? It means that, brought up in a world of dominant masculinity, she must work throughout her life, in small things as in great, to discriminate her feelings, her eros values, from all the conventional opinions and second-hand convictions which beset her animus and freeze her womanhood, and at the same time she must affirm the great gulf which lies between eros and the possessive concupiscence into which her instinctual emotions can so easily drive her. She will need great courage if she is to recognize and confront the half-conscious plotting and scheming of the animus in order to get her own way, prove herself in the right. Thus she enters on the quest for her true identity as an individual woman. The way will bring her into darkness and loneliness, through fire and water, but at the last she will begin to discover consciously that unpossessive love between persons which brings renewal of faith in life itself and finally the *agape* of wholeness. The modern woman, deeply threatened as she is by the power of present day collective unconscious forces, cannot possibly achieve this mission unless she wields the sword of the *imaginative* spirit as Eowyn did. We must never forget that, in the words of Rollo May, "Imagination is the life-blood of Eros," and that without Imagination in its true sense, there is no creative spirit, and no harmony between instinct and intellect is possible.

Robert Grinnell, in his book, *Alchemy of a Modern Woman*, says that a woman of today who has lost contact with her feminine nature will find herself

> in the situation of trying to be a hero-animus, and so, having blocked Eros and the approaches to her feeling, she is over-shadowed by the monster, the archaic feminine. . . . But it is the hero-animus who must lead her forth from a mythological destiny into life and awaken awareness of her anima nature. Only so can she become a leader of man's soul.

In another place Grinnell writes that a modern woman's "transformational activity has a certain bisexual quality which is mercurial rather than strictly feminine. She performs heroic tasks. But these have something of the character of ancient ceremonies and rituals rather than raiding expeditions."

These passages beautifully illuminate the meaning of Eowyn's story. Her hero-animus had blocked her feeling as long as she identified with him. But standing on the field of battle she declares herself a woman with tears of love for Theoden in her eyes, and wielding the sword of the animus power within her she performs her heroic task. It does indeed have the quality of a ritual, transforming act, and is far removed from the imagery of the conquering hero.

Eowyn was carried into Gondor and lay near death. But then came Aragorn, whose image she had truly loved with all the idealistic generosity of her heart. Aragorn is the king, and the true king, symbol of the Self as known to men, has healing hands; and he calls her back from the borders of despair and death; for in confronting the evil thing one is inevitably infected by it. Her devotion to the royal image within her, to the highest and noblest attitude she knew, now draws her back into life. Eowyn does not yet know the change that has been wrought in her, as so often we do not know at first. She still believes, as she slowly regains strength, that there is no meaning in life for her but to seek death in battle like a man. But when so deep an inner change has taken place, there comes always the event from outside which brings the new birth into consciousness.

Faramir, too, is recovering from his wound and his terrifying experience. He and Eowyn are left behind in Gondor and must wait, inactive, while the last battle is fought. And now in the shadow of their near certainty of the end of all they have loved in the world, Eowyn discovers at last that she is fully and completely a woman. Love awakens in her — not for a hero figure but for a flesh-and-blood man on this earth. The ice round her heart is melted, and in their whole and conscious commitment to each other, we recognize in Faramir and Eowyn a man whose heart is alive with feminine sensitivity and a woman whose masculine courage and intelligence have been tried in the fire. They are equals in every true sense of the word, but Faramir is a man; Eowyn is a woman — there is no mixing. They are an image of the marriage of Heaven and Earth, within themselves and with each other.

No effort of all the men of good-will, essential as it is, would have sufficed to save the world without the spirit of Eowyn, the woman; and if the shield maiden of Rohan had not passed through those long years during which the sword of her spirit was forged while her natural femininity lay submerged, the vital blow at the root of despair could not have been struck.

C h a p t e r   F o u r

Orual

IN HIS NOVEL *Till We Have Faces*, C.S. Lewis has re-examined the ancient myth of Eros and Psyche, incorporating into it the character of Orual, a woman whose nature and character we cannot fail to recognize as contemporary. Her story concerns a woman's long search for her true face, for her identity as a person. Like most of us, she runs from this discovery for the greater part of her life: she lives behind a veil, and she refuses to hear the innermost voice of her soul. Only when she comes to that moment when she stands in a dream before the divine judge does she hear the hidden words by which she has evaded reality and the meaning of love for so long, and only then can she finally know her own face:

> The complaint [against the gods] was the answer. To have heard myself making it was to be answered. Lightly men talk of saying what they mean. . . . When the time comes to you at which you will be forced at last to utter the speech which has lain at the center of your soul for years, which you have, all that time, idiot-like, been saying over and over, you'll not talk about joy of words. I saw well why the gods do not speak to us openly, nor let us answer. Till that word can be dug out of us, why should they hear the babble that we think we mean? How can they meet us face to face till we have faces? (p. 294)

The first part of the book consists of Orual's life-long complaint against the gods. She is, as it were, a female Job, and she dares what we must all dare if we are to know the reality of God. The second part of the story, written just before her death, is only about 50 pages long compared with the 250 of the first part. In it the facts of her life, told with such searching honesty in the first part, unite with the myth and are filled with conscious meaning. So it is that, seeing her innermost self at last, she stands face to face with Eros, with Love itself.

At the beginning of this second part Orual says:

What began the change was the very writing itself. Let no one lightly set about such a work. . . . The change which the writing wrought in me . . . was only a beginning—only to prepare me for the gods' surgery. They used my own pen to probe my wound. (pp. 253-54)

A modern woman in this world of alienation from eros must take up this work or succumb to possession by the animus; and she must take it up with the same kind of honesty that Orual achieved, and which is of all things the most difficult for a woman caught by the inferior masculine spirit in her unconscious life.

This work is not necessarily the actual writing of one's life story in a literal sense; that may or may not be a part of it. But there must be a creative battle with "the word" in some form or other, for the word is the power of conscious definition and discrimination, while at the same time all language is symbolic. Nothing kills the symbolic life so quickly as words reduced to mere information or mindless chatter. There can be no awareness of the uniting myth without this battle to discriminate and to separate, but if women leave this work to the animus disconnected from their womanhood, then they never glimpse their true story. In the Christian myth, the Word, the Logos, must become flesh if man is to stand face to face with God, and this, a fact so consistently forgotten, is an impossibility unless he is conceived and brought to birth by woman.

The ancient way of unconscious mediation by woman of the inner wisdom is no longer enough for us today. The word in modern woman must become flesh within her own psyche by conscious creative work through her imagination, undertaken in *partnership* with the animus who relates her to her hitherto unconscious powers of discrimination. The form of this work no one can dictate. It must be discovered by the individual herself, and it may be something very simple. It is not necessarily a matter of becoming a notable artist or writer, but nevertheless, it is a task demanding immense courage and perseverance in the teeth of weakness, failure, and even despair until, as in Orual, the surgery is finished. Then indeed will come the "death before death" of which the god spoke to Orual. Myth and fact will then be known as one; her sister Psyche, whose name tells us her meaning, will be transformed and the god revealed.

In the long journey of Orual from childhood to old age, we can see the terrible blows that wounded her feminine nature, her attempt to deny the numinous, her retreat into the masculine, her fight with the gods — and through it all the integrity and courage that brought her to her final beauty and wholeness.

Orual was the elder of two daughters of the king of Glome; the story begins, symbolically enough, with the death of her mother. The small kingdom of Glome was remote and primitive, still worshipping the ancient mother goddess Ungit, and had been little changed by the civilization of Greece. Her father was a rough, crude chieftain; his passion was the hunt. By the standards of that time he was a strong king, respected if not loved. He married again — this time a delicate, gentle princess. A slave had been brought to court, a man of Greece, and the king had appointed him to teach the arts and knowledge of Greece to his two small daughters — to "practice" on them until such time as he, the king, should beget a prince, a worthy pupil. We are given a hint that Orual's face was extremely ugly. "Learning is all she will ever be good for," said her father.

So Orual acquired a second father: a wise and gentle man, a philosopher, a rationalist, the best kind of humanist who thought he had outgrown belief in the old gods and their superstitions. The king had named him the Fox. To him the child, motherless and despised by her father, gave the devotion of both her heart and of her expanding mind. Redival, her younger sister, however, deprived now not only of her mother but of her sister's attention as well, and delivered over to a crude and self-seeking nurse, grew up with nothing to love but her own pretty face.

The collective consciousness of the surrounding culture was in process of emerging from a primitive identity with the unconscious, the goddess Ungit. In the coming of the Fox, we feel the penetration of the light of consciousness into the darkness of Ungit, and the king himself came to depend more and more on the Fox's clear thinking.

The king's contempt for women and for his daughters demonstrates, as always, the negative side of man's struggle to free himself from the devouring aspect of the feminine unconscious, of the mother goddess. There is no true human woman in Orual's environment. The mother is dead, the stepmother is so weak she only lives a year. The nurse is out for what she can get. The absence of eros is seen in the wild rages of the king, in the greed of Batta the nurse, in the vanity of Redival, in the superstitions into which the worship of the mother goddess is deteriorating during this time of transition.

The Fox is truly kind and human, but he too misses the significance of the feminine. His way, with its rejection of the gods by the reasoning mind, is seen clearly as powerless to control the forces of barbarism.

Yet into the discord and decay at the court of Glome, as always at such moments of tension, the true miracle comes—the birth of the redeeming child. Historically, this was represented by the coming of the Buddha and the Christ; in mythology, by the dying and resurrecting of the gods; in legend, by the Grail hero and so many others; in individuals, by the intuition of redemption. All are born in such times. But in this story, in contrast to all those myths and legends, the child is a girlchild, whose name is Psyche. The repressed feminine psyche is reborn as a great new possibility of redemption and transformation, which can only grow to conscious maturity in a new kind of woman who, like Orual, has learned the way of Logos and, at great cost, has held or returned to her own feminine devotion to eros.

The fury of the king on the birth of another girl was murderous. In his rage he actually stabbed to death a young boy who carried a cup of wine to him, and swore he would send the Fox to work in the mines. His contempt for the feminine not only breaks the cup and spills the wine; it also kills the boy, the promise of growing manhood, who offered the cup, and, further, it seeks to banish the bringer of the new light of reason and humanity down underground. The king's wife has died giving birth to the child. The king's hope of sons to carry on *his* way has gone; yet, in spite of his rage, his unconscious recognized the new-born child, for he called her Istra, which in Greek is Psyche.

The child had a kind of beauty that caused even the Fox in his rationalism to speak of the divine. To Orual she brought a joy beyond anything she had dreamed of. Still a child herself, she became overnight a mother to the new baby. She found a peasant woman to suckle the child and spent days and nights rejoicing in the beauty and innocence of Psyche. It was not just physical beauty; it was beauty in all its aspects.

After the ominous scene at the birth of Psyche, the years passed in deceptive peace. The king ignored his daughters; he relied more and more on the Fox in his affairs but continued on his unconscious way. Redival started a secret love affair with an officer of the guard; the king discovered them, had the young man castrated on the spot, and sold him as a eunuch slave (again it is growing young manhood that is destroyed). He blamed the Fox and Orual and ordered them to keep Redival with them always. Then one day Redival struck Psyche, and Orual's fury was such that she almost strangled Redival and had to be pulled off by the Fox.

All of Redival's values centered on her physical appearance and on her attractiveness to men, so she can be seen as a projection of Orual's shadow side. Redival was fiercely jealous of Psyche. We see later that Orual, while despising Redival's vanity and meanness, displayed these buried qualities in herself. She could not stand the ugliness of her own face and covered it with a veil — thus showing her over-valuation of superficial appearances, her refusal to face herself as she was. Her love for Psyche was so jealous a love that when in danger of losing her she dealt Psyche a blow far more deadly than any Redival could have struck. For the moment the Fox's rational arguments and tolerance could simulate peace, but the storm was brewing.

The year after Orual's fight with her sister brought the first of the bad harvests and also the first sign that the common people were beginning to identify Psyche as a goddess. People were dying like flies, and the sick began to call for Psyche to heal them, having heard that she had once nursed the Fox back to health.

The people thronged to the gates of the palace, projecting onto Psyche the divine power of innocence to heal, and the king sent her out among the sick, for he would do anything to avert a threat to himself and his power. She gave of herself wholly, and her absolute devotion brought healing, as that kind of innocence always does, but she caught the fever herself, and later in the city more and more people died. Such mass projection, as usual, turned into its opposite, and Psyche was now called the Accursed and held to be the cause of the famine and sickness. And the people threatened the palace, demanding bread.

Meanwhile the priest of Ungit himself had become ill with the fever and was for long inactive, but Redival in her malice carried news of Psyche's "deification" to him. The priest recovered and met with the leaders of the people, who reported that the "Shadowbrute" had been seen in the land: the dark god who demanded human sacrifice. The priest was of the old religion, selflessly dedicated, and he heard the voice of Ungit, the voice of the unconscious, demanding "the great offering"—the sacrifice of the best and purest in the land to the god and goddess. In the temple of Ungit, he performed the ritual of the casting of lots, and the lot fell upon Psyche. She was to be given in marriage to the son of Ungit, the god who was known to many as the Shadowbrute—and to the very few as Eros. Tied to a tree far away on the holy mountain, dressed as a bride, she would be left alone for her brute lover to take.

Orual then offered to be the victim herself. The king contemptuously showed her ugly face in the mirror. She was no bride for a god. Orual's reaction seems much more noble than the king's. In terror, he resisted giving up his ego to the god. She in equal terror and blindness resisted giving up the person she most loves, which is the hardest of all sacrifices for a woman.

When Psyche herself embraces the idea of sacrifice, Orual can only feel hurt and humiliated. She feels Psyche ought to be crying on her shoulder in fear and distress; she is angry with her for this acceptance of necessity, for this faith in the meaning of her fate. Orual has always been the strong one on whom Psyche had relied for all her needs, physical and emotional. She cannot let go, cannot rejoice in her sister's new freedom, because *she* has not set her free.

Her last words to Psyche at that parting on the eve of the sacrifice were to haunt her throughout her life. Psyche had said in her intuitive wisdom, "All my life the god of the mountain has been wooing me. O look up once at least before the end and wish me joy. . . ." Orual replied, "I only see that you have never loved me. . . . It may well be you are going to the gods. You are becoming cruel like them." (p. 76)

This is no remote image. It is very near to us on many levels. Countless mothers in effect do say this to their children, wives to husbands, friends to friends, when faced with another's inner growth or with separation from those they love: "You have never loved me." Moreover the highly rational educated woman of today approaches her own inmost feminine wisdom in this spirit. She, like Orual, will not allow her Psyche to connect her with the gods, with the irrational eternal paradoxes of life, with the Fool beyond reason—she sees only the cruel negative side of the sacrifice—that "making holy" of her inmost self—and she panics at the threat it brings to her determination to save the world and all the people around her through her *own* newly acquired masculine reasoning and activity. The "oughts" and "shoulds" of the animus are in fact a passionate feminine possessiveness.

This then is the Great Offering—the giving of that which is most loved to the god who is as yet unknown. A woman makes this offering when she is willing to risk the loss of a relationship rather than make possessive demands on the person loved. A man makes it when he will sacrifice his achievements in the world rather than betray his deeper values. To both that offering brings the experience of Eros, the god of Love.

The sacrifice then is the offering to the god of that which is most loved; it is also the end of the ego's greed. Yet this is, of course, still too rational a definition. The oneness of the best and the worst remains a mystery—for only a mystery, in the true sense of the word, redeems. Indeed behind this mystery of the offering of the accursed and the blessed lies an even greater one—the mystery of the god who is both Love *and* the Shadowbrute. Most people, especially Christians, affirm the one truth without the other. Psyche, in the story, still young and untried, is able to look the whole reality in the face, however little she yet understands, and thereby she transcends all the rational wisdom of the Fox and accepts the unknown way she must tread: "To be eaten and to be married to the god might not be so different." For the Fox the gods are allegories of man's best qualities; for Orual they are all Shadowbrutes; therefore neither has access to the reconciling symbol of the "holy."

This paradox of the accursed and the blessed has been proclaimed in the rituals of all the religions of the world from the animal and human sacrifices of primitives to the symbolic sacrifice of the Mass; the victim had to be the best, the purest, and yet was also the scapegoat carrying the sins of the people; and always in these rituals the victim is eaten by the god and the priest, and often by all the worshippers. Thus the people were connected through the unconscious to the great paradox.

This thought returns us to our main theme—the responsibility of modern women, whose feminine values are squeezed out between the fine reasoning of the Fox and the mindless contempt of the king, to find their way back through conscious imaginative work to their intuitive awareness of the meaning of the sacrifice, and so to the "Kingdom of God."

Psyche is the innermost innocence and beauty of Orual's being—that which knows but does not fully know it knows. She exists in all of us, however deeply buried under layer upon layer of ego-centered greed and one-sided conventional opinions. She is sometimes altogether forgotten and rejected; but most often in people of good will she is recognized as a great, even *the* great value, but is totally misunderstood by the conscious mind. Often she becomes an ideal pursued in all the wrong directions—either projected into the sky or onto ideas of progress or onto the people whom we love. Like Orual we then grasp at these people or ideas with a smothering intensity, unconscious of the fact that we are at bottom holding desperately to the lost vision of our own childlike innocence. Fundamentally we are determined to cling to the *un*-conscious Paradise, to possess it forever, to refuse to the child within the agony of conscious growth. For Psyche to grow, she must be "sacrificed," and our projections must be torn away from us.

The priests then took Psyche in the ancient ritual and led her far away to the Holy Mountain and tied her to a tree. There she was abandoned. Meanwhile Orual lay for many days sick and raving in her bed. And in her dreams—a thing she could not understand—Psyche was the enemy; Psyche pursued her with jeers, and Psyche was leagued with Redival and looked like the king her father. None of this is surprising, for, as always, possessiveness contains its opposite—rejection. She had rejected her own truth, and that which we reject we meet always in dreams transformed into the enemy. Her dreams indeed foretold her life. Her double possessiveness and rejection of Psyche, and so of her own face, meant that her feminine instincts were blocked. She would find no man to love her as a woman. And so, like Tolkien's Eowyn, she took to herself the disguise of a man among men.

Still, she remained a woman, and, try as she would, she could not simply accept the Fox's reasonings as the only truth. So she fell into the most painful of all the tortures which spring from the split between the truths of the head and the truth of myth and imagination. She tried hard to believe the Fox, to live by his teaching, but, since intuitively she knew the gods existed, she saw them as wholly evil, imposing on man the most horrible cruelties just to indulge their whims. As in many women of the finest quality, the whole of her feminine unconscious turned negative.

The very day of the sacrifice, the wind changed, and very soon came rain. The plague was over; the kingdom was for the moment relieved from threats of invasion. For Orual this was a bitter joke on the part of the gods; for the Fox it was a most unfortunate coincidence tending to confirm the superstitions of the ignorant. For neither of them was there any meaning in this synchronicity; and if we refuse this meaning, we can know nothing of the inner rain whereby true grief and joy are united in a human heart. But in Orual, the woman, the refusal was a far more damaging thing than in the Fox, because of her woman's instinctive knowledge of the unconscious. She *knew* that meaning was there, but refused it.

Orual was now determined to go to the mountain and bury the bones of her sister, and she persuaded Bardia, the captain of the king's guard, to go with her. As they traveled through the great silence and beauty of the fresh green land after the rain, Orual was shocked to find that her heart was tempted to dance with delight.

They arrived at the tree of sacrifice; the chains, the iron girdle hung there, but there was no trace whatever of bones, rags of clothing, or any thing at all. No beast could have made so clean a sweep, no wandering shepherd would have had tools to release her. For Bardia it was no problem: the god had taken his beloved. For Orual it was a further horror undermining her rational thoughts.

They went on and down the unknown side of the mountain into the secret valley of the gods, and there on the other side of a river stood Psyche herself. Orual felt first terror, then overwhelming joy. Psyche was in rags but obviously radiant and glowing with well-being. She welcomed Orual with great delight and invited her across the stream. Together they sat and rejoiced—but only for a brief moment. Orual saw only the empty green valley, the stream, and Psyche in rags; but Psyche now told of the beautiful palace in which she lived, of the invisible hands that tended her and brought her food and wine, and of the god, who was the West Wind, who had lifted her out of her chains from the tree and brought her here, and of the greater god who had become her bridegroom, coming to lie with her at night. She was deeply happy, with only one flaw; the god had never shown himself to her. He came only in darkness and had forbidden her to make any attempt to see his face.

Orual listened in growing dismay. She could not see the palace; the wine Psyche offered her was nothing but water from the stream.

When the sisters realized this difference of viewpoints, there was a terrible moment. Enmity arose between them. We see two levels of truth at war, bitterly opposed to each other. Would Psyche succumb to the "nothing but" attitude? Or would she reject Orual's truth in fury? She did neither—for already she knew intuitively the god Eros, even though she had never seen him. She accepted her sister's lack of vision with compassion.

For Orual, Psyche was either mad or deluded. But nevertheless for a brief moment she admitted that there might be things in that other dimension that she could not see.

It was at this moment of near belief that she made, in Dante's words, "the great refusal." It is a moment that comes to us all—in a dream, in an outside event, or more often, in both, when we are offered a choice—a chance to accept that unknown reality which we cannot yet see. She even had a brief vision of the towers of the palace but dismissed them as shapes in the mist. Orual refused her chance; she rejected the truth of her own psyche. She tried to force Psyche to return with her to Glome, and then recognized with anger and resentment that she no longer had any control over her young sister.

In rage she returned alone to Glome, and, reinforced by the Fox's argument that there must be a coarse, brutal man who was seducing Psyche, she traveled once more to the valley taking with her a lamp. She was determined to persuade Psyche to disobey her lover, to light the lamp when he was asleep and look upon his face—sure that the credulous child would be disillusioned. In this plan she succeeded by a piece of blackmail so cruel that Psyche gave in. She plunged a dagger into her own arm and threatened to kill herself if Psyche would not consent. Psyche did so, but not weakly. So once more she became the great sacrifice—this time consciously for an individual person whom she loved. She was no longer the innocent victim playing a mythological role; she was a human being consciously embracing her fate.

Back across the stream Orual waited through the night. She saw the lamplight shine out across the water in the stillness—and then the calm was broken, a great voice sounded and she heard the terrible weeping of Psyche. Lightning flashed, thunder roared, and the storm tossed rocks high in the air and turned the river to a torrent. And then there came a still clear light and in it a figure with a face so beautiful and remote that she could not bear it for more than an instant; and she heard a voice "unmoved and sweet." "Now Psyche goes out in exile," it said. "Now she must hunger and thirst and tread hard roads. Those against whom I cannot fight must do their will upon her. You, woman, shall know yourself and your work. You also shall be Psyche." (pp. 173-74)

It is now that the paradoxes, incredible to the reasoning mind, of the way to individuation break through to us, and we begin to sense how without the worst in us, the best would remain in an unconscious state, unable to "know that she knows." Orual horribly betrayed her love for Psyche; but without that betrayal Psyche herself would have continued to exist in an infantile paradise of innocence remote from human life. We have to doubt the god, insist upon seeing him, refuse to continue in childish states of projection and vague awareness, no matter what it costs. Usually we must be forced to this disobedience by the worst in ourselves. "O happy fault" — the *felix culpa* of Eve. And yet, of course, the fault remains a fault and must be paid for in full.

Orual imagined that the god's words, "You also shall be Psyche," meant that she would be exiled from Glome and wander the world hungry and homeless, like her sister. In accord with her attitude to life, she could only conceive of being punished by the gods — she could only feel that unmoved remoteness of Eros as a cold cruelty and contempt. It was impossible for her to recognize and will the necessity of the bitter separation from her own soul and the terrible loneliness it brings. Thus she did not hear what the god had actually said. For in truth he had spoken no word of condemnation; beyond all emotion, he had uttered the greatest promise any woman can hear. "You shall know yourself and your work. You also shall be Psyche." Her unconscious mind then threw up an image which her conscious mind could not grasp. His voice, she said, was like "a bird singing on the branch above a hanged man." Those who can deeply experience the joy of the bird and the horror of the hanged man as one reality have said yes to life and to the "dreadful beauty" of the god. Orual was to do so much later in her old age, but in this moment she rejected both bird and hanged man and closed her eyes to that prophecy of individuation and promise of wholeness.

Back in Glome, having refused meaning and repressed her guilt, Orual now entered upon a new way of life. Bardia had realized when she drew a sword on him, as he stood guard outside Psyche's room on the night before the sacrifice, that she had a natural skill with a weapon. Seeing her terrible grief and apathy after Psyche's going, he offered to teach her to fence, knowing in his simple way the healing power of a physical exercise which required concentration of mind and discipline of body together. Thus Orual spent many hours with him and became a first class swordsman. It was a great turning point, for it meant she had consented to live, to fight, and to suffer. At the same time she began working hard for the king, together with the Fox, on all the business of government. Significantly, Redival—her shadow—had been consigned wholly to the care of Batta, the crude old nurse.

Thus Orual was cut off from every feminine influence or concern. Moreover she had done something crucial on her return from the hidden valley: she had put a veil over her face, which she was to wear in public for the rest of her life, until at the very end she consented to look upon her true face. Thus indeed do all women who plunge wholly into a masculine role. Having cut off their essential feminine individuality, they have no real "faces." Psyche is in exile, wandering, weeping in the unconscious, searching for Eros. Such women hide this weeping from themselves and others, but it troubles their dreams and, like Orual, they cannot shut it wholly away.

Nevertheless, now, as we read of Orual's new masculine life, we have the extraordinarily moving experience of realizing how the god's promise to Orual is at work within her. Deeper than her conscious attitudes, deeper than her bitter emotions, the true devotion and superb courage of her essential being are fundamentally in touch with the god, and so give meaning as yet unrealized to it all. She is learning to "know herself and her work" as he promised. To feel this in Orual is to realize with wonder and joy how mysterious are the patterns of our lives, in which the dark discordant threads are interwoven with those we see as bright and shining, to make at last a whole design; we recognize how blind we are in our cause-and-effect thinking, in our thin rationalistic attitudes.

The essential commitment to her love for Psyche was not shaken by her inner blindness, nor by her sin of possessiveness. She rejected that which she most loved because she could no longer own it; she rejected her own face, her own nature as woman, but she did not reject the gods themselves. She hated them; she dared to curse them for their inhumanity, which is quite a different thing from denial. It is indeed a terrific affirmation. In India, is has been said that those who hate God are considerably nearer to him than those who love him.

Orual's essential commitment, then, shows through in the courage with which she now set herself to do, as well as she knew how, the work that was laid upon her. She retreated behind a veil but she did not retreat from life. She thought she was working hard merely to smother her bitterness and grief, but the all-important thing was that she *worked*. She trained her body and her mind to take up the extremely heavy responsibilities that lay ahead of her. She had challenged the gods; she would not weakly cry out against her life as it was, but would make clear choices with such consciousness as she had. So her life became a story. She was not identical with her fate any longer; she related to it. The Fox's clear-sighted humanity was strong within her. She would stand on her human values and defy the gods.

The first sign of her new strength was that she was now able to face her father as an equal; never again would he strike and bully her. She felt herself equal to man on his own ground, but her contempt for herself as woman grew stronger.

As always when a new attitude emerges into consciousness, the outer events synchronized. Her father had a stroke and lay for some time mindless and helpless. At the same moment the old priest was known to be mortally ill and the next priest took over. Orual discovered in herself her own strong masculine authority and stepped into her father's place. She astonished Bardia and the Fox by her wise judgment and her sudden independence.

It was at this juncture that Trunia the young prince of Phars, a neighboring kingdom, took refuge at the court from the armies of his elder brother. He too was a man of tolerance and humanity, fighting to replace the old barbarism. Argan, his brother, had invaded Glome demanding the return of Trunia, and Glome, still weakened by the recent famine and plague, could not risk war. Yet to give up Trunia would equally have subjected Glome to the power of Argan, and, what was perhaps more important for Orual—still inwardly a woman as was Eowyn—it would have been an unforgivable personal betrayal. So she sent a personal challenge to Argan, proposing a duel with a champion from Glome to decide the issue. She herself would fight this duel. Bardia had told her that as a swordsman she surpassed even himself.

It was at the moment of her preparation for the fight that the king and the old priest both died. Orual was now queen, and Arnom, the new priest, was a man far more influenced by the wisdom of the Greeks, far less close to the unconscious than his predecessor. The new era was on the threshold, but all would disappear in a new barbarism if Argan were not defeated.

Orual confronted the enemy in very much the same state of mind as Eowyn. She would do her utmost to defeat the dark threat to Trunia and to her world but she half-hoped she would herself be killed — for to the woman without contact with her femininity life is a weary desert. She fought and Argan was killed. Both kingdoms now had new rulers who would bring prosperity and peace to their lands in the following years.

Once again here is a woman on whose sword depended the future of her civilization. Like Eowyn, Orual wields her sword in a personal encounter which is at the same time a blow at the roots of despair. Again it has the quality of a ritual. It is also, like Eowyn's, a fight to save a single person. Unlike Eowyn, Orual wielded her sword in the wars of her country for many years after the duel, but she herself said that the only fight in which her sword achieved anything was on the one occasion when Bardia's life was in danger and she saved him. So she remained a woman at heart, and, delude herself as she might, it was basically in the cause of her love and concern for persons that she used it.

Working for many years to make sure that her victory over Argan and the forces he represented would bear fruit, Orual continued magnificently to use the sword of her masculine discrimination and authority to ensure the welfare of her people. Nevertheless because, unlike Eowyn, she continued to delude herself, continued to despise her womanhood and to refuse Psyche to the god, the devouring side of the goddess took over her emotional life. Only at the end would she realize the terrible things she had unconsciously done to the people she most loved — not only to Psyche herself, but to Bardia, to the Fox, and to Redival.

All this is made plain in the second part of the book. But there is another vital element in Orual's journey before her awakening — the experience of love and desire for a man. From the time of her first fencing lessons, Orual had realized that Bardia thought of her more and more as though she was a man—and this both grieved and pleased her. What she did not at first realize was that as a woman she was falling deeply in love with him. Some women have an extraordinary capacity for repressing this fact when they know that their love will not be returned. In Orual the full awareness of it did not break through until the moment when after her victory in the duel, Bardia did not stay for the banquet but asked to go home as his wife was in labor, and he used the words, "Queen, the day's work is over. You'll not need me now." "I understood," said Orual, "in that moment all my father's rages." But she was not her father; she controlled her rage and was gracious. Bardia would never know what he had done to her by those words. She looked the fact in the face that she was simply "his work"—a queen, yes, but not a human woman to him, and she knew her love for him and her terrible jealousy of his wife.

This happened on the very day on which, of all others, she had been acclaimed as a hero in an exclusively masculine field of activity. She had conquered with a sword. And now, as though her unconscious would not tolerate this, she was pierced through and through as a woman by her love for Bardia. She was now to discover the agony of instinctive desire, an experience without which no man or woman can reach maturity. It is well to affirm here that, contrary to popular belief, the physical consummation of such desire is not essential to maturity. The instincts may sometimes be even more deeply experienced without that consummation, as Orual's story makes clear.

On that night of achievement and bitterness she drank too much wine at the banquet and here is her account of how she felt when she went to her lonely bed:

> My double loneliness, for Bardia, for Psyche. Not separable. The picture, the impossible fool's dream, was that all should have been different from the very beginning and he would have been my husband and Psyche our daughter. Then I would have been in labor . . . with Psyche . . . and to me he would have been coming home. But now I discovered the wonderful power of wine . . . not at all that it blotted out these sorrows—but that it made them seem glorious and noble, like sad music, and I somehow great and reverend for feeling them. I was a great, sad queen in a song. I did not check the big tears that rose in my eyes. I enjoyed them. (p. 224)

These last sentences reveal the negative side of the realization of one's life as a story. It is a pitfall few can avoid at one time or another. We are inflated by our own suffering and the ego identifies then with the victim of "the sacrifice." There are people who positively insist on being victims, over and over again.

Orual goes on to tell us how she heard the chains swinging in the well, the sound of which always brought to her the illusion of Psyche crying, cold and hungry, outside. Her love for Bardia and for Psyche are in fact manifestations of one love, but in her present state they are simply mixed—"not separable"—and therefore, of course, very definitely not in harmony, and this is so because Orual herself is not a woman *united* to the masculine spirit within her. She is an undifferentiated man-woman. She wants Bardia to love her as a woman, Psyche to love her as a man; and in the midst of all this her personal emotions become unendurable. How powerful is the symbolism of the chains creaking in the well—the sound of Psyche weeping which she cannot shut out! The chains are an image which brings to mind the essential bondage of the commitment of real love through which a woman draws up the water of the unconscious for man. They are creaking unused in the winds of Orual's spirit, and, meanwhile, her true psyche weeps as she searches for the god. For love brings us freedom only when we accept its binding nature: "I locked up Orual or laid her asleep as best I could somewhere deep down inside me; she lay curled there. It was like being with child, but reversed; the thing I carried in me grew slowly smaller and less alive." (p. 226)

The Fox grew old and died. Orual had freed him before her encounter with Argan, and she never allowed herself to realize how great was the sacrifice he had made for her sake when he decided to stay in Glome and not return to his beloved Greece. His service to her had been beyond price, but in his extreme old age his thinking grew confused; his intellect gave way to unclear images and to too much talk. It is indeed what happens to over-rational thinking, especially that of the animus in women.

Meanwhile the queen locked away her memory of the god she had heard in the valley, and she thought she had almost succeeded in substituting the Fox's philosophy for all concern with the gods. Nevertheless she had to build thick stone walls around the well in the courtyard with the creaking chains, in order to shut out the weeping of Psyche.

She had two strengths, she said, in her queenship. The first was the wisdom of her two councilors, the Fox and Bardia, and the fact that they treated her like a man; her second was her veil. For this gave her an aura of mystery which carried great power. People began to notice the beauty of her voice and her figure, and to tell all sorts of stories about what lay behind the veil. It is well for us to think of how often in daily living we unconsciously use this hiding of our identity behind a veil as a kind of power mechanism. It is a different thing from the persona. When we retire behind a veil we deliberately hide our true faces, our essential attitudes and values. The persona is a necessary shield between a person and the world. At best it expresses a person's truth, while protecting him from invasion; at worst, it is a collective personality which takes over his truth or is used by him to deceive. A veil offers nothing in place of the truth. Hence its power to incur projections.

Through the years Orual necessarily met Ansit, Bardia's wife, from time to time, and jealousy tortured her. She tried to comfort herself with her knowledge of being part of his man's life, but it did not ease her; neither did the thought of Bardia's simple, whole-hearted devotion to both queen and wife. She wrote, "This is what it is to be a man. The one sin the gods never forgive us is that of being born woman." (p. 233) How appalling a point of view this sounds to a modern woman! Yet in fact it is a deeply repressed belief which is at the root of the behavior of so many women whose values have turned masculine at the expense of their womanhood.

After the death of the Fox, Orual was restless. There was peace and prosperity in the kingdom and she decided to go on a journey through her own and neighboring lands, after which she hoped that she and Bardia could rest more and delegate the work. It was on the way back from this outer journey that the event happened which precipitated her writing her book, her complaint against the gods, and so started her inner journey to self-knowledge.

She came one day upon a little temple in the woods with a small wooden statue of a goddess whose face was covered with a veil. It was cool, clean, and light in the temple. The priest, a quiet old man, came to speak to her and she asked about the goddess. He replied that she was a very young goddess whose name was Istra. And he told her then the sacred story of Psyche and Eros, as it has been told through the centuries. As Orual listened to her own story, as she thought, she grew more and more angry at what she called the half-truths. Most of all she exclaimed against the statement that the two ugly sisters in the story had *seen* the palace in the valley. "But why did she—they— want to separate her from the god, if they had seen the palace?" They wanted, said the priest, to destroy her *because* they had seen the palace and were jealous. Instantly Orual resolved to write her book. She would tell the real story and expose the lie that she had seen the palace. She could shut out the gods no longer; she would face them and tell the truth about the cruelty: "I could never be at peace again until I had written my charge against the gods. It burned me from within. It quickened; I was with book, as a woman is with child." (p. 247) Through her book, the child which was her true self was conceived and would in due time come to birth and maturity.

A dream came to her at this time. It reproduced the first task of Psyche in the myth—the sorting of the seeds. In it she sat before an immense pile of mixed seeds which must be sorted before morning. Failure would bring disaster, and she knew in her dream that success was humanly impossible. Near despair, she nevertheless set to work—and then in her dream she saw herself as a tiny ant carrying a seed on her back and staggering under the weight of it. Not until the end was she to realize that it was the work of the ants which enabled Psyche to succeed.

Her book was, of course, the sorting of the seeds—the immensely painful task of discrimination, of complete honesty, as far as she was capable of it, about the thoughts, feelings, and actions of her life. It is the first necessity of the way to consciousness for women.

Thus the first part of her book was written; only after that came the brief fifty pages in which Orual's transformation breaks through into her life. The change begins with the first real encounter on equal terms that she had ever had in her life with a truly feminine woman.

Bardia was dead. He had been sick for a while, but it seemed not a serious thing except that he had no strength to rally from it and gradually weakened and died. Orual, overwhelmed with grief, went to visit Ansit, Bardia's widow, with bitter jealousy in her heart, but trying to accept the other's sorrow. She spoke to Ansit of Bardia's seemingly light sickness, and then the formalities between them crumbled. Ansit told of her bitterness—of how Bardia's strength had been slowly eaten away by the weight of the responsibilities which the queen had laid upon him, by the demands upon his time and attention year after year, by day and by night. And she, Ansit, had waited for the short times he could spend at home, had watched his weariness, his unflinching loyalty to the queen. At first Orual defended herself. Ansit has had all—husband, children—she nothing. "I'll not deny it," said Ansit. "I had what you left of him."

At this Orual lifted her veil. It was a turning point in her life. She stood exposed and face to face with the woman who was her enemy. "Are you jealous of this?" she asked; and Ansit looking into Orual's true face, into her eyes, recognized for a moment the love and suffering there. "You loved him. You've suffered, too." They wept for a few blessed moments in each others' arms.

The moment could not last. Each regressed into her own shadow side again; Orual resumed her veil, Ansit her bitterness. Orual spoke again. "You made me little better than the Lord Bardia's murderer. . . . did you believe what you said?"

"Believe? I do not believe, I know that your queenship drank up his blood year by year and ate out his life." Ansit still differentiates between the suffering woman and the queen.

Orual had succeeded all too well in her aim after her rejection of Psyche and the god—her aim which was, as she had written it, "to build up more and more that strength, hard and joyless, which had come to me when I heard the god's sentence; by learning, fighting, and laboring, to drive all the woman out of me." The natural joy in being a woman, repressed into the unconscious, drinks the blood, eats the life out of those around such a woman.

Ansit then says, "Oh, Queen Orual, I begin to think you know nothing of love. Or no; I'll not say that. Yours is Queen's love, not commoners'. Perhaps you who spring from the gods love like the gods. Like the Shadowbrute. They say the loving and the devouring are all one, don't they?" (pp. 264-65)

Here is the great irony! Orual's whole adult life had been lived in bitter rebellion against just those words spoken by Psyche before her sacrifice: "To be eaten and to be married to the god might not be so different." Orual had cried out in fury that the love of the gods was nothing but horrible cruelty. And now out of the mouth of the human woman whom Bardia had loved came the same words applied to her own love. She herself is the one who has loved with the cruelty of the gods. Because she was unable to accept that the vision of Eros in his true form included the Shadowbrute, the devouring and the being devoured, she was doomed to live out these things unconsciously, split off from her conscious love. She would have bitterly rejected the words of St. Ignatius of Antioch on the way to the arena. "Let me be ground by the teeth of the wild beasts that I may be found a true bread." For St. Ignatius the beast was as true a manifestation of the divine as the angel. He had his levels clear. A terrible cruelty on one level did not destroy for him the beauty of the bird singing beside the hanged man.

Orual has come to her second great moment of choice. Ansit, though mature where Orual was unconscious, was weak where Orual was strong. She fell into a cruel personal bitterness, and her last words to Orual were, "You're full fed. Gorged with other men's lives, women's too: Bardia's, mine, the Fox's, your sisters'—both your sisters." Orual, though filled with a blinding fury in which she, the queen, could have delivered Ansit over to torture and death, in reprisal, did not give in to her instinctual rage. Her long discipline and her love of human justice bore fruit; but even these things would not have been enough, if she had not been touched at last by that other dimension of truth which she had so often rejected. For the first time she was able to say, "Something (if it was the gods, I bless their name) made me unable to do this"—and in a few days' time she knew "those divine Surgeons had me tied down and were at work. . . . it was all true—truer than Ansit could know."

Ansit's words were, of course, only one side of the double truth, but because Orual had refused the knowledge of it for so long she had to experience it first as the only truth. In the hours and nights that followed she faced the horror of looking on that which she had called love and seeing only its other face—the hatred which had poisoned it from first to last.

During the long process of the purging of love we all must come to know the empty desert which accompanies the death of a craving which we recognize at last for what it is. How much in all our loves is a demand to be fed by other people's lives—not an acceptance of food freely given? Those men and women who give their lives consciously to be "eaten" without thought of return are indeed fed by the god within, but Orual was gorged and starving.

That which came to her in one stark moment of truth comes more often to us in smaller moments of insight interspersed with regressions; for we cannot at first stand the sense of nothingness for long, and we hasten to fill it with new cravings. In Orual's story, however, we see the life-long process with great clarity, condensed into a few years, or months, perhaps, at the end of her life. She has become, she says, "a gap"—and only in that gap can the divine surgeons do their work. It is important to realize the quality of her disillusionment, since it is so very easy for us to confuse the real experience with the absolutely opposite experience of self-disgust which can delude us by simulating the emptiness. The latter merely drives us into a despairing guilt which is the opposite face of our ego pride. Self-justification and escape inevitably follow.

The three words which tell us that Orual has truly accepted the bitter truth are in parenthesis. "My love for Bardia (not Bardia himself) had become to me a sickening thing." "Not Bardia himself." The self-disgust which simulates the true facing of the shadow never brings such a clear distinction between the craving and the thing craved for, however much we may cover up this fact—"It is all my fault" we say, usually meaning just the opposite. The three words tell us that Orual for the first time is seeing Bardia as separate from herself—as his own man, not as her possession, and it is this that guarantees her honesty and gives her strength to stay still in the emptiness.

The shock which awakened Orual had come from an outer event, and, because she accepted this bitter fact with the whole of herself as far as she yet knew that self, the drama now moves into the inner world and the gods began to speak to her "face to face" in a series of great dreams and visions which completed her life and showed her the vision of immortality. She began to recognize not simply facts, but to know the truth which comes only with the awakening of the creative imagination.

We, for the most part, experience the shocks and visions alternately, working for long years outwardly and inwardly to recognize the myth and the meaning. Yet surely it often happens in Orual's way, perhaps more frequently than we realize. She had spent most of the years of her life in an inner hell of her own making, and she was quite unaware of the purgation which she passed through at the same time, nor did she realize the real significance of her book. The breakthrough of vision, of consciousness, which now came to her before her death took place in the space of a very few weeks. The timing is after all not important, for life is a circle, a sphere, and will be known as such only when we have wholly accepted the straight lines of time and mortality.

The process of individuation was now forcing itself up into Orual's consciousness. She felt stripped of everything, but still she clung desperately to the last fortress of her egocentricity. She asserted vehemently that she had truly loved Psyche, that in this one thing she had been blameless, had suffered terrible injustice from the gods. We each have a last fortress of this kind—"in this one thing at least," we tell ourselves, "I have been wholly blameless, all good." Over and over again the cry is heard, "Why do I make no progress when I long so sincerely to grow?" The answer of course is that the longing is still, like Orual's, a demand to possess. There is no progress *towards* wholeness—only a preparation for death and rebirth.

We come now to a final great vision in which Orual is brought to the ultimate stripping—to the death before death in which at last she is unmade and recreated. The god's prophecy is about to be fulfilled: she will know herself as Psyche while at the same time she remains uniquely and forever Orual.

She knew with certainty that the vision was not a dream. It included her conscious self, like the "active imagination" of Jung's terminology. It began with her setting forth over a parched desert, knowing she must find the water of death and bring it to Ungit. Orual thought she was carrying a bowl as she labored on for, it seemed, hundreds of years, her throat parched with terrible thirst. Sometimes the sand rose over her ankles and all the time the pitiless sun beat down from exactly overhead so that she cast no shadow; there were no shadows at all. It is a terrifying image of the life of consciousness cut off entirely from the unconscious, from the darkness and mystery of life, from the waters which bring death and healing, but Orual was at last truly searching for the waters though still unaware of their meaning or of the nature of her true goal. Her thirst was now so desperate that she would drink of any water, however bitter; she longed simply for relief from the terrible sunlight. But she came only to a new horror, to unscalable mountains crawling with serpents and scorpions, and in the heart of these mountains, she knew, lay the well of water that she sought.

She had come to the end of any possible effort, sitting on the burning sands. She was at the meeting place of opposites, for the cold-blooded instinctive poison of snake and scorpion is at the opposite pole from the burning aridity of one-sided intellect. There came now a shadow in the sky, and Orual prayed that it might be a cloud, a blessed cloud bringing rain. But it was not. Then, "though the terrible light seemed to bore through my eyeballs into my brain," she saw that the small dark shape was an eagle, a great eagle of the gods, and it came to rest beside her.

To remember the symbolism of the eagle at this point greatly enhances the impact of the vision. The eagle is the messenger of the gods; he is an image of the true spirit soaring above the earth, yet resting upon it, and casting a blessed shadow. He redeems from the autonomous intellect, from the pride of man's spirit cut off from the shadows and from the waters of the unconscious. For Charles Williams, Tolkien and Lewis, all three, the eagle was the savior in man's extremity of need.

He comes to each one, it seems, only when every possible effort of which the ego is capable has been made. It was he who took Psyche's bowl, in the myth, when she was about to despair, and brought to her the water of death. To Orual he now came at last, but he could bring no water because, as she now discovered to her horror, she carried in her hands not a bowl but a book — the book in which she had written her complaint against the gods.

All Orual's hopes fell in ruins about her. Yet in reading what follows we feel an extraordinary excitement. Far from rebuking her and casting her away the great bird cried out as it were in joy. "She's come at last. . . . the woman who has a complaint against the gods." The spirit in a woman such as Orual, who has lived by the masculine principle, cannot bring her the water she seeks, but nevertheless, because of her long devotion and suffering he can and does lead her to the experience through which she will find her bowl, her womanhood, again. It is as though the masculine spirit itself rejoices in the coming of this new woman to her great moment.

At the eagle's voice the souls of the dead rise out of the mountain to greet her. They are buried images of her ancestors, her heritage, the gathered experiences of humanity itself: "Here is the woman. Bring her in. Bring her into court. . . . To the judge, to the judge." She cannot yet find the water, but she who has loved and served human justice has found the place of ultimate justice.

The great image of the eagle in Dante symbolized above all else divine justice. In the great eagle of souls in the Heaven of Jupiter, all speak with one voice but the voice proceeds not from a collective "we" but from a thousand "I's" in the final unity of judgment which is not a choice between this and that but a recognition of the whole.

Justice is the greatest manifestation of the Logos principle on earth, and the hardest thing for the feminine psyche to learn. Orual sought it with all the energies of her mind and heart, and in doing so exclusively she lost her feminine instinctive roots, and therefore her vision of the nature of the divine. In this moment of Orual's story when we hear the eagle's glad cry, "She's come. . . . the woman who has a complaint against the gods," we realize that what such a woman has sought with the devotion of her whole being she finds (for what we wholly seek we inevitably find); and that when she recognizes and accepts its logic in her own life at last, it will be to her the opening of the door to all that she has rejected. She will know the true nature of mercy and love.

Orual was seized upon by many hands, pushing her, lifting her towards a great hole in the heart of the mountain. She was plunged into the cold and dark out of the burning light and found herself alone, standing on a rock, while around her in a grey light a sea of faces—thousands upon thousands of the souls of the dead—stretched away out of her sight. Near her feet were the faces of her own dead—the Fox, her father, Batta, Argan—and far away there was a veiled figure cloaked in black (whether male or female she could not tell) sitting on a rock raised above the others. It was the judge; and he spoke saying, "Uncover her." Hands reached up and stripped off her veil and every stitch of clothing, leaving her old body and her Ungit face exposed to the vast concourse of souls. Only her book remained in her hand, and it was small and tattered—not at all like the great book she felt she had written. "No thread to cover me, no bowl in my hand to hold the water of death, only my book."

"Read your complaint," said the judge. Another agonizing and final choice was before her, and she almost yielded to the last temptation. Seeing the poor shabby thing she held, she thought she would fling it down and trample on it—tell them her true work had been stolen. And as she unrolled the parchment and saw the mean and vile scribble—a writing so unlike her own—she wanted desperately to repudiate her work, to deny that it was truly hers and refuse to read it.

It is a moment of great danger. When the time comes that we are stripped to the bone and suddenly it appears to us how poor and shabby is the work we have done into which we have poured all that we thought best and purest in us, then indeed we may feel an overwhelming temptation to betray our own truth. We cannot stand the exposure of our despicable pride and so we long to deny responsibility for our own story for what we are, good or bad, right or wrong.

"Whatever they do to me, I will never read out this stuff," thought Orual. "But already I heard myself reading it." She was ready in her depths to accept the whole truth in spite of shame and disillusionment, ready to let go of her last fortress of pride and possessiveness.

So she laid bare the whole of her complaint against the gods—the ultimate protest of human rationality and ugly possessive love:

> You'll say I was jealous. Jealous of Psyche? Not while she was mine. If you'd gone the other way to work—if it was my eyes you had opened— you'd soon have seen how I would have shown her and told her and taught her and led her up to my level. . . . There should be no gods at all, there's our misery and bitter wrong. . . . *We want to be our own.*[italics added] I was my own and Psyche was mine and no one else had any right to her. Oh, you'll say you took her away into bliss and joy such as I could never have given her, and I ought to have been glad of it for her sake. Why? What should I care for some horrible, new happiness which I hadn't given her and which separated her from me? Do you think I wanted her to be happy, that way? . . . She was mine. *Mine.* . . . (pp. 291-92)

"Enough," said the judge at last. Silence fell; and Orual knew that she had been reading the same thing over and over again. Suddenly she heard her voice strange to her ears: "There was given to me a certainty that this, at last, was my own voice." All projection was at an end. Never again could blame be laid on any one, any circumstance, any god. The silence was long and profound. At last the judge spoke. "Are you answered?" "Yes," said Orual.

We have arrived at the last chapter. It begins with the words I quoted at the beginning: "The complaint was the answer. To have heard myself making it was to be answered." This is the inexorable justice of the god. Our thinking may long have outgrown the pro-

jected image of an avenging god meting out rewards and punish-
ments from his judgment seat; and yet the attitude remains in the
unconscious as powerful as ever, because our thinking has not encompassed the true nature of justice. To be in hell is to refuse the
tension of the opposites and therefore all self-knowledge; to be in
purgatory is to accept that tension and to enter the long struggle for
the knowledge of who we are, a struggle which involves the passionate integrity whereby we stand by our own truth even against the
gods on whatever level of awareness we may be. The emergence from
purgatory into the heaven of wholeness will come, as it did to Statius
in the *Divine Comedy*, and as it came to Orual in the place of judgment, when we have suffered the tension long enough and deeply
enough to find ourselves suddenly through and beyond it as we hear
and accept our own voices, our own faces, exactly as they are.

Orual did not yet know what had happened. It was no great
emotional experience of new insight. She knew only that her complaint was finally answered because she had at last *heard* it. Still with
her rational mind she expected judgment and punishment—but *this*
trial was over. She had accused the gods and was answered. She had
been the plaintiff; it remained, she thought, for the gods to accuse
her, for she was still unaware of the nature of the divine mercy.

This then is the woman's test: to go straight to the goal of her spirit
against all the deepest feminine instincts. The crucial test of the man
is exactly the opposite. Will he respond to the promptings of the
heart and turn aside from his goals to help another in need? If he
does not do so he is lost. It is not, however, so simple an issue for
modern men and women half way to the realization of the contrasexual principle in themselves. Each has a double test, for the animus
must learn compassion and the anima must find strength to emerge
from the moods which so easily turn the man aside from his way.
Orual understood now how she herself, the woman who refused the
way of all women and who mistook the meaning of the new masculine strength she felt in herself, had almost wrecked Psyche's
chance of wholeness. Her animus had set for her a rational, opinio-
nated goal and held to it, shutting out compassion but demanding it
from others. Nevertheless deep down in her unconscious her true
feminine psyche was true to her way because, no matter how distorted, Orual's love was a true love at its root, and her quest was for
truth at all costs.

Orual had at last understood the whole of Psyche's myth and had seen the pattern of her own life within it. She accepted every last shred of responsibility for her own story and it was almost time now for her final realization.

But first, there is another aspect here which raises a deep question. In almost all fairy stories and novels of the Christian era until very recent times, the transforming love in human beings has been heterosexual. For two thousand years our one-sided drive for ego-consciousness and the resultant eclipse of the feminine has caused the love of man for man, which presupposes a feminine element in the male, to be regarded as criminal, while the love of woman for woman has been for the most part simply ignored as insignificant. When Radclyffe Hall wrote *The Well of Loneliness* at the beginning of the twentieth century, the collective reaction of horror was extreme. We may find this strange today, when these things are openly discussed, and novels such as those of Mary Renault are accorded the high praise they deserve. But free intellectual discussion and even the creative imagination of the few are very far from the perception of meaning by the general public. There is a long way to go before love—love, not lust—between persons of the same sex is accepted and respected to the same degree as heterosexual love. Any love, for anyone, if it goes deep enough may be the way to transformation. The extraordinary interest of Lewis' myth in this context lies in the fact that Orual is a woman with normal heterosexual instincts, whose deepest love is nevertheless given to a woman. Though she truly loves and desires Bardia, Psyche is her heart's beloved. Tentatively I would ask whether this does not point to a little-recognized inner truth for women of today who are seeking individuation.

Any person of insight would surely agree that if a woman or a man is unable to relate satisfactorily to others of the same sex, it is proof of a state of undifferentiated consciousness. But the love of Orual for Psyche points at something more powerful than the capacity for this kind of relatedness. It is *through* her love for a woman that she finds at last the reconciling symbol and is united to the god.

It is, I believe, true that for a woman who has a strong androgynous nature, her love for another woman can sometimes lift her to greater heights and plunge her into deeper pain than her love for a man. There is certainly no question about this in the case of Orual's two great loves. It can be, in fact, a deeply religious experience when the symbolic meaning breaks through.

It is easy to explain these things in terms of mother and father complexes and so on, and end up by killing the potential beauty of such relationships. The emergence of the contrasexual element in both men and women in this age will increasingly mean that a maturing person will know love for both sexes. The experience of love and desire between persons of the same sex need not necessarily include a physical outlet—indeed the release of tension on the physical level, since it is symbolically devoid of potential creativity, may destroy the meaning of the experience in such relationships. As with all new shoots of consciousness, however, the dangers of misunderstanding and misplacement of levels are very great. These things belong to the secret life of the individual in whom, through love—to repeat Jung's words—"the fire of suffering" will melt those "incompatible substances, the male and the female," until the goal of life is known in the *hierosgamos* of Psyche, the human being, and Eros, the god.

I have never felt altogether at ease with the statement we so often read in Jungian books that the symbol of the Self appears to us usually as someone of our own sex. It can be misleading. Psyche in the story is not in herself a symbol of the Self even at the end; neither is Eros. God though he is, he is still under the domination of the mother—imprisoned in the unconscious—until the human Psyche has done her part. Then *he* becomes incarnate and *she* is lifted up to the divine. The true symbol of the Self is always a union of opposites. It is clearer perhaps to say that we may first glimpse the Self through an androgynous image of our own sex. Therefore, while we project the image of the animus or anima onto the opposite sex, we are apt to project the Self onto our own, and it is this that makes love for someone of our own sex extremely dangerous as well as an intensely creative opportunity. On the one hand it can become auto-eroticism and lead to a deadly kind of possession through identification with the archetype—a thing which kills all true human feeling; on the other it can become the experience which leads through the purging of our possessiveness to the vision of the *hierosgamos*.

Orual's love for Psyche, both the danger, which almost destroyed her, and the transformation which it wrought in her, are clear before us in unforgettable images. Hard as was her awakening to the greed of her love for Bardia, it was far harder for her to let go of her possessive love for Psyche, who was an image of her very self.

There is, however, a great difference between the love of a woman for a woman and that of a man for a man, a difference which derives first from the mystery of the mother-daughter relationship, as with Demeter and Kore, and second from the differing natures of the animus and the anima. Irene de Castillejo has written of this last fact, which is too little stressed in Jungian thought. She points out that the animus is very different in its function from the anima, in that the anima *is* in a sense his experience of the feminine unconscious, whereas the animus is the image who enables a woman to differentiate herself *from* the eternally feminine unconscious. In its negative form, of course, the animus cuts the woman off from this, while the negative anima simply drags a man into it. The point is that the inspiration, the numinous ground of the unconscious to which the masculine gives form, in either man or woman, is feminine.

May Sarton, in her novel *Mrs. Stevens Hears the Mermaids Singing,* has written of this same thing. Mrs. Stevens is an old woman who is a well known poet. In the book she is interviewed by a young man and woman for the press, and she looks back over her whole life. As she does so she realizes that, much as she has owed to the men she has loved, the inspiration of her creative spirit did not come from them. It sprang rather from her passionate loves for a few women, from her childhood onwards, and from the suffering and joy that such loving brought her. The Muses, she rightly concludes, are feminine not only for men but for women also. Sappho, that very great woman poet, was likewise a lover of women.

A woman must hear the mermaids' song from the sea, if she is to make contact with her creative imagination. When she has heard it, then the work of the animus begins — the hard work of bringing to focus, defining, giving expression to that song from her feminine depths.

We have now reached the moment in Orual's story when she is about to meet her beloved again:

Now I knew that she was a goddess indeed. Her hands burned me (a painless burning) when they met mine. The air that came from her clothes and limbs and hair was wild and sweet; youth seemed to come into my breast as I breathed it. And yet . . . with all this, even because of all this, she was the old Psyche still; a thousand times more her very self than she had been before the Offering. For all that had then but flashed out in a glance or a gesture, all that one meant most when one spoke her name, was now wholly present, not to be gathered up from hints nor in shreds, not some of it in one moment and some in another. Goddess? I had never seen a real woman before. (p. 306)

Orual was silent in the fullness of her joy. But it was not the end: "Suddenly . . . I knew that all this had been only a preparation. Some far greater matter was upon us." She heard again unseen voices. "He is coming," they said. "The god is coming into his house. The god comes to judge Orual."

No joy without terror; no beauty without dread—Orual knew it now as the arrows of the god pierced her through and through. She was standing beside Psyche at the edge of the water, the water transfigured by fire. She cast down her eyes and saw—not her old ugly face beside Psyche's beauty, as in the old king's mirror. She saw in the mirror of the water of life and death two Psyches, both "beautiful beyond all imagining"—though it no longer mattered in those terms—the same and yet not the same, for still, though "unmade" and recreated, still she was Orual.

Then came the great voice once more. "You also are Psyche," it said. This was the final judgment. This time it was no distant promise; it was eternal reality, and as she heard it Orual had courage to raise her eyes and she saw—gloriously and finally she saw—no god and no pillared court but her own garden and her own book in her human hand, the simple daily realities of her life, transformed now by the union of Psyche with the god.

Orual knew that she was very near to her physical death and was content. Her circle was complete. Touchingly she wondered why those around her should weep for her when she had done so little to give them cause to love her. She died as she wrote the last sentence of her story.

There is a brief epilogue written by Arnom, the priest: "This book was all written by Queen Orual of Glome, who was the most wise, just, valiant, fortunate and merciful of all the princes known in our parts of the world." She was indeed a great prince in spirit, and in the end a great and simple human woman, whole and complete.

Chapter   Five

Dindrane

C.G. JUNG, WRITING of archetypes dormant in the unconscious, says that they are activated when one-sided attitudes prevalent at a particular time and place are in urgent need of a
compensatory image. By the end of the first millennium of the Christian era, the rejection of the body, of the feminine, of matter itself,
had reached a peak. There were some who actually believed that the
material world was a creation of the Devil, and earlier there had even
been an unsuccessful movement within Christianity denying that
women had souls. In a letter written in 1953, Jung said that the
twelfth and early thirteenth centuries saw "the beginning of Latin
alchemy and of the natural sciences and also of a feminine religious
symbol, the Holy Grail."[1]

The Grail itself is indeed a supreme symbol of the lost values; for
without the vessel of the feminine all the "ten thousand things" must
exist in a state of unrelatedness to each other — a chaos without
meaning. The Grail is the cup from which each individual life receives its essential food and drink: it is the chalice containing the
mystery of blood and spirit: it is a maternal womb, the body of Mary
herself. Without a vessel no transformation on any level can take
place — no cooking of ingredients in a kitchen, no chemical experiments or alchemical search for "gold," no *metanoia* in a human soul,
no incarnation of the Word to dwell among us.

Almost another millennium has passed since the Grail legends
rose from the unconscious, and their vitality has never faded. Again
and again poets and storytellers have breathed new life into them —
have, indeed, re-created them. The need for the affirmation of the
feminine has not lessened since the twelfth century and has become
particularly insistent in our own technological age.

The many legends surrounding the Grail image are for the most
part concerned with the adventures of the knights, of the men who
seek to find its meaning in their own souls. But the liberation of

73

woman and the fight to establish her equality with men in hitherto masculine fields of work and thought has meant that she too has great need of a much more conscious awareness of the symbols of her own deepest feminine roots. Many women today are even contemptuous of the nature of the feminine being—of that which contains and nurtures and is still, which responds to people and things without any will to use or manipulate them, which guards in silence the mystery of life. If women do not themselves take up the quest of the Grail within, it is certain that their new-found equality in the masculine sphere will lose its meaning and become another "wasteland." A great hope for the future lies in the fact that so many individual women are now entering upon that quest.

Charles Williams, who died in 1945, was one of the great re-creators of the Grail myth in our century. His Arthurian poems are not easy to read—they are, indeed, often so obscure that even C. S. Lewis, his friend, who wrote a commentary on them,[2] had occasionally to admit defeat, but the more often one returns to them, the more vividly they speak to the imagination, particularly through the poet's profound insight into the fundamental nature of woman; and we are left with shining and unforgettable images.

Before discussing two of these poems, "Taliessin in the Rose Garden" (from *The Region of the Summer Stars*, Oxford University Press, 1950) and "The Last Voyage" (*Taliessin Through Logres*, Oxford University Press, 1938)[3], it is first necessary to say something of the characters from the Grail legends who appear in these poems. Dindrane is Sir Percivale's sister; she appears briefly in the *Morte d'Arthur* of Sir Thomas Malory, though Malory does not name her. Williams called her sometimes Dindrane (from Welsh sources) and sometimes Blanchefleur (from the French poems). Taliessin does not appear in Malory; he was the legendary Welsh bard and seer—the twice-born child who tasted some drops from the cauldron of wisdom of the mother goddess, Ceridwen. Williams made him the central figure of many of his poems (as the king's poet at Arthur's court). Taliessin in Williams' story loves and is loved by Dindrane; it is a total commitment on all levels, but it is not consummated in the flesh since both have freely and consciously chosen celibate vocations.

Guinevere in the Rose Garden poem is, of course, Arthur's queen, through whose love for the king's friend, Lancelot, the fellowship of the Round Table was finally split and Arthur brought to his death. In the other poem, among the last of the cycle, we meet Sir Galahad, Sir Percivale, and Sir Bors. These are the three knights who, in Malory, achieved the Grail and took ship with it on its voyage to Sarras, the eternal place, where it was withdrawn from the war-torn kingdom of Logres. (Logres is the temporal kingdom of Britain; the forest of Broceliande is, in Jung's language, the unconscious; Caucasia, for Williams, stands for the flesh, and Carbonek for the spirit; Camelot is the temporal city.)

There is one phrase that recurs in the poems whereby Williams defines the wholeness of such a woman as Dindrane: "Flesh knows what spirit knows but spirit knows it knows." It expresses the truth that the material, the instinctual, world remains innocent, at one with itself—every stone, plant, insect, and animal fulfilling unconsciously its nature as it was created to be. But since consciousness dawned in man (as in the myth of the Fall), he has been split between the opposites, between light and dark, male and female, conscious and unconscious, good and evil—all in opposition to each other. The feminine was identified with flesh, the masculine with spirit, but the woman who is one-in-herself in full consciousness is the woman who "knows she knows." She has integrated the life of the spirit with the instinctive life of her flesh through the living in this world on all levels of the love which is the way of conscious return to the unity of all the opposites. The same integration, of course, applies to man, but he more usually must approach it from the opposite end of the spectrum.

As the poem "Taliessin in the Rose Garden" opens, the king's poet is walking among the roses making poetry and he sees three women at the entry to the long garden path: Queen Guinevere talking to Dindrane and a maid doing garden work beyond. The sparkling red of the queen's great ruby ring and the glowing red of the roses unite in Taliessin's imagination with the red of falling blood and there follows a long meditation on the nature of woman.

Guinevere was a queen; on her was laid the great responsibility of carrying for her country the symbol of the feminine side of the holy marriage between Heaven and Earth, the symbol of humanity united to God, of the flesh infused by the spirit—giving birth in due time to the new king:

Glorious over Logres, let the headship of the queen
be seen, as Caucasia to Carbonek, as Logres to Sarras

But Guinevere had betrayed her vocation:

under her brow she looked for the King's friend
Lancelot

Here at the outset Taliessin foresees that the Queen's betrayal of
her feminine wholeness, her refusal to accept her great responsibility for the symbolic image which she carries as queen (the "con-
summate earth of Logres," he calls her) will mean that the "falling
blood," which could have been the redemptive blood of sacrifice,
will become the blood of war, bringing destruction of the kingdom
when finally the king is forced into awareness by his own misbegot-
ten son Mordred and makes war on his friend Lancelot to his own
undoing. Thus any civilization is doomed when the queen (the
leading feminine principle, the dominant attitude in women) loses
integrity of heart and succumbs to what someone has called "love as
a release of tension" in place of commitment to the relatedness of the
true eros.

We may here ask why it is that through the ages adultery in a
woman has been regarded as so much more terrible a thing than in a
man. For centuries and in many places a woman was put to death if
discovered in adultery. It is not enough to answer that the domination of men over women has been the sole cause of this attitude.
There is also a profound psychological reason.

Nature is equally promiscuous, whether it be male or female, but
since woman is so much closer to the unconscious than man, she is far
more likely to be swallowed by the instinctive life and so lose her
humanity if she separates her body from her feeling values. Because
the flesh is symbolically feminine, man has projected onto woman his
deep fear of the chaos and lack of order with which the growth of
human consciousness is always threatened. This projection is mercifully waning, and the extreme cruelties visited upon a promiscuous woman are a thing of the past in most cultures. But an
individual modern woman ignores at her peril the fact that very real
damage may be done to her psyche if she gives her body indis-
criminately without a commitment to relationship of heart and
mind. Whether this commitment is lived through a life-long mar-

riage or for one night only is not the point. Depth of feeling, not frequency, is the vital thing. It is not a matter of conventional taboos or moral condemnation; it is a question of the fundamental difference between the masculine and feminine psyches.

I am not, of course, implying that a man is absolved from a similar feeling of commitment; far from it. No person of either sex can come to wholeness without full consciousness of the values of eros and willingness to accept the ties and the sacrifices which all true relatedness demands. Because, however, these values are the dominant principle for a woman, she is in much greater danger of disintegration if she betrays them than is a man, and the effects of her betrayal on the environment are deadly. It was Guinevere, not Lancelot, who bore the greater responsibility for the final disaster.

In the story of Lancelot and Elayne, and of his begetting of the Grail hero upon her, we can feel at once these distinctions. Lancelot was tricked into spending a night with Elayne, thinking that he was lying with Guinevere. It was therefore an inevitable fate, and Lancelot remains morally innocent. It is inconceivable that Galahad, the High Prince, the whole man who "achieves" the Grail, could have been born from a union of Guinevere and some great knight with whom she might have lain, unconscious of his identity. Symbolically that would be so false that we find the very thought revolting. Elayne, Galahad's mother, loved Lancelot that night and ever after with all her heart and soul as well as her body, even though she could never be with him again, and she accepted the pain of this knowledge. Our reason replies that so also did Guinevere love Lancelot—both he and she were equally guilty of betraying the king, her husband and his friend. Both of them were equally faithful on another level to their love for each other. Why then if Lancelot could father the Grail Prince could not Guinevere have been his mother? First, of course, because Guinevere, while accepting Lancelot, was at the same time pretending to be faithful to her husband—she wanted to have her cake and eat it, too. Her devotion was never whole, and she betrayed her symbolic feminine vocation as queen, as well as betraying her husband. But still more important, it is an ultimate necessity for a woman that in the instinctual area she be *conscious of what she is doing*, as was Elayne, if she is to give birth to the divine hero within— conscious, not in the rational analytical sense, but in the sense of awareness of her own feelings, and of a responsible commitment of her body and heart together. If she were to be tricked in this area, she would be less than woman—merely female (or possibly, in these days, an imitation man).

There is a trinity of women at the beginning of "Taliessin in the Rose Garden," the three being a queen, a virgin soon to become a contemplative nun, and an ordinary working woman. In all women this trinity exists, lived or unlived, either positively or negatively. We may know and live the "queen" through our sense of responsibility, not only for those around us but for all mankind. "Through words and deeds the superior man moves heaven and earth—even if he abides in his room," says Confucius. This is the royal quality—awareness of the symbolic power of everything we are. Or, for we are free to choose, we may identify with the queen and demand to be first all the time, to be served and protected and personally admired. The working woman is equally essential: to live in the present and do each task as it comes, tending the growing things, both of the earth and in the psyche. Without this we are no longer human; but again, if the work we do, whether with hands or minds, absorbs our whole personalities, it becomes one of the most seemingly virtuous ways to evade reality. These two persons of the trinity are easily understood.

But what of the virgin? In our time it has become almost a shameful word. I was told the other day of a boy aged twelve who said to his mother, talking of a girl his own age, "She's nothing but a virgin." Asked what he meant by this, he replied, "Oh, a virgin means a complete dud, boring and dull."

A young woman who is still a virgin at twenty often has a miserable sense of inferiority on this account. A "virgin" in common speech means a woman who has never had intercourse with a man, but in its more ancient and deeper meaning a virgin is a woman who, whether she has had intercourse or not, has no *need* to unite physically with a man in order to become whole, one-in-herself, for she has known intercourse with the god within. This has always been the symbolic meaning of the life of a nun. As the bride of Christ, she seeks the inner marriage of the human and the divine. It is easy, however, to see how the affirmation of a vocation to prayer and contemplation can sink into the negative repression of the sexual desires themselves. Chastity, which means purity of heart, has come all too frequently to mean a denial of the purity of instinct itself. No one can become "virgin" in the true sense without going through the fire of instinctual emotion. This experience, however, does not necessarily include fruition on the physical level, and the time has surely come not only for a resurrection of the true meaning of the word "virgin" but for a return of respect for those whose inner truth may demand virginity in the ordinary physical sense.

Robert Grinnell, in his book *Alchemy in a Modern Woman*,[4] writing of a woman patient who suffered from frigidity, says that this problem in a woman may come from her high ideals in the realm of eros, together with a mistaken interpretation of them through a typical masculine over-valuation of physical sex. Grinnell adds that eros in a woman may be called a "sort of feminine conscience" which takes her beyond the demands of the ego and lifts her out of her momentary desires. Thus the natural woman is transformed into the woman who "knows she knows."

Virginity and the quest for the holy marriage within are emerging from behind the walls of the cloisters, which through so many centuries have guarded that great symbol, and in our time, only individual women can give it new life. To one the god may come through her sexual fruition, to another through suffering its absence — and both are "virgin" in the deep sense.

To return to the poem, Taliessin, musing on these things — the glowing ruby ring of Guinevere, the red roses in the garden, the imagined falling blood — and on their meaning in woman, sees a great vision of the Zodiac. Each of the twelve houses, he says, is a door to the whole, "All coalesced in each." But Cain, by killing Abel, split the Zodiac at a single blow, and through the incoherence of the houses at war with themselves the blood flowed and the way of return "climbed beside the timed and falling blood." The shedding of blood can only be redeemed by the offering of blood. Then, as Taliessin looked on the stricken world, he heard:

> The women everywhere throughout it sob with the curse
> and the altars of Christ everywhere offer the grails.
> Well are women warned from serving the altar
> who by the nature of their creature, from Caucasia to Carbonek,
> share with the Sacrifice the victimization of blood.

The woman's monthly shedding of blood is the outer sign and an inner symbol of her female capacity to give birth. Williams means, I believe, that the menstrual blood of woman is a continual reminder of the truth that after the Fall, after the split in creation, there can be no "return," no healing of the split, without sacrifice, without the giving of blood. If the woman or the feminine in man does not "bleed," there is no creation in this world. Therefore, he says that women "share with the Sacrifice the victimization of blood." The piercing of Christ's side was the wound in the heart of his feeling nature. (The liver was thought by the ancients to be the seat of the emotions and is on the right side).

I do not know any other writer, theologian, or psychologist who has given this very profound, yet very simple and, once seen, obvious explanation of the intuitive revulsion which many feel at the thought of a woman priest celebrating the Mass. If a truly mature woman, fully aware of her animus (the masculine aspect of her unconscious) were to read services and preach sermons, it would not offend. The Mass, however, is a *symbolic* rite, and no matter how developed her spirit may be a woman remains biologically female. Since her shedding of blood, says Williams, is in her flesh an equivalent of the blood of the victim, therefore, if *in her flesh* she offers the blood of Christ, she usurps on the wrong level the function of the spirit. "Flesh knows what spirit knows," Williams goes on, "but spirit knows it knows." In this, of course, he is emphatically *not* saying that individual women cannot know they know; indeed he goes on to show this with great clarity. He is speaking only of her symbolic feminine role in a ritual, not of her individual being. A symbol is, of course, that which makes one the two levels of reality—spirit and matter, inner and outer truth.

There is usually a symbolic meaning hidden behind an old wives' tale. During the Second World War, I lived in a small village in Berkshire, England, where a local woman cooked for our family. I remember that she told me she never tried to make jams during the days of her menstrual period since it was well known to be useless; the jam or jelly simply would not set! In other words, no *transformation* could take place at these times: the separate ingredients, the fruit and sugar, could be mixed, but could never transform into the third thing—that which is both and neither. The relevance to the transformation of the bread and wine on that other level of the Mass is plain. Projected onto such things as the making of jam, it may seem nonsensical in the light of our scientific knowledge, but the ancient symbolic truths which express the mysteries of being have always been preserved both in folklore and in the rituals of the great religions.

Though in the ancient world there were everywhere priestesses, they were never, I believe, charged with the actual killing of the sacrificial animal or offering its blood. The tearing to pieces of victims by the women in the Dionysian rites was not a priestly act but a ritually contained release of instinctual frenzy. The priestesses served as links to the unconscious through their mediumistic power — the sibyls, for instance — they tended the sacred fire, as did the vestal virgins, fulfilling the great religious functions of woman; but they did not wield the knife of sacrifice or offer the blood. Rather it is their task to draw up the waters under the earth from the well of the unconscious that all may drink of the *aqua permanens*, as the alchemists called the water of life. It is the measure of the masculine one-sidedness of our culture that there have never been priestesses of this kind in institutional Christianity.

It would be useless for the Church at this stage to attempt to introduce new rituals for priestesses. A true rite is born, not made, and if consciously contrived is merely sentimental. Nor does the answer lie in the current urge to admit women to the priest's role. Nevertheless, we cannot put the clock back in a mood of nostalgia. In most Protestant sects, the communion service is not a symbolic transformation rite but a commemorative meal, so that there should be no objection whatever to women ministers. Only to the Catholic, Orthodox, and Anglican rites do the words of Charles Williams apply. But the demand for women in the priesthood is perhaps one of the indicators that for growing numbers of people the symbolic life is slowly being pushed out of the collective institutions as such. In the coming age, as Jung frequently pointed out, the symbols must come to birth in the individual soul, in the man or woman who enters on the lonely quest for the Grail within, and this applies to church members as profoundly as to anyone else. It was always in the legends a quest that must be undertaken alone, but it is never achieved without the discovery of objective relatedness to others, as opposed to the all-too-easy unconscious "mixing," or the "togetherness" which submerges any true meeting between human beings.

As C. S. Lewis points out in his commentary on Williams' poems, the menstrual blood of women differs from the blood of animals in heat. For animals it is the only time at which they can conceive. In human beings it is the proof of the possibility of motherhood, as in nature, but there is a major difference in that conception can take place at any time. The beginning of the monthly flow at puberty is, moreover, a sign in the body of the psychic split—that is, of the "Fall" which was the beginning of the conscious "way of return" for Eve as for Adam. The innocent wholeness of childhood, of Eden, is over. At puberty the longing begins for completion by physical union with the other sex, a longing which continues (symbolically) until the "stanching" at the menopause. In Plato's image, the original human being is a sphere which, being cut in two, forever seeks to reunite with its other half.

At a later point in the poem, Williams hints at the inner identification of the woman's menstrual blood, which tells her that she has not yet conceived, with the blood of the wounded Grail king, bleeding because he cannot bring to life the new consciousness of the Christ, the Self. In some beautiful lines Taliessin speaks of how woman may consciously give birth to the new keeper of the Grail, within herself, and so heal the wound in the psyche.

First, however, Williams speaks of the natural woman living instinctively the One way:

women's flesh lives the quest of the Grail
in the change from Camelot to Carbonek and from Carbonek to
      Sarras,
puberty to Carbonek, and the stanching, and Carbonek to death.
Blessed is she who gives herself to the journey.

Camelot is the city of men, the life of this world, which is entered at puberty—the potentially creative blood begins to flow, and primitive woman already begins her vocation as wife and mother. She cleaves to her man and receives the seed, she gives birth in pain, she is the earth without which the creative seed is sterile. But when this flow of her blood is stanched at the menopause and she must let go of her desire to conceive and give birth to a physical child, then her lifelong experience of "Camelot" can bring her to that instinctive wisdom which we still may find in old women of this simple kind who have given themselves to the journey—who accept the "stanching," as they have accepted the pains and joys of motherhood. They come to Carbonek, the place where the holy is glimpsed and from it go on in peace to the goal of death. By the generous, rich living of her feminine nature such a woman is whole, but without knowing that she knows.

Taliessin, making poetry in the Rose Garden, having sung of the quest of the Grail in the flesh of woman — of the blessedness of those who give themselves with the simple diffuse awareness of the natural woman to life's journey, goes on in the next stanza to sing of the blessedness of the conscious woman on the same journey:

> The phosphor of Percivale's philosophical star
> shines down the roads of Logres and Broceliande;
> happy the woman who in the light of Percivale
> feels Galahad, the companion of Percivale, rise
> in her flesh, and her flesh bright in Carbonek with Christ,
> in the turn of her body, in the turn of her flesh, in the turn
> of the Heart that heals itself for the healing of others,
> the only Heart that healed itself without others, when
> our Lord recovered the Scorpion and restored the zodiac.
> Blessed is she who can know the Dolorous Blow,
> healed in the flesh of Pelles, the flesh of women;

The philosophical star of Percivale — the image of the wisdom in the heavens, the light of man's soaring spirit — shines on the roads of this world and penetrates into Broceliande, the darkness of the feminine unconscious. Happy the woman, says Williams, who is flooded by this light of consciousness, and who then feels "Galahad," the new whole man, stir to life within her. We are carried perhaps for an instant into the thought of a woman rising above the earth and *becoming* a sort of female Galahad, but the next line jerks us firmly back to the true blessedness of the new vision for woman. She feels Galahad rise in her flesh; the point is that she feels him *consciously* in the actuality of her feminine nature and so reaches full awareness of the truth of the heart, of the love that is both personal and rooted in the transpersonal life. Her spirit then reaches maturity and "she knows that she knows."

Only in the Heart of the Self is the split healed. The use of the word "heart" here is vital in our context. As James Hillman has so compellingly shown in his essay on the feeling function, the desperate need of our time is for the discovery of eros, of feeling values. Emotional experiences for their own sake and theoretical truths we have in plenty, but true feeling which leads to the perception of the abiding values is still rare in our time. It is for individual, conscious women to lead the way. How difficult it is for men, who are so dangerously exposed in this age to possession by the intellect, by technology, or by their inferior unintegrated femininity, to find the meaning of eros without this mediation of true women who do not only live these things instinctively, but "know that they know."

How horrifying, on the other hand, is the attitude of those many women who are so busy doing things and demanding their rights, personally or collectively, that they reject altogether that "precious beaker," the Grail of the feminine being which receives the wine of the mystery so that in due time many may drink.

Let us now return to those strange words, "Blessed is she who can know the Dolorous Blow / healed in the flesh of Pelles, the flesh of woman." The so-called Dolorous Blow caused the wound in the thigh of the Grail King Pelles, which bled without healing until the coming of the new man, Galahad. The wounded state of the king was reflected in the sterility of the surrounding wasteland. What lies behind these images? C. S. Lewis, in his commentary, is silent. There is, of course, the obvious connection with what has gone before; the stanching at the menopause of the shedding of blood is a symbol of the making whole of wounded humanity in a natural woman, who, her task of rearing children over, turns towards death with a sense of joy and acceptance during those last years — acceptance which only comes to those who have given themselves freely to the experience of the dark as well as of the light. "Blessed is she who gives herself to the journey," says Taliessin. But the second blessing is different. "Blessed is she who can know" the meaning of these things.

It is significant that so many modern women suffer acute and painful problems, both physical and psychic, at the menopause, and that it often drags on for years causing all sorts of disturbances. It is beautifully called "the change of life," but how many women do in fact change their lives — change their attitudes, turn inward to find meanings and to prepare for death, and so enter consciously on the new phase of the journey, from Carbonek to Sarras? Very few; the majority cling desperately to Camelot because they have never fully given themselves to that phase of the journey, and so the energy released by the biological change, instead of flowering into a creative activity of the Logos within her, into an imaginative confrontation with the meaning of death, is eaten up by the unassimilated drives of the animus, the masculine component of her psyche which turns destructive instead of connecting her to the spirit within. The wound inflicted by the Dolorous Blow—that is, the split between spirit and flesh—is not healed in such women but bleeds more freely than ever in the psyche. So the wasteland spreads and the heart shrivels. We see all around us the plight of middle-aged women substituting ever-increasing outer activity for the inner life, or searching miserably for a man, any man, or his equivalent, to fill the void by preserving the illusion of youth.

"Blessed is she who can know the healing of the Dolorous Blow." In such a woman the shedding of blood and its stanching both become conscious sacrifice and are filled with meaning. She is aware of the "change of life" on every level and embraces it with her whole heart.

Those words of Williams about the Dolorous Blow surely derive from the strangest of all the legends in Malory's *Morte d'Arthur*. As the three knights Galahad, Percivale, and Bors approach the end of their quest they are joined by Percivale's sister, who, as has been said, is not named by the earlier writer, but is called either Blanchefleur or Dindrane by Williams. Malory tells of how this "noblewoman" led Sir Galahad to the "ship of Solomon," which was later to carry the Grail and the three knights away from Logres to Sarras. Here they found Sir Percivale and Sir Bors waiting, and the lady, fulfilling her role of link to the unconscious, revealed to them the story of the ship, and of the sword which Sir Galahad found there. She was not recognized even by her brother Percivale until she revealed herself as a daughter of King Pellinore. Then all four set forth on the last phase of the quest.

As they journeyed they came to a castle from which armed knights emerged, who tried to seize the princess, Percivale's sister. There was a battle, but finally the travellers were induced to listen to the reason for the seizure. The lady of the castle was very sick and had long lain in a coma, and it had been foretold that she could only find healing through the blood of a princess of royal descent who was also a virgin; therefore every noblewoman who passed that way was seized in hope that she might fulfill these conditions. When Percivale's sister heard this she said at once that she was both a princess and a virgin and offered freely to give her blood to the lady. "Who will let my blood?" she said. One of the ladies-in-waiting stepped forward and made an incision in Dindrane's arm and the blood gushed out into a bowl. So much blood did she lose that she knew she would die, and she spoke to the three knights bidding them not to bury her but to put her in a ship at the next harbor and set it adrift. "And when you come to Sarras," she said, "you will find this ship with my body in it waiting for you, and there you shall bury me."

And so she died, and the other lady rose from her sick bed and lived. The three knights obeyed her and leaving her body in the ship they came to Carbonek, the Grail city, and Galahad healed the wounded king. From thence they came to the sea and boarded the ship of Solomon, to which the Grail had removed itself; and without sail or oar they were borne over the sea to Sarras.

This legend is the basis of Williams' poem, "The Last Voyage." In his own re-creation of the story he significantly shows us the body of Dindrane, the woman, travelling in the same ship with the Grail and with the three knights — Galahad, the "alchemical infant," the holy child; Percivale, the star of wisdom; Bors, the ordinary practical human being. There is now a quaternity in this ship. All four are carried to the "spiritual place" where, in the unconscious, two of the knights and the dead woman will remain with the Grail until the time of its rediscovery, while Bors alone returns at once to the world. The ages of growing emphasis on man and his works were ahead — the Renaissance, the Enlightenment, followed by the industrial revolution and our century of technological materialism. This is the great significance of Bors' solitary return: Galahad's intuition, Percivale's inner wisdom, and the feminine values of Dindrane are all removed into the unconscious.

Bors is in Williams' poems the husband and father, the down-to-earth householder, the extravert. The poet sees him as the guardian of the Grail vision during the coming centuries, but we have watched the gradual eclipse of simple human values of Bors by the sterility of intellect and technology divorced from feeling. Now surely the time is ripe for the emerging of the Grail from Sarras — for the resurrection of Dindrane.

Malory's story of Percivale's sister and of her shedding of blood for another and her close connection with the Grail is unique, as far as I know, in the versions of the legend. No one took much notice of it, it seems, until suddenly in Williams' poetry it moves into the center of that last picture of the swiftly receding Grail:

Before the helm the ascending-descending sun
lay in quadrilateral covers of a saffron pall
over the bier and the pale body of Blanchefleur,
mother of the nature of lovers, creature of exchange;
drained there of blood by the thighed wound,
she died another's death, another lived her life.
Where it was still to-night, in the last candles of Logres,
a lady danced, to please the sight of her friends;
her cheeks were stained from the arteries of Percivale's sister.
Between them they trod the measure of heaven and earth,
and the dead woman waited the turn and throe of the dance
where, rafting and undershafting the quadruplicate sacrum,
below the saffron pall, the joyous woe of Blanchefleur,
the ship of Solomon (blessed be he) drove on.

To me these lines are some of the most powerful in the whole cycle of poems; they vibrate with meaning, if only we can bring to them a "total response," in Jung's words.

In Williams' experience of the myth, springing from the hints in Malory, Blanchefleur or Dindrane is above all "virgin," one-in-herself, the companion of the poet Taliessin, on all levels—body and heart, mind and spirit; she is the foster-mother of Galahad, the sister of Percivale—the feminine wisdom which is essential to his "philosophical star." But Logres, the collective culture of that era, was not ready for the "new woman" who shines briefly through the story. Woman collectively would remain subject through many centuries to the dominant male, largely unconscious of that which her flesh always knows. Nevertheless, the lady, "mother of the nature of lovers, creature of exchange" had, before her disappearance with the Grail, given her life's blood so that an ordinary woman of this world might carry her life in her bloodstream and transmit it to the future. The sick woman had been in a coma—the "flesh," the earth, had been too long despised in Christianity. The blood of Dindrane, the whole woman, gave her the possibility of renewal, and the lady was able to dance in the simple delights of human exchange, carrying in her veins—unconsciously in the depths of her being—the life of the "dead" woman whose "exchanges" encompassed heaven and the whole world.

She, Dindrane, waited in the unconscious of women for the day when one here, one there, would awaken her from her sleep. She

awaited "the throe of the dance," and a throe means a pang of
anguish, and more particularly a pang of childbirth. And the place
where she lay in the poem was the ship of Solomon, that Solomon
whose image carries the meaning of the wise and understanding
heart. She is held as in a womb, the fourth in the "quadruplicate
sacrum" of the Grail.

There is one other line which as yet we have not looked at,
"drained there of blood by the thighed wound." By the use of the
word "thighed," Williams links the sacrifice of Dindrane to the
wound of the maimed king, soon to be healed by Galahad. (It will be
remembered he had also likened the menstrual blood of the natural
woman to the blood of the Grail king in the Rose Garden poem.) The
extraordinary interest of this passage lies in the fact that the actual
wound of Percivale's sister was cut into her *arm*. The arm is a symbol
of creative activity in this world; the thigh indicates male sexual
power. The Grail King is wounded, his masculine strength is
maimed so that he is unable to beget any new vision. The woman on
the other hand is drained of blood from her arm, and her potentially
active creativity sinks down again into the unconscious to await "the
throe of the dance"—those birth pangs which have come indeed to
woman in the last one hundred years. It is immediately after this
shedding of Dindrane's blood that Galahad, her foster son, symbol
of the whole man, heals the Grail King, but the great vision fails to
become incarnate in the world precisely because the values of the
whole woman could not yet be accepted. The Grail is withdrawn and
with it Dindrane, the "seeing" woman.

All this may be read as a symbolic statement of the situation in the
middle years of this century—when the poet was writing—and also
of the inner quest of every conscious woman, whether Williams was
aware of this or not. If a woman's true creativity in the realm of Logos
is wounded—if her "arm" activity is used to manipulate instead of
create, then man is emasculated. (It is not, of course, fundamentally a
matter of cause and effect, but of synchronicity.) If, however, her
wound becomes sacrifice (the willing death for another which is the
giving up of the animus-possessed demands of her ego), there will
follow the rebirth. She returns in the "throe" of the dance, in the true
"exchange" encompassing both earth and heaven, and with her she
brings the long hidden Grail.

The human arm is that which distinguishes man from the animal and it symbolizes, as has been said, his relatedness to life. Dindrane gave blood from her arm and life to another. The dancing lady with the blood of Dindrane in her veins was the feminine counterpart of Bors, the husband and householder, who transmitted to his sons, as she to her daughters, the hidden intuition of the Grail, down through the centuries of growing humanism. With the dawning of the age of Aquarius, the age of seeing, which is contemplation, the age of the carrier of the water of life in a vessel, may we not see indeed the awakening of Dindrane, the woman consciously one-in-herself, no longer secluded from this world, but walking the streets of the City of God and mankind. So, in the words of Taliessin in the Rose Garden, she may "bring to a flash of seeing the women in the world's base."

NOTES

1. C. G. Jung, *Collected Works* (Princeton: Princeton University Press, Bollingen Series, 1955), vol. 18, p. 678.
2. C. S. Lewis, *Arthurian Torso* (Oxford: Oxford University Press, 1948).
3. All of Williams' Arthurian poems have been republished in *Arthurian Poets: Charles Williams*, edited and introduced by David Llewellyn Dodds (Bury St. Edmunds, Suffolk: The Boydell Press, 1991).
4. Spring Publications, Dallas, 1973, p. 52.

Chapter Six

Brunhilde

AT THE END of the last act of the final opera in Richard Wagner's massive *Ring of the Nibelungs* cycle, the warrior heroine Brunhilde orders a great funeral pyre to be raised so that she and Grane, the horse she had given to Siegfried, may join the dead champion in the flames. She sings of her love of the great hero, who, truest of all, was forced to betray her so that she might finally learn wisdom; then she speaks to her father Wotan, the chief deity in Norse mythology, sending home his ravens with the news "both feared and longed for"—the end of the gods proclaimed in the opera's German title, *Götterdämmerung*.

She draws from Siegfried's finger the Ring which has been the driving force in this long epic of greed and redemption, then calls on the Rhinemaidens, who had guarded the original gold from which it was fashioned, to reclaim it from the ashes. "May the fire that burns me cleanse the Ring from its curse!" cries Brunhilde. "Dissolve it in the stream and ever keep safe the pure shining gold whose theft wrought such evil!" She throws a flaming brand into the pyre and speaks to Grane, her horse and Siegfried's: "My friend, do you know whither I lead you—are you neighing to follow your friend?" Joyfully she mounts and together they plunge into the fire. The Rhine rises, and on the flood come the Rhinemaidens, who hold up the Ring which Brunhilde has flung to them. In the heavens, Valhalla and all the gods within it are consumed in the flames.

Wagner had begun the four-opera cycle with another scene featuring the Rhinemaidens, in which he made clear the origin and nature of the Ring of power: gold hidden in the depths of the unconscious, where there is no differentiation of good and evil. This gold, this treasure, lies in the womb of the great mother; her daughters, the Rhinemaidens, collective anima figures of man's psyche, play and disport themselves around it, basking in the light of its beauty. They are its guardians and from them it must be stolen if it is to reach the light of day, emerge into consciousness. In every age some individuals have dared consciously to descend and to take this gold, forging it into the circle of wholeness, of the Self, but for the most part it is stolen by the collective shadow of mankind, of which Alberich the Dwarf is the symbol (as are his brother Mime and his son Hagen later in the cycle). By Alberich the gold is also forged into a symbol of the totality, but through his denial of eros, love, it becomes the small and exclusive Ring, which may be used and possessed only by one owner. Just as the individual, singly not collectively, may come to wholeness only when he has found that to be finally alone is to include all, so just one man at a time can possess the Ring of Alberich, identifying the totality with his personal will to power and excluding all that is other.

The circle of wholeness and the Ring of Alberich are basically one and the same—the positive and negatives poles of the Self. That which determines the nature of the power bestowed by the Ring is the degree of consciousness with which each and every one of us responds to that love which is both "center and circumference." He who has reached the stage of "Love and do what you will" is completely free from any temptation whatsoever to *use* the Ring whether for good or evil purpose, whereas he who rejects love and does what he wills is delivered over to possession by the Ring, and so to ultimate destruction. For if this first opera—indeed if the whole cycle—makes anything clear, it is above all this: that the finding of the gold, the Ring's forging, its passage from hand to hand, the manner of the curse's operation on everyone who carries it or covets it, are all determined by the individual's relationship to eros, and to the meaning of love.

At the outset the gold is in the possession of the anima, of the unconscious, feminine principle in man. Alberich finds it when he is moved by lust of the lowest kind, but nevertheless the object of his lust is the beauty of the Rhinemaidens. Through it he glimpses the beauty of the gold in the unconscious, and through it he learns that the Ring can only be forged by a man who has renounced love. This is true both of the Ring of world domination and the circle of wholeness, though in opposite senses. The seeker after the truth of love, just as the seeker after personal power, can only find the gold through the experience of his passionate, instinctive nature, and from this experience he learns that when his desire is purged of all possessiveness, all demand, he will be able to forge the Ring of wholeness. For him this purging of eros is the way to that love which is beyond desire, the love of which Jung is speaking when he says that only when a man can renounce any and every desire without a moment's hesitation has he found the Self. Nevertheless, only *through* desire can desire be transcended.

For Alberich, on the other hand, the renunciation of love means the total rejection of all the feminine values of relationship, of all tenderness and kindness, of all respect for the individual—a total exclusion of all but his own will.

In our own time, we see this murder of eros values on every side. It reveals itself in the deification of the collective "good," so-called, and the justification of every conceivable horror in its service—and not only in Nazi and Communist countries, as people so often comfortably assume. The energy of eros, repressed and rejected, is turned invariably, in small matters as in great, into the insatiable pursuit of power; whereas its full acceptance and transformation through conscious sacrifice of the ego's will gives birth to the power of that love which is perfect freedom from desire. We have only to look about us and into our own hearts. Wherever we see a demand that things should go our own way; whenever we try to push people into behaving in the way we imagine to be right, we are forging the eros gold into a Ring of personal exclusive power.

While Alberich was renouncing eros and forging the Ring under the earth, Wotan the god in the sky was in a semi-conscious way also busy betraying the values of the heart in the service of his own pride. He had employed the giants to build Valhalla for him, a magnificent palace and stronghold, and he had bribed them with an infamous promise. A vast structure of self-glorification in consciousness parallels the similar process down below. The giants symbolize Wotan's own inflated idea of himself, and an inflation, if indulged in and used to enhance personal glory or safety, exacts precisely the price which Wotan had undertaken to pay—that is, his own wife's sister, the goddess Freia, she whose Golden Apples are the only food which could keep him and the rest of the gods alive. Every inflation is followed by depression, apathy, and loss of energy, a failure of the life-giving food of the goddess, the nourishment which comes to man through human relationship. Wotan, like Alberich, had promised to give up eros, but unlike Alberich, he is ashamed of his promise and wants to get out of it. He is the ruling principle of consciousness in the myth and he wants to have his cake and eat it, too. He made the promise without facing the fact that he might really have to fulfill it one day, trusting in the god Loki (the trickster, the Lucifer of the myth) to find a way out when the time came. How familiar this sounds! Indeed, all the ambivalent goings on of Wotan are immediately recognizable as a picture of the self-deceptions, the generosities and meannesses, the nobility and cowardice, which live side by side in us all.

The giants are coming to claim the goddess as their payment. Loki has produced as yet no solution, and that other goddess, Fricka, Wotan's wife, the protector of marriage and respectability, upbraids Wotan for his betrayal of Freia. He protests, however, that she was as anxious as he to build the castle, in order to keep him at home with her. When a ruling principle is dying, feeling regresses into possessiveness and conventionality. It will be seen later how Fricka undermines and almost destroys Wotan's true feeling, symbolized by Brunhilde, his daughter by another woman, the earth-goddess Erda.

The giants demand immediate payment, Freia appeals desperately to Wotan, and now Loki appears with his solution. The giants must be offered something they will value more highly than the goddess, so that they will freely give up their claim to her. It must be remembered that there is one sin Wotan cannot commit without losing his power forever: he cannot break his given word, symbolized by his spear, by which he rules the world and on which are graven all the solemn vows he makes. If ever he is untrue to such a vow, he knows the spear will break in pieces and his power will be shattered. It is indeed true that if the ruling principle of consciousness betrays its own nature, its *word* in this basic sense, it must inevitably crumble — we do not trust it any more and so its power to rule is gone. So Wotan can plan every kind of trick except this one, and Loki, his shadow, must find a way out without risking this betrayal.

Loki now tells of the Ring of power which Alberich has forged. If Wotan can obtain this Ring and give it to the giants they will relinquish Freia. It is an irony that in order to keep his word and with it his world domination, he must give into the hands of the giants the Ring which will give them precisely that same power which he is trying (with one side of himself) to save. Wotan, however, is not an

Alberich. He will not in the end betray eros for the sake of power, and finally, with great reluctance, he hands the Ring to the giants.

Thus the Ring, taken from Alberich by a trick, is brought up from the underworld into the light of day and passes into the hands of the giants, who in their turn have renounced eros, their lusting after Freia, in order to obtain it. The curse is immediately demonstrated. Only one man can wear the Ring and all who have turned their backs on love must covet it. Fasolt and Fafnir fight and Fasolt is killed. But Fafnir is stupid. He has immense physical strength and the devouring greed of instinct, but he is incapable of using the Ring. So the Ring possesses him, and he regresses into the form of a dragon, buries the treasure and the Ring in a cave, and spends his life hanging on to it.

But this situation cannot last and so the Ring is at last brought out into the open by a human being of good will into whose hands passes the fate of the world. Siegfried defeats the dragon and takes the Ring for his own, but he is not aware of its meaning. He carries it lightheartedly and for some time is protected from its curse because of his fundamental good will.

Siegfried is the son of Siegmund and Sieglinde, a brother and sister begotten by Wotan on a mortal woman in an attempt to create a new human race which will provide a hero who will be able to defy the gods and become a whole and free individual on his own. Here we see the double nature of the unconscious at its most profound — for the urge to wholeness which is constantly pushing us towards consciousness is balanced by the immensely strong pull backwards into inertia and darkness. Wotan demonstrates this ambivalence at his every appearance in the story. Human parents, insofar as they are themselves unconscious, repeat this pattern, pushing their child with pride and joy, often much too fast, towards growth and maturity, and then, at the least sign of an independence which threatens their ascendancy, pulling him back into an infantile dependence.

Wotan proceeds to do just this. He has set the stage for the meeting of Siegmund with Sieglinde (the sister from whom he was separated in early youth) — and has left the great sword Nothung for him to find and draw from the tree in the house of Hunding, the man who kidnapped Sieglinde and married her. Siegmund, unknowingly meeting his sister-anima again at last, finds at the same time his manhood, his sword. The free man in Siegmund defies the laws of the gods and men in the service of his true love, and the evil Hunding will inevitably go down before the magic weapon. Wotan is pleased and proud of his son until Fricka, his hide-bound conventional wife-anima, who will make life exceedingly uncomfortable for him if he condones any kind of rebellion against the time-honored laws of the gods (especially incest, since Fricka is the goddess of marriage), absolutely forbids him to allow Siegmund to win the fight. Weakly Wotan gives in and sends for his warrior daughter Brunhilde and tells her to see to it that Hunding shall be victorious. Says Wotan, "Boldly I brought him up to flaunt the laws of the gods. Why did I want to break myself in this way? How wisely Fricka found out the fraud. She saw right through me, all to my shame. I must yield my will to her purpose." Brunhilde is horrified at all this and for the first time in her life she dares to disobey her father. She will carry out what she knows to be his real desire and defy his conventional orders.

Brunhilde's rebellion is a symbol of the crucial turning point in the psyche of every woman. It is the moment when she first stands by her own feeling, defying the father, the external authority by which she has lived. Brunhilde stands also for the true feeling of the father himself, which is why he is so excessively furious with her. She does not succeed in saving Siegmund, for Wotan himself, like so many human fathers, shatters with his spear the sword he himself had given to his son, but she does save Sieglinde and her unborn son— and the parts of the shattered sword—before Wotan can stop her. Wotan's rejected feeling side fails to save his first attempt to create a free man, but she nevertheless makes possible a second chance in the future. She must now pay the price.

Brunhilde was the daughter of Wotan and Erda, the earth mother, but she, like Siegfried, had evidently been taken from her mother and brought up entirely by a man, her father Wotan. Her other dealings with men consisted solely in collecting dead warriors from the battlefield and bringing them to Valhalla for the greater glory of her father. So a woman whose animus remains identified with an immensely powerful father image will have no use for a living man, and will unconsciously turn all her relationships with men into a sterile repetition of her tie to her father. She is indeed a true Valkyrie: bringing dead heroes to Valhalla, her free creativity stifled, she gives out a feeling of not living quite on this earth. So also the father who binds his daughter to him with unconscious chains is using his potential creative feeling to protect himself from reality, and continually attempts to bolster up his prestige through obeying his Fricka anima. Brunhilde, however, rebels. She will not betray her own truth. In disobeying she is true not only to herself but to her father. How it recurs, this theme! Disobedience to authority, *at the right moment*, is the essential of any and every breakthrough of new awareness; disobedience with a condition, however. It is senseless and meaningless rebellion if it is not inspired by a real devotion to a conscious value and if there is not complete willingness at the same time to suffer the consequences, whatever they may be. Brunhilde knew that her disobedience would probably be punished by death. Wotan instead condemns her to a long sleep—on a high mountain peak, surrounding and protected by flames—and to an awakening which, if it happens, can only deprive her of her divinity.

Dr. Marie-Louise von Franz has said that there are women who are "asleep" and who often remain so for many years. As in the fairy tale of the Sleeping Beauty, nothing can awaken them except the seemingly fortuitous arrival of the "Prince." She points out that this sleep of woman, both collectively and individually, is caused by a devaluation of the feminine principle. For instance, a woman whose mother's animus has dominated her childhood may have grown up in the belief that she is quite worthless—that her personality has no meaning, and she simply stays out of life, goes to sleep. If she is wholly identified with her father's anima, the same sense of non-existence as an individual holds sway. Collectively it is the same; the rejection of the feminine values, the attitude that women are inferior creatures, that they are in some way the source of all evil, from the serpent and Eve onwards, has been a dominant feature of our culture for centuries, and the central theme of this myth is the sterility and near disaster which this rejection brings in the long run, the rejection of eros which forges the Ring of power and from which the world can only be saved by woman redeemed and conscious.

In this context we see clearly how significant it is that both Siegfried and Brunhilde have been nurtured by men, without mothers. Erda is certainly around, but she only rises up sleepily out of the earth from time to time and keeps asking Wotan to stop pestering her! The earth mother herself is sleeping. It is surely a man's world. The Germany of Hitler was the violent eruption into society of the absolute supremacy of the masculine; small wonder that the Nazis gave precedence to this myth over Christianity.

Brunhilde's disobedience, her stand for real feeling, is the seed of the re-emergence of the feminine—but like all such seeds it takes a long time to ripen. The new attitude rises for a moment in us and asserts itself in some act of rebellion, perhaps, but as yet it is too weak to live in the conscious world. The authorities who dominate this world push it down again and it must sleep and wait. We may remember such a moment when we stood by our feelings in the teeth of all the generally accepted laws of our world, but were not strong enough to maintain the barely glimpsed freedom. Now the woman lies sleeping, but not dead, and she is surrounded by fire. Only one who will fearlessly experience the fires of his own emotional nature can reach and wake her. A man's dormant capacity for conscious relationship is awakened only when he has passed through this fire.

The third part of the drama is the story of Siegfried's coming to manhood in the cave of the dwarf smith, Mime. Sieglinde having died when he was born, the boy had grown up in ignorance that such a thing as a mother existed—and his presumed father, Mime, certainly provided him with no heroic image. In such a situation he learned nothing of tenderness and love except from watching the birds and beasts, and it is interesting at this point to note the difference between Siegfried's education and that of Parsifal, in the opera based on the Grail legend, which Wagner wrote after the Ring cycle. The quest of the Grail was for Wagner a symbol of new birth, one possible only after the sacrifice of Brunhilde and Siegfried. Parsifal, in contrast to Siegfried, grew up without a father, alone in the woods with his adoring mother, and his need as a youth was to break away from his mother's apron strings, from too much femininity. He was too shy, too naive in his feelings, too much afraid of offending. He failed to ask the right question on his first trip to the Grail castle because he had been told that it was not polite to ask questions. Siegfried, on the other hand, could most certainly never be accused of a surfeit of courtesy. He is brash and boastful, and, contemptible as Mime is, one is left feeling irritated at Siegfried's constant and overbearing rudeness. His need is to find the meaning of kindness and forbearance. He had never even met a woman. So it appears that the Siegfried type of hero who has grown up unloved and must seek for all the unknown values of the heart, remains at the mercy of the unconscious, in spite of all his courage, in spite of Brunhilde even, falling blindly into eros traps until the light breaks through at the moment of his death.

Siegfried, having reforged his father's sword (from the shards rescued by Brunhilde after Siegmund's death and given to Sieglinde and, in turn, Mime), is goaded by Mime's clever insinuations into a determination to find out what fear is, and he storms off, shouting some more boasts, to find the dragon Fafnir. Here is no chivalrous knight, spending a night in lonely vigil, before taking up his dragon-slaying task as a grown man; no simple primitive going through the pains of initiation to manhood in his tribe. Siegfried is rather the young adolescent male, aggressive, self-confident, bent only on getting, however idealistic his aim, what *he* wants, insensitive at first to anything else.

Jung in his autobiography tells the dream which came to him at the great turning point, after his parting from Freud, when he first began to confront the unconscious. He and a little primitive man together shot and killed Siegfried, who was driving at great speed a chariot made of the bones of the dead. The dreamer had an unbearable feeling of guilt and sorrow at what he had done and when he awoke, there was a sense of great urgency, so great that he knew he must understand this dream or kill *himself*. Then he saw that Siegfried stood for the German determination heroically to impose their will, have their own way, and that he had been secretly identified with that attitude himself. Hence his grief in the dream over the death of the heroic idealism of the ego and its demand to conquer, which can be a thing of great beauty. But Siegfried was driving a chariot made of dead bones. His time was over. If Jung had in fact gone down into those deep places of the unconscious with the old Siegfried attitude of bending everything to his will, he would indeed have been lost. Hence the terrible urgency.

Only a hero without fear is able to kill Fafnir. Innocence alone is wholly free from fear, whether it be the unconscious innocence of childhood or the final innocence of the Self, and in face of it all conflict is done away. "The wolf also shall dwell with the lamb, and the leopard shall lie down with the kid; and the calf and the young lion and the fatling together; and a little child shall lead them" (Isaiah 11:6). Siegfried is still in a state of innocence because although he is already a young man, he has not yet experienced the split in his nature. Impulse and act are still one thing, everything is external and just what it seems; there are no shadows, no questions. Life is a simple, "I want" or "I don't want." Such a man has an enormous strength—of a kind—for none of his energy is drained off into doubts and questioning. He does not kill the dragon for the sake of riches and power, nor for the sake of some ideal, nor because he is in danger. He simply kills the dragon because it is there in his way.

There are stirrings, however, in Siegfried. He has heard of this mysterious thing called fear, and he is determined to find it. It is his first "quest"—and rightly, for without the experience of fear there is no fall and no redemption. Then just before he meets the dragon comes a moment of quiet (the first time he stops rushing about and roaring, it seems!) and he dreams of his mother and father, and on awakening listens to a bird singing and is carried out of himself by a longing to understand what the bird is saying—that is, he has recognized that there is a language other than his own. He kills the dragon and he drinks the drop of blood, and with it the poison enters his being and his ears are opened to this new language. Siegfried experiences the Fall; he enters the split, and conscious experience begins, the knowledge of good and evil. In every myth and legend in every human life it is the same. The poison must enter into us, we must emerge from the infantile paradise, before we can ever set foot on the way to that which Blake calls "Four-fold Vision." We must drink a little of that which is poison to the conscious ego, but not too much, for it we drink too much we *become* the dragon, are swallowed by the unconscious.

The bird, the voice from within, now speaks to Siegfried, and in the manner of our dreams it both warns him of his danger and points the way to his next task. The poison of the archetypal dragon has entered his blood stream and its immediate effect is to protect him against an actual attempted poisoning by Mime. (It is the same principle as that of inoculation in medicine.) Innocently he would have fallen into the trap without the warning of the bird, but his innocence is broken. He destroys his enemy, defeats Mime, the personal shadow, and then discovers that he is lonely. It is this discovery of loneliness which sends a man off in search of his other side, his feminine soul; he has half-consciously recognized the need for relationship. So Siegfried goes to seek the fire through which he must pass to find both fear and love.

It is at this point, wearing the Ring from the dragon's hoard, although quite unconscious of its power, that he meets Wotan, who is travelling in disguise, and breaks the god's spear. The fight with the shadow always leads to this; the old ruling principle of consciousness which opposes the new way is challenged and its authority broken. From this moment it is clear that the downfall of the gods has begun. What remains in doubt is the manner of it and the succession.

Siegfried having shattered authority, passes through the emotional storms of youth, no longer innocent. He experiences, it may be imagined, his own passionate nature, and having shirked nothing he comes to the opportunity of love. Siegfried is the young man who braves the emotional fires to find his first glimpse of responsible feeling.

This, however, is no story of the Prince who wakes his Sleeping Beauty so that they may live happily ever after; on the contrary, it is the beginning of Siegfried's experience of manhood, and of Brunhilde's experience of mortality. Hitherto Siegfried has been a boy; now through the awakening of his first love comes the glimpse afar off of the beauty of the end, the final unity, and with the possession of the Ring comes the beginning of responsibility. One night he spends with Brunhilde, and then he leaves her to prove himself as a man, giving her the Ring to keep as a pledge of his love. This gift is the certain proof that Siegfried values love, undifferentiated though it still is for him, above power. The weakness and sin into which he now falls are not therefore a basic betrayal, they are a failure to grow *through* the personal romantic love into that other love which includes and transcends it. The gift of the Ring to his personal love shows indeed his freedom from the power drive, but it also symbolizes his unconscious identification of his beloved with the totality, and his failure to take up the real responsibility of consciousness. This is the experience through which all young men of generous heart must pass when they fall in love. Then come the years of learning how to withdraw the projection without rejecting their love. And most, like Siegfried, must regress before the vital breakthrough to consciousness can be made. It comes to Siegfried only at the moment of his death.

In Brunhilde, too, the same pattern is clear. Warned by one of her Valkyrie sisters that if she does not part from the Ring it will bring

disaster on gods and men, she refuses to listen. The Ring is Siegfried's pledge of love and nothing else matters. Her personal love
is the *whole* to her—no other value can possibly transcend it, and to
women this is a more frequent danger than to men. Nevertheless,
until a man or a woman has passed through this overwhelming
experience of personal love in some form or other, he or she does not
even set foot on the way to individuation. Nothing can be
sacrificed—that is, transformed, made holy, purged of personal
demand—unless it has first been fully possessed.

Like most of us, then, Siegfried and Brunhilde proceed to learn
the hard way. Siegfried has never confronted the shadow more than
half-consciously. He has simply swept him out of the way imper-
iously with his all-conquering sword, with his personal will, brush-
ing aside everything he does not understand. He killed Mime and the
dragon, and broke Wotan's spear, all without a moment's reflection.
He then goes to his meeting with Hagen, the son of Alberich, in a
castle by the Rhine and fails to recognize this new enemy, who traps
him exactly as Mime had tried to trap him—with a doctored drink.
As an innocent boy, he heard the warning of the bird in his heart.
This time he no longer hears. He drinks the potion, forgets the love
of his heart, and is gripped by sensual passion for the first woman in
sight—Gutrune, Hagen's half-sister and the sister of King Gunther.
Not only that, but he proceeds to betray Brunhilde by impersonating
Gunther to her and trying to force her likewise into accepting a
lesser love, as King Gunther's bride. In this he does not succeed
fully: Brunhilde agrees to marry Gunther not out of love, but only
out of hatred for Siegfried himself and his betrayal of her, which she
cannot comprehend, not knowing of the potion. Therefore she reveals to Hagen Siegfried's one weak spot—his back—and is thus
responsible for his death. It is the course of many a relationship,
falling from the high promise of the first vision. As the beauty of the
projection fades, it is called "nothing but" and so betrayed. It is not
consciously sacrificed so that its reality may be reborn through the
hard work of learning separateness and objective love.

Gunther and Gutrune are good, simple people. They agree to the
fulfillment of their desires which Siegfried plans for them. How
could such a great hero be wrong? But they are uneasy nevertheless.
So is the truth of the simple humanity within us betrayed when the

inner vision of beauty is pushed down into the unconscious by the wiles of the shadow unrecognized.

Siegfried falls lower yet. On the banks of the river, he greets the Rhinemaidens, who rise up and plead for the Ring, which Siegfried, disguised as Gunther, forcibly took back from Brunhilde. He refuses them the Ring and then indulges in fantasies about possessing one of these beautiful women, "if only he were not true to Gutrune." The maidens then threaten him with the consequences of keeping the Ring for his personal use—and he at once regresses to his childish boasting about how fearless he is. We have a feeling he has hit bottom, and it is indeed so.

At the request of Hagen, of the shadow himself, as so often, he begins at last to *reflect* and his memory returns. He remembers the birds and speaks his first words of humility: "Since I heard women singing, I have quite forgotten the birds." Most of us hear the birds singing in our youth and most of us allow the loud songs of our emotional involvements to replace the sound of the birds. Only when we hear again the still small voice do all the songs of the world become a great harmony. For Siegfried this moment comes when Hagen stabs him in the back. As so often, the shadow is the final instrument of full awakening. He has paid for all with his life, but he is awake, conscious at last of *meaning*. Brunhilde, aroused from sleep *within* him this time, is his forever as he dies. Hagen is powerless to take the Ring, and it remains for Brunhilde to return it to the unconscious.

The fall of the gods is an inevitable outcome of the story of the Ring. The manner of the fall is the vital theme, as we said earlier. The Ring in the hands of the collective shadow would have utterly destroyed the old gods, but through Brunhilde's conscious sacrifice, they are burned in a fierce purging fire, and there is a hope of rebirth. Nevertheless, there is something unsatisfying about Brunhilde's leap into the fire with Grane, the horse. Brunhilde is an image of immature womanhood, however noble her sacrifice. She was incapable of consenting to a life of loneliness, to the bearing of Siegfried's child without either projected gods or personal love to help her carry the burden, and so the most she could do was to return the Ring to the water maidens in the unconscious to be their plaything until the next theft and the next forging.

But Brunhilde, too, has a second awakening, though it cannot live as yet in this world. As the feminine principle in the myth, she never in fact finds her place in the ground of being. It is she at the last who is playing the active role. The man, the spirit, has refused to part with the Ring and so has died by treachery. The woman completes his task and *deliberately* enters the fire, taking Grane, their horse, symbol of man's basic libido, with her. We are left with the feeling that the whole cycle has ended in destruction—that everything has taken place in the unconscious. Nothing has won through to incarnation. It has been a tremendous and magnificent attempt, and no such attempt can be called a failure, because in fact the Ring was saved from those who would use it to destroy consciousness; but on the other hand, it is only a negative success. Siegfried, the man, has gone under, and his anima must inevitably go with him. Brunhilde's dramatic immolation of herself is yet another image of the devaluation of the feminine principle. Hindu women were burned on their husband's funeral pyre because they were of value only as appendages of men, had no existence in their own right. As long as this attitude remains there can be no *hierosgamos*, no conscious union of male and female, no final end to the rule of ego power.

Siegfried and Brunhilde are great symbols of the generous enthusiasms of youth; the tragedy lies in their inability to grow to maturity. Jung wrote of the desperate need of western man for this taking up of the conscious search for wholeness at the midpoint of life. At this time, if we are not to follow Siegfried into his decline, when his innocence became childish gullibility and the voice of the bird was no longer heard in his heart, we must "kill" Siegfried, the golden hero of youth, as Jung killed him in his dream.

At the end of *Götterdämmerung*, only one person remains alive: Gutrune, the ordinary human woman who has been throughout a simple-hearted victim of the doings of hero, heroine, and villains alike. She fades into the background before the climax and is easy to forget, but she is there, a human being who can begin again.

Chapter Seven

The Cat Archetype

WHAT DOES THE cat mean in the psyche of man that she has acquired such a numinous quality? She inspires the most violent reactions in some people—either of attraction or repulsion, and there are not many other creatures which arouse this same kind of irrational emotion—snakes, spiders, rats, and bats come to mind, but the extreme reaction to these is nearly always one of revulsion only, except in the case of a very few passionate snake-lovers. They have one thing in common: they are all creatures of the dark, of the night, and carry the mystery and *mana* of the unknown. The snake is the most powerful of all animal symbols, the incarnation of evil, the Devil, or of light and healing, the Christ ("As Moses lifted up the Serpent in the wilderness so must the Son of Man be lifted up"—John 3:14), and the legends of the cat also have this double nature. Whereas, however, the snake is cold-blooded—cold with the deathly cold of evil, or cold in the utter conscious aloneness of the Cross—the cat is warm-blooded; her symbolism lies in the realm of the instinctive emotions, much nearer to the everyday struggles of our lives. She differs from all the other animals mentioned above in that while remaining a creature of the night and essentially remote and mysterious, she is also a creature of the day, welcomed into the house, fed by us, warmed by us, but, unless we delude ourselves, never possessed by us.

What are her qualities? She is an image of the enchanting beauty and grace and precision of natural movement and of the "play" instinct. She has the extreme patience and swiftness of the hunter, and her complete power of relaxation is unique among the animals close to man. Above all she is the only domesticated animal which has retained through all the centuries her qualities of wildness and independence. Kipling's *Just So* story of "The Cat That Walked by Himself" profoundly and delightfully expresses this truth. The horse becomes man's willing servant and the dog becomes man's "first friend," but the cat becomes neither servant nor friend, she simply makes a bargain with the woman [note: *woman*]. She will kill mice, she will purr, she will play with the baby, and in return, the woman will feed her and give her a place by the fire, but always and always she retains her right to say, "I am the cat that walks by himself and all creatures are alike to me." And so, as Konrad Lorenz says, even if a cat goes for walks with you, you always know that it is because *she* chooses, not because you wish it. You cannot train her—at best she will acquiesce in your wishes if it suits her. All genuine cat lovers (not the sentimental cat humanizers) respond with a similar detached respect. (see T.S. Eliot's poem "The Ad-dressing of Cats"—an unknown cat must be approached with much form and ceremony, never with the "old fellow" attitude as with a dog!)

The cat, then, represents in the human psyche the beauty and integrity of our warm-blooded instincts in all their wild independence, to which, if we will, we can relate in our homes, in our consciousness, and which, if we respect and feed them will protect us from the unseen rats and mice in the dark places of the unconscious which nibble away at our souls. She is the bridge between the wildness of the jungle and our consciousness. The cat, like all pure instinct, is amoral, but until we can learn to accept this essential part of our humanity, to see its beauty and terror and accept it without repressing it or distorting it with sentimental names, then we can never come to any true morality, never come to the discipline and freedom of a whole man. We shall remain conventionally "good" on the outside and given over to *im*morality in the unconscious. We shall have broken the pact of humanity with the cat, and as we give her no food or warmth or respect she will leave our house, our mice and rats will multiply and her untamed wildness will be rampant in the dark. Of her negative aspects we will talk more later.

Why is the cat more specifically a feminine symbol? All that independence and the hunting instinct might be superficially thought to be masculine qualities. But the aggressiveness of the bull or the roar of the male lion are very different in kind from the softness, the stillness, followed by the pounce, of the cat (and it is the lioness, not the male lion, who generally hunts for food). The gentleness of the cat's soft paw and the sudden claw are truly feminine! On the positive side, the cat's independence can typify for the woman her emotional freedom, if she will refuse to cling to people or illusions, and will refuse to lie to herself. It can also warn her of the potential coldness and fierceness of her instinctual reactions under their soft feminine exterior: to draw strength and healing from them, she must meet them with her human heart, and with the austerity and detachment and lack of sentimentality of the true woman. Then the fierceness of those instincts can become her strength, her claws can be used not to scratch and tear at others or at herself but to destroy the rats in the dark, and her softness can become real warmth and tenderness instead of the fawning and weakness which too often possess her. Then she has accepted and related to the cat within. (In a man, of course, all this relates to his instinctive anima. The cat qualities are manifest in his moods and she is more remote a symbol for him.)

Finally the cat's capacity to see in the dark connects our conscious values to the life of the unconscious. In this aspect she is an image of the instinctive intuition of the woman, the mediumistic Sybil quality, which can either be a dangerous possession by the dark forces or a great gift of insight and sympathy.

In Egypt the name for cat means "to see," and Bast, the Cat Goddess, was identified with the eyes of Horus, the Sky God. Horus had a sun-eye and a moon-eye, which stood for healing and protection. The cat can see in the dark and she was honored in Egypt for the killing of snakes, so Bast brought protection against both natural and supernatural evil. This belief has persisted through the ages and in Scotland there is a saying that when a person is deluded, one should "cast the cat over him." In folklore the head of the black cat, when burnt to ashes, was believe to heal blindness — the ashes being blown into a person's eyes three times a day. The tail was, however, held to be the most potent healing agent. Rubbing a sty with a cat's tail was common, and the blood from the tail was used for skin troubles. Sometimes a black cat's tail was buried under the doorstep of a house and was supposed to ward off all disease. The cat's tail has the particular meaning of balance, restoration of equilibrium.

It was told that the Devil's mouse had nibbled a hole in a dark corner of Noah's Ark, and the water was about to rush in when God's cat pounced and killed him and God's frog then sat in the hole and blocked it. In Italy there was a story that St. Francis was praying in his hermitage when hundreds of mice from the Devil jumped out of his sleeves and began to nibble at his feet, to eat him up. But God's

holy cat appeared in the nick of time, put the mice to flight, killing all
of them except two which escaped into a crevice. The descendents
of the holy cat, concludes the story, have ever afterwards sat motionless beside holes in the wall, waiting to catch those two fugitives!

Mice and rats are carriers of disease. They represent the problem
of uncontrollable hordes, the fragmentation of the collective unconscious invading and devouring us unseen. We have great need of the
"holy cat." In the personal sphere, there are people who identify
with the mouse mentality. They are the "pounced upon," the constantly "victimized," filled with self-disgust and really *wanting* the
worst to happen. Others are "pouncers," identified with (not related
to) the cat and pouncing on everyone weaker than themselves. The
first kind have the destructive cat in their shadow, the second are
"mice" underneath their aggression. All of us have a degree of this
cat-mouse symbiosis and need to find the holy cat's eye within us to
bring things to light.

There are also images of the cat in her negative forms, as the
incarnation of evil. It was in the Middle Ages that she became the
symbol of destruction instead of healing, and the opposite pole of
the archetype came to the fore. The witch cult and the witch hunt
arose, we know, in inevitable response to the over-idealization of the
feminine, expressed in the sentimentalized worship of the Virgin
Mary shorn of her true humanity, and in the extremes of the cult of
the "perfect lady" in courtly love. As always, the unconscious threw
up the extreme opposite—the woman who was supposed to be totally given over to evil, to have made a pact with the Devil, her will
completely possessed by him.

I am indebted to a lecture given some years ago by Patricia Dale-
Green at the Guild of Pastoral Psychology, London, for the following legends. She spoke of the pact of the witch and pointed out that
the most coveted gift of the Devil was the power of *revenge.* To
implement her revenge, the witch would transform herself into a
black cat, but more often she used a real cat as an instrument—her
cat-familiar. This was a cat she had bound to her by feeding it with
her own blood or with milk from her own breasts—thus establishing
an unbreakable identification with the animal. As the witch was
bound to the Devil (who himself often appeared as a black cat) by
sexual intercourse with him, the "coldness" of his seed breeding
hatred and insatiable passion for revenge, so the true animal cat was

bound to her and made to serve her evil will, thus destroying that basic freedom of the natural cat of which we have spoken.

All this may seem remote from us, but it is more common than we are easily willing to admit. Insofar as we refuse to see our shadow side, covering it over with sugary so-called "goodness" and conventional facades, evading the starkness of true fact, we constellate the "witch" in the unconscious. If we will not accept and suffer the pain of becoming aware of our natural desires and instincts and of relating to them, consciously and with respect, then the witch inside us will, in the words of the lecture, "fly off in black fantasies on the back of the black cat," and, unseen, we will be possessed by the desire for revenge, and will act under compulsion, completely at the mercy of the instinct which we repress and hold in contempt.

It is surely through this desire for revenge that we can spot the hidden workings of the witch in us. Whenever we find ourselves violently blaming circumstances, other people, bad luck, etc., for our troubles and failures, then we are *revenging* ourselves for the pain of facts, usually facts about ourselves. The claws of the cat are out underneath, no matter how sweet our exterior, and they will be tearing and rending at people around us or at our own souls. The more unconscious this process is the more deadly. The witch, unrecognized, casts spells with the greatest ease. We are now "playing" in the vicious sense with our victims—not playing blamelessly as nature plays—but letting the cat instinct possess us and drown out all humanity. The moment we *use* the cat, use any instinct for personal power or for indulgence of *cold-hearted* intercourse, psychological or physical, then in binding her to us we are delivered over to her unbridled cruelty. If she is not free, she is deadly, her beauty destroyed, her healing night-vision turned into the uncanny ability to sense the weak spots in others and use them for her own ends or for the mere pleasure of hurting. These things must be stated in this extreme way if we are to watch for the little things that start up such a process, the little hole made by one mouse, which could end by destroying the whole Ark (the totality of life on the earth, in the legend). Our cat, if she is free, will come quickly to the rescue.

There are concrete ways to invoke the help of our "cat." In times when we feel invaded by vague depressions or tensions it is literally as though a hole has been nibbled in our psyche by a mouse out of sight in the dark, and if we will then be very still and allow ourselves to be flooded by whatever emotional reaction is uppermost at that moment—whether of fear, resentment, desire, jealousy, love or hate—plunging right into it without the censorship of guilt or shame—we will very often find that, on emerging, that little hole has been plugged. The cat has put the mouse to flight. We have set free our emotion (our cat) to be what it is and immediately we are able to see it in its true perspective, to relate it to all our other conscious values, and our energy will flow out into life again. It should be emphasized that such an experience must be given *form*—written, or painted, exactly as it came to us—so it is contained, and we relate to it and are freed from its domination.

There is one more interesting story Dale-Green told which illustrates another aspect of the cat symbol. It concerns the cat vampire, which figures largely in both European and Eastern folklore. A Japanese legend tells of a prince whose concubine was one night killed and buried by a huge cat, which then assumed her form. The prince, knowing nothing of this, continued to make love to the disguised demon, and day by day he grew weaker and weaker as the cat vampire drained his strength away. Servants watched with him at night to try and discover the cause of this but always they were overcome by sleep, until one young soldier asked to be allowed to sit with him. This man, when he began to be drowsy, thrust a dagger into his own thigh to keep himself awake and succeeded in discovering the vampire. His gaze was enough to render her powerless, so she turned back into a cat and escaped to the mountains. The prince quickly recovered.

Here is a picture of the possession of man's anima, or feminine side, by the cat. The man is then completely at the mercy of every mood and has a sense of being drained of all energy. We all know, too, how some people, whose unconscious is in the grip of a destructive attitude, can drain away the strength of those around them. Their negativity feeds on our creative energy. Psychic exhaustion comes always from some degree of "vampire" possession, which sucks our life blood, delivering us over to the forces which fight to destroy consciousness. It is only when we are "asleep" that this can happen. When we are ready and willing to suffer acute pain, as did the soldier in the story, in the effort to stay awake, to be constantly aware, then the spell is broken and we are free.

Ghosts and vampires are unconscious contents which we have "killed," totally rejected, or, alternatively, attitudes which we have in truth outgrown, but which we refuse to bury. They are dead but we still cling to the corpses and so are haunted, drained of blood. The horror of all primitives of an unburied corpse is well-founded in psychic reality—the ghost then walks and saps our life.

As Dale-Green concluded, "The power of the sacred eye of the Cat Goddess is stronger than that of the evil eye of the witch. The witch-cat may poison people's minds, infect their bodies and inflict both with blindness, but the Cat Goddess is a destroyer of poison, a healer of blindness, and a bringer of good health."

The Way
of
Discrimination

Chapter Eight

The Secret and the Open

THE ANCIENT CHINESE saying from Lao Tzu's *Tao Te Ching*, "He who knows does not speak: he who speaks does not know," is very well known and often quoted. But most of us pass on from the particular piece of verbiage or bad taste that has brought these words to our minds and do not pause to consider their profundity. We do not ask ourselves the essential question as to what kind of knowledge the sage is speaking of, nor do we seek to discriminate the opposite truth that silence and secrecy in the wrong places may nourish a deadly kind of ignorance or deceit.

This kind of discrimination, on every level of being, is becoming more and more urgent in our age of instant communications, of competitive "networks" concerned only with the speed with which every event from all over the world can be spread to the largest possible number of people. There seems to be not the slightest pause for considerations of a right to privacy or of the often false impressions spread by instant reporting without any responsible thought. This is obvious on the collective level—less so in the life of an individual; yet it is only through increase of conscious discrimination in the lives of enough individuals that the values of a society can be changed.

In the course of many years spent in listening to the problems of men and women suffering deeply from wrecked or endangered relationships of all kinds, it has become clear to me how much damage may be done by a well-intentioned but false conception of the meaning of honesty. For that most essential of all qualities of spirit is not a simple matter of never telling a lie; and most certainly it does not imply a blind assumption that one must never have a secret and that when anything is hidden from those whose lives are close to ours we are culpably practicing deceit.

Thus, both collectively and individually we are threatened today by something very like a frenzied worship of publicity on all levels.

All sense of meaning in our lives is undermined when this worship invades "the secret place of the most High,"(Psalms 91:1) and destroys the mystery, the awe, the wonder without which "the people die."

The danger of corrupt and truly dishonest secrecy is, of course, inevitably constellated when reverence for the essential secret places of the soul is lost. It has become commonplace to hear almost every day news of corruption, of lies and cover-ups among those who have been chosen and entrusted with responsibility for the welfare of millions. The real criminals among these people are less terrifying than the assumptions of so many that something they conceive of as "good" can be pursued legitimately against the law and without any attention to ethical values and the *consensus gentium*, so long as it is adequately covered up. I read recently that the facts of Watergate are being passed over almost in silence by certain modern history books used in our schools.

The loss of ethical values has become so great a danger, however, that at last more and more voices are being raised in protest against such pretended "objectivity." People are beginning to worry about what it may mean for the future of our children if schools do not teach the ethical values of the heart. The opposite approach, the fundamentalist schools where the so-called values taught breed intolerance and control over the minds of others, is equally disturbing.

These collective trends, however, are symptoms and not causes. There can be no return to the rigid moral standards—"this action is right and this wrong for everyone alike"—so often upheld by our churches. This attitude merely creates a swing to its opposite—a so-called freedom which is as enslaving and dishonest as conventional morality. Our task today is far more difficult. It is the opening of the long, hard journey to the freedom of the fundamental honesty which comes to the individual soul when he or she has found an inner guide—one who makes conscious the responsibility of our ethical choices which alone can lead us to their roots in the wholeness of the Self. Here they may be freed from *all* the selfish preferences of the ego.

So we each need to define for ourselves as far as may be possible the truths so wonderfully expressed by T.S. Eliot in *The Four Quartets*, quoting Dame Julian of Norwich, "All shall be well and all manner of thing shall be well . . ." and, continuing with his own words, "by the purification of the motive in the ground of our beseeching."

The ego will resist, often for years, our longing to uncover the motives in the ground of our being—in the Self in which the ego's demands have no power over us. Most difficult of all the sacrifices of the ego's demands is the letting go of his or her desire to achieve a state of what we conceive to be "spiritual" goodness.

As is the inevitable pattern in linear time, the collective *Zeitgeist* swings from extreme to extreme. The hypocritical extremes of Victorian prudery and the secrecy of moralistic fear have inevitably created in our century the modern worship of publicity and our evasions of ethical responsibility. As ever, the baby has been thrown out with the bathwater, and the terrible result is the loss in our society of the true meaning of a binding commitment. For instance, in most church marriages, and even in the civil ceremonies, the same or similar beautiful words of commitment are spoken, but the unspoken assumption is lurking below and invalidates the meaning. Divorce is no longer a last resort for a marriage which, after long and sincere work on the changing relationship, is finally proved to be dead and becomes an unreal tie. Most often divorce has become a quick way to avoid all the pain of real honesty with oneself, and with one's partner. The spirit of honesty can never be lived when reverence for the secret, the mystery at the center of life, has been lost, and it follows that the spontaneous openness of the child, who is not yet invaded by the inevitable "shoulds" and "should nots" of man-made laws, also disappears. Only if the secret remains inviolate in the inner life can the growing boy or girl, the adult man or woman, remain true to the values of the heart.

At first this truth, if it survives collective standards, remains in the head, and only in later life the individual may find instinctively the strength to perceive and to recognize that which must be hidden and that which must be revealed in our daily lives and relationships. It takes a deep wisdom to know when a secret must be preserved even by a lie on one level in order to save a far more essential truth on another level of being and loving. We must abide by the law until, in Jesus' apocryphal words, we "know what we are doing."

In her book, *Projection and Recollection in Jungian Psychology* (Open Court, 1980), Marie-Louse von Franz wrote a phrase which touches the essence of a great mystery. " . . . bonds with other people," she says, "are created by the Self and are *very exactly regulated as to distance and closeness.*" She goes on to quote Jung on the "central secret" of the objective cognition which is hidden behind emotional attachments and repulsions, behind the "magical dependence" which these projections engender. Only when projections are withdrawn does the beauty of the pattern of "acausal order" in our relationships appear. Also we easily forget that projections cannot be withdrawn by any act of will; for the ego does not *make* its projections—they inevitably possess us to the degree that we are not yet able to accept the consciousness of the Self as the essential place where, as Christ affirmed in his life and work, alone the prayer is born which transforms the soul. Without this secret we can never learn the discrimination which makes us free to be open—to speak freely of facts, feelings, emotions, thoughts, at the right times and in the right ways; and to be silent when the truth of the Self so guides us.

In an anthology edited by C.S. Lewis from George MacDonald's writings (Collier Books, MacMillan Publishing Co., New York, 1986), we find the following:

The Secret in Man

For each, God has a different response. With every man He has a secret—the secret of a new name. In every man there is a loneliness, an inner chamber of peculiar life into which God only can enter. I say not it is the *innermost chamber.*

The Secrets in God

There is a chamber also . . . a chamber in God Himself, into which none can enter but the one, the individual, the peculiar man—out of which chamber that man has to bring revelation and strength for his creation. This is that for which he was made—to reveal the secret things of the Father.

But if anyone rushes to reveal his glimpses of that first secret place in himself to all and sundry, without the long discipline of discrimination, he or she will assuredly never enter the *innermost* secret chamber, where the whole, unique life of a conscious being brings to others revelation and strength beyond any words and without any effort of the will.

That the words quoted came from George MacDonald, who was one of the great writers of classic children's stories, is of particular interest in our time; for there are a growing number of signs that those great children's books and stories, which are read and reread with joy and delight by adults who have not crushed the child within, are enjoying a kind of renaissance. Not long ago there was an article on the contemplative life in the *Review for Religious*, by Clifford Stevens, who wrote:

> The most contemplative piece of writing I have read recently is contained in Clifton Fadiman's three volumes, *The World's Treasury of Children's Literature*. . . . One becomes a contemplative because he is struck by a sense of wonder: the wonder of life itself, the wonder of God's ways with human beings. . . . Contemplatives are the children of history, the clowns of God, and their contemplative play it is that keeps the world sane for another generation.

He quotes John Garvey in *Commonweal* as saying that:

> A true contemplative monastery is a playground for children where some deep secret keeps laughter alive, a laughter that returns the human spirit to that sense of wonder, without which it very quickly dies.

The point is that all these and many other writers of profound insight always insist that there can be no wonder, no transforming laughter, no true play that is not born from a "deep secret" in the psyche—a secret which must be preserved at all costs, never revealed to any who cannot be trusted to understand and to preserve it inviolate.

I have recently read that enduring children's story written by Frances Hodgson Burnett and first published in 1911, *The Secret Garden*. That which many all-too-sophisticated children of this century may have rejected as sentimentality is often seen more clearly by an adult reader whose inner child is reborn. He or she recognizes, to use Rumer Godden's words about the book, "a blend of power, beauty, vivid interest and honest goodness," and feels the magic touch of wonder and the transforming springtime of the soul that is found in all our secret gardens. It is the child Mary's impassioned determination to keep the garden she has found an inviolable secret that brings the possibility of rebirth to three lost and miserable souls. Mary, aged ten, has of course no thoughts about "rebirth," but the child has the instinctive certainty of absolute disaster should this kind of secret become known to someone she could not trust "for sure, for sure," to keep the secret.

This instinct for the vital secret is as ancient and profound as the "religious" instinct itself. All religions from the most primitive to Christianity itself have mystery at their heart, and the ancient "mysteries," such as those of Eleusis, revealed only to the carefully prepared initiates, involved an oath of secrecy so closely kept by thousands over hundreds of years that to this day their nature is only fragmentarily known.

It was said that at the death of Christ on the cross, "the veil of the temple was rent in twain," symbolizing the opening of the mysteries to all men and women, not only to the chosen few. But this did not mean that everything was to be exposed and explained rationally, as the churches nowadays more and more generally seem to convey. On the contrary, it meant that the guardianship of the mystery must eventually pass from the "institution" of the temple, from the collective carriers of ritual and symbol, to every individual—"For each, God has a different response. With every man he has a secret. . . ." The secret of the new name is written in the white stone, "which no man knoweth but he that receiveth it." (Revelation 2:17)

Through the two thousand years since that moment, all Christians have had access to the sacramental meal, but that is not enough. The churches have indeed guarded and preserved the mystery, but during this extraordinary century of ours, in the dimension of time, we are in the midst of another essential awakening—a growing realization in more and more men and women, inside as well as outside the institutional churches, of the ultimate message of the incarnation. The secret remains: it is One and universal at the center in which we all may finally know the unity, and at the same time it is unique in each one of us—as, on another level, the pattern of every snowflake is unique.

Children, far more often than we know, have each their extraordinary secret; they do not understand it, but have no doubt at all, like Mary and her garden, of the essential nature of this "secret."

C.G. Jung, in his autobiography, tells of his pencil box in which, as a child, he had hidden a manikin he had carved and a little stone. This gave him the courage and sense of meaning in his childhood that he desperately needed. He knew that once discovered or spoken of, it would lose its power. Only in his maturity did he come to understand the archetypal meanings of this long forgotten secret treasure of his childhood and how it had preserved his soul.

Today even many who have great insight encourage the immediate exposure of dreams and visions in artificially composed groups. By doing this their power to nourish is immediately lost because they belong in the secret place where alone a transformation of the psyche may take place. Worse still, those who speak of them in public, or even to a friend who is not him or herself an "initiate," are invaded by the unconscious responses evoked and the ego thus becomes dangerously inflated (or deflated). Worst of all there may arise from such small beginnings the numerous cult leaders who identify with a powerful vision thus publicized. Thereafter they attract followers hungry for meaning; and finally minds and hearts of thousands may be dominated by the hubris of the leader so that they are completely blinded to the goal by money and power masquerading as religious power.

There is, however, an essential kind of sharing with the right people on the right levels. Russell Lockhart, in his book, *Words As Eggs*, affirms this necessity of "telling" in the essential work of eros in the psyche of the individual, as she or he grows in self-knowledge. There is, however, a paragraph towards the end of the introduction to this book which is a beautiful summing up of the two necessities of wholeness that I have been discussing. It brings wonder to the heart.

> In this work I have discovered that the words "self," "ethics," and "secret" are inescapably intertwined. Following the lead of these words I argue that "the deeper purpose of secrecy is not to cover up what the ego wants to hide but to bring the ego into connection with the Self where, in secret, it comes to learn of its ethical obligations." And I took a step beyond my earlier expression the "eros means telling" by seeing that "ego's unconsciousness heals frequently through revelation and telling of secrets. But the secret connection with Self is revealed not through telling but through enactment of ethical obligations learned and remembered in *secret* consort with the self. . . ." [italics added]

This is the incarnation in every man and woman.

Chapter Nine

Choice

CHOICE IS THE conscious exercise of free will, and the nature of a man's choices is the measure of his growth to maturity. The great majority of choices made by human beings are really not properly so called at all, but are mere acquiescence in a compulsive desire from the unconscious. "I don't choose to do this or that" is very often a synonym for "I don't want to do this or that," or, "I am afraid to do it," or, "I can't be bothered." Such a phrase is usually heard in the negative form, and unconsciously the speaker announces a profound truth. Indeed, as he says, he does not choose. If he really had made the conscious decision he means to convey, he might then say, "I choose not to do so and so," instead of "I don't choose." This kind of choice may often look very decisive and mature but is in fact on the same level as the choices of a child who obeys or disobeys his elders either because he is afraid, or rebellious, or because he is compelled by outer forces or by his instinctive urges.

At the other end of the scale is the free choice of the mature man, made with the highest degree of consciousness possible to that particular individual and with complete acceptance of responsibility for its consequences whatever they may be. This taking of responsibility must of course include the recognition that, insofar as we are still possessed by unconscious contents, our choice is not wholly free and will therefore have unseen consequences which we cannot reject. Nevertheless, if we have made the truest effort of which we are capable to discriminate the motives, the choice, no matter how "mistaken," will lead to a situation in which we may be shaken into greater awareness. As Jung says, although it would be nonsense to attribute to the unconscious a "purpose" in our conscious sense, yet the evidence is overwhelming that, provided we will confront it consciously, with the courage to listen, it will constantly offer us that which we need for the next step towards individuation and wholeness. The one fatal thing is to sit on the fence, playing for safety by making no choice at all when we are in doubt.

This brings us to the crucial matter of what we may call a man's basic choice. A young man said recently, "What does it mean to be chosen? I don't believe anyone is chosen." He was talking of the Jews as the "chosen people." The answer surely is that a man (or a people at a certain moment in its history) is chosen because he *has chosen*, because he has made his fundamental choice between drifting with the many or relating *as an individual* to the collective forces of consciousness or of the unconscious, of opinion or instinct. The Jews were a chosen people because, in a hostile world, they had glimpsed the one God and held to their vision through all persecution and backsliding. A man is chosen, is one of "the elect" because he chooses to follow the One by the way of individual consciousness. Immediately, however, a great temptation arises. To be chosen in this sense is confused with being set above one's fellows, with being "special," not in the true sense of the word, which means simply "of a particular kind, distinct from the generality," but in the sense of being specially good or meritorious. The extreme dangers of this are seen in the excesses of the Calvinistic doctrine of the elect, the saved. Once a man was pronounced "saved" — perhaps after a most genuine inner experience, he was beyond the law and could slip into justifying himself no matter how unconscious his following choices. "Love and do what you will!" But when a man feels in himself, after a glimpse of the real nature of Love, that he has made his fundamental choice, he must immediately remind himself that his choice is not a sudden release from responsibility but, on the contrary, imposes on him the necessity for a life-long effort to renew daily this choice in every smallest detail. He may more safely say to himself, "I have chosen to learn what love is, and therefore for a very long time I must *give up* doing what I will — that is, making unconscious compulsive choices — on the superficial level, in order to follow this deepest will in me to love, to be true to my individual way for which I am chosen, set apart." Only when individuation is achieved will come the state in which the innocence of the child and the conscious will become one thing. Most of those who have made this basic choice can remember a major turning point in their lives when it became a fully conscious act of will, though we may not have realized the crucial nature of the decision until afterwards. For it may concern a choice about something which from outside does not appear to be a vital matter at all.

> To some among us comes that implacable day
> Demanding that we stand our ground and utter
> By choice of will the great Yea or Nay.
>
> —*C.P. Cavafy*

By choice of conscious love, not by choice of desire or fear.

Chapter Ten

The Sense of Humor

IT IS IMPOSSIBLE to define that which we call "a sense of humor." Yet perhaps by playing around it in the imagination, we may bring to light a little of the wonder, the mystery, of that divine and human gift. Barbara Hannah wrote of C.G. Jung that he often used to quote Schopenhauer who said, "a sense of humor is the only divine quality of man."[1]

"Humor" itself is a word of many meanings. In the Middle Ages and through the Renaissance it meant, among other things, one of the four principle body fluids that determined human dispositions and health (sanguine, phlegmatic, choleric, melancholic); and in physiology it still means "any clear or hyaline [transparent] body fluid such as blood, lymph or bile." Some other definitions in *The American Heritage Dictionary* are: "the quality of being laughable or comical;" "a state of mind, mood, spirit;" "a sudden unanticipated whim." The root of the word is the Latin "umor" meaning liquid, fluid. Humor, therefore, on all levels is something that flows, resembling water itself, and symbolizes the movement of unconscious forces gradually evolving into basic characteristics of the individual human being, which express themselves in the body, in moods and emotional reactions, in qualities of feeling, of mind, and of spirit.

The *sense* of humor, however, has a far more elusive meaning. *The American Heritage Dictionary*, in defining "sense," after mentioning the five senses we share with the animals, continues, "Intuitive or acquired perception or ability to estimate (a sense of timing). A capacity to appreciate or understand (a sense of humor). Recognition or perception either through the senses or the intellect (a sense of guilt)."

Our humors, therefore, are unconscious drives or reactions, but without consciousness there can be no *sense* of humor at all, however much we may enjoy jokes and absurdities. It is especially interesting that the kind of sense or perception defined as a capacity "to appreciate and understand" is illustrated by a reference to "a sense of humor." The other definitions speak of the senses or the intellect or intuition; only "appreciation and understanding" are words that bring the heart into the matter. This may be a hint to us that the wisdom and compassion of the understanding heart are indeed the core of the laughter that is born from the mature sense of humor.

Most people do not think about the essential difference between a sense of humor and mere reactions to any kind of comical situation. All such things *may* induce laughter whether we have a real sense of humor or not. But the quality of the laughter is very different in those who "appreciate and understand." Those without that kind of perception do not penetrate to the "laughter at the heart of things" of which T.S. Eliot spoke in his introduction to Charles Williams' last novel, *All Hallow's Eve*.[2]

Eliot writes of Williams' stories that even for people who never read a novel more than once they are good entertainment, and continues:

> I believe that is how Williams himself would like them to be read, the first time; for he was a gay and simple man with a keen sense of entertainment and drollery. The deeper things are there just because they belonged to the world he lived in and he could not have kept them out. For the reader who can appreciate them there are terrors in the pit of darkness into which he can make us look; but in the end, we are brought nearer to what another modern explorer of the darkness has called 'the laughter at the heart of things.'

Eliot does not name that other modern explorer, but his words express a fundamental truth about those people of whom we can truly say that they possess and communicate a sense of humor. Unless a man or woman has experienced the darkness of the soul, he or she can know nothing of that transforming laughter without which no hint of the ultimate unity of opposites can be faintly intuited.

In all the greatest poets, mystics, and storytellers this sense of humor shines, even when not expressed recognizably in words and images that inspire laughter — even when they are conveying tragedy and sorrow and the darkest experiences of human life. For a very little consideration will show us clearly that the sense of humor is always born of a *sense of proportion*, both in the inner world and in the outer. The sense or perception of proportion means the capacity to discriminate and respond to (to "understand and appreciate") the relationship of the parts of anything to the whole. "Proportion is the desirable, correct or perfect relationship of parts within a whole," according to *The American Heritage Dictionary*. If we come to the point of retaining a sense of proportion in the midst of all the smallest as well as in the most profound of human emotions, we shall also discover that at the center of every experience is that laughter of God which Meister Eckhart, among many, affirmed with such delight.

There are so many kinds of laughter, and often it conceals a bitterly destructive rejection or contempt. When we yield to that, we are cut off altogether from the sense of humor which always strengthens the compassion in which all our pains and joys become whole. Hurt vanity, our own or another's, personal resentments or anger, humiliations or demands for some change in another—the antics of our alternately inflated or deflated egos—can be accepted with pain and known also as occasions for the laughter that heals. In this laughter we recognize them at once as a temporary loss of "relationship to the whole," to the center that is everywhere. Charles Williams has a wonderful phrase, "the excellent absurdity," refer- ring to any achievement of leadership or power. A man's fate, the meaning of his individual life on earth, is simply to live fully his own particular small part in the pattern of the whole, whether seemingly great or seemingly most ordinary, retaining always that blessed sense of humor about its importance to ourselves or to others with at least the "intention of Joy" (another Williams phrase) even in the midst of emotional pain.

Humility is without question closely related to the sense of humor. The one surely cannot exist without the other. T.S. Eliot, writing about Charles Williams in the introduction to *All Hallow's Eve*, states:

> He appeared completely at ease in surroundings . . . which had in- timidated many; and at the same time was modest and unassuming to the point of humility: that unconscious humility, one discovered later, was in him a natural quality, one he possessed to a degree which made one, in time, feel very humble oneself in his presence . . .[3]

Eliot is expressing here the identity of a sense of humor with the
sense of *proportion* and the humility which this engenders.

C.G. Jung was another, and one of the greatest, explorers of the
darkness in this century. He consciously entered the "pit of darkness" in the unconscious, and, evading no fact of evil and its horrors,
found also the "laughter at the heart of things." Many who knew him
well have testified to the quality of his sense of humor and of his
laughter, and Laurens van der Post in his biography of Jung[4] wrote a
beautiful tribute. He compared Jung's laughter to the laughter of the
Bushmen of Africa, thus linking it to the instinctive gaiety of the
natural man, of the child, who has not lost his original unity with
nature. (Williams also spoke of this gaiety in *The Greater Trumps* as
an intrinsic attribute of natural intelligence.) But this natural laughter must surely die when the growth of ego-consciousness plunges
the individual into the terrible conflicts of the human condition
before it is given back at the birth of joy. In between lies "the ethical
phase—endurance and action," as Jung once expressed it in a letter.[5]
This is the phase of exploration, of purgatorial choices and con-
frontations, in which we learn to behave "as if" we knew joy without
ever disguising to ourselves the actual state of our emotions: then,
sooner or later, the true gift of that laughter will come to us, when we
least expect it, through the response to life which is a sense of
humor—the realization of proportion.

The original gaiety of the natural man had certainly undergone a
night-sea-journey in Jung as it must in every one seeking conscious
wholeness. The adolescent ego must go through the struggle to
establish its identity as separate from parents and the
environment—a process often prolonged throughout a lifetime. In
this inner struggle we are frequently caught in a sense of the earth-
shaking importance of our achievements, which is a normal phase in
the young. But the individual may tragically remain into adult years
obsessed with his or her superiority or inferiority as the case may be.
Nothing more quickly kills the ability to laugh at oneself which is the
sure mark of a sense of humor. We are then left with the sterile
moralities of convention, a kind of solemn and possessive pursuit of
"spirituality" from which the wind that "bloweth where it listeth"
and its laughter are entirely absent. The opposites of these
moralities—senseless rebellion, violence, license, greed, and

corruption—can never be controlled by such attitudes. Only the far more difficult search for the ethics of individual freedom and joy can avail in our predicament.

A sense of humor is in fact the royal road to this freedom and this joy. One who has it is always ready to laugh at all the pretensions of the ego in him or herself or in another. This at once differentiates it from intellectual wit and superficial joking and, still more obviously, from the forced cheerfulness of some who are determined always to do "good," to improve the ego and the world.

Without this kind of humor no one can experience the laughter of the reborn child within, for it brings with it a recognition of the fundamental validity of the "other," of object and subject as one. People who lack this perception may laugh in the same situations, but there is a subtle difference in their laughter, for it does not spring from the heart and the belly; at its worst it often contains hidden barbs directed at another, since it is a protective armor for a frightened ego. We all laugh at the foibles of those around us, but those with a sense of humor do not laugh *at* a person; there is simply a feeling of delight in the ridiculous wherever it is manifest, and such laughter does not condemn the other or oneself but simply enjoys the sudden recognition of the loss of proportion in all our human conflicts and contradictions. It is a healing, not a destructive thing—a delight in life, in its comedies and tragedies, its seriousness and absurdities—the "excellent absurdities" that Williams loved.

"There are many ways of laughing," wrote van der Post of Jung's laugh, "but the greatest is that which comes from the joy of seeing disproportion restored to proportion. His laughter was delight, sheer and uncompromising, in the triumph of the significance of the small over the unreality of excess and disproportion in the established great, and so pure a rejoicing in another enlargement, however minute, of the dominion of proportion."[6] And proportion is, once more, "the perfect relationship of the parts to the whole."

It is a sad, even a dangerous loss to Christianity that the Gospels and so many of their interpreters never convey the sense of humor that Jesus must certainly have manifested in his life, and we are told nothing of the laughter that must have been so often heard from him and with him. But if one listens imaginatively to some of the stories and sayings it is clearly to be heard. After his ultimate exploration of darkness and the "descent into Hell," it ripples and flows with such

joy in the Resurrection stories that the absence of specific references
to it cannot hide it. When in later centuries the lives of saints and
sages have been described, how often their laughter lifts our hearts.
St. Teresa's autobiography, for instance, dances with it.

There is, in fact, no real "spirituality" (a much misunderstood
term in these days) without the laughter which the sense of humor
brings. It is not to be confused with frivolity and it cannot exist in
anyone who is not a serious person able to explore the darkness and
suffering in life. The lack of this quality in the soul may also reveal
itself among those who seek to lighten the solemnity of their religious beliefs by *mixing* the funny and the serious, making jokes
either silly or embarrassing, *about* the deep realities. The sense of
humor, the laughter of the Self, never *mixes* things in that way, thus
destroying both the serious and the gay. It simply begets in men and
women a true perception of all the suffering and the joy, the tears and
laughter, the seriousness and the fun, inherent in our experience.
When all these opposites are clearly discriminated, they may then be
known as one in the unity of the laughter and the tragic darkness of
being.

In the diaries of Etty Hillesum,[7] a young Dutch Jewish woman,
writing during the occupation of Holland by the Nazis, told of the
horrible suffering of those who, including herself, were waiting in a
camp for transportation to Auschwitz (where she was to die). Her
compassion, not only for the victims but for the Germans who
inflicted the suffering, shines out from the book, but most moving of
all are her words in the midst of the horrors, about her experience of
the deepest and most radiant inner joy she had ever known. She tells
how she realized what a very little thing all this misery was in the
glorious wholeness of the universe. Her joy was the dawning of the
sense of proportion, the relationship of every part, however dark, to
the whole.

As we wonder how we could possibly have endured such a fate, we
are nevertheless inspired by these great ones urgently to seek in our
everyday lives a fuller realization of this joy, this laughter. The
humdrum tasks, the endless repetitions of the daily round, are often
much more difficult to recognize as occasions for this kind of vivid
living in the moment than are the more dramatic events of our lives.
We hurry through the so-called boring things in order to attend to
that which we deem more important and interesting. Perhaps the

final freedom will be a recognition that every thing in every moment is *"essential"* and that nothing at all is *"important"*!

The first step on this way is to learn all over again that natural gift of the small child—the gift of "play," which is so conspicuously absent from our society. The natural gaiety and laughter of the child within us is lost in exact proportion to the loss of our ability to play; and it is fascinating to remember the many contexts in which that word is used. We use it unconsciously without any thought of its fundamental meaning and therefore the word so often loses its connection with that natural joy. Every kind of dramatic performance is called a play, and all actors are players, as are all musicians, and all ball and game players. Tragedy, comedy, farce, and all kinds of music—Bach, Plainsong, Jazz or Rock and Roll—are brought to us by players, among whom there are those who appreciate and understand the nature of play and so convey the joy of it to their audiences whether through their "playing" of dark truths or light. But there are so many who have no perception of the meaning of play and whose striving motives are to acquire fame and money or self-satisfaction by sensational performances, often in productions without meaning—the opposite of play.

It is even more obvious in sports—which carry for so many the spirit of true play—but which in our day are becoming swallowed up in the atmosphere of big business. The players are, of course, truly playing when they put out all their skill and strength to win, thus reflecting archetypal conflicts. And there still remains in many great individual players and coaches the recognition that without the experience of defeat as well as the exhilaration of victory there can be no real meaning in play. But victory at all costs—secret drugging, violence, corruption, and greed—threatens all sports, and indeed all our activities that cease to be games but become competition for the satisfaction of any kind of demand of the ego. The enormous popularity of sports is a symptom of the deep yearning in all of us for the spirit of play. Through the enjoyment of such things we may discover at last that until our whole lives, whether working or at leisure, are infused by the joy and laughter of play for its own sake—never for the sake of gain—we are not truly alive at all. Work and play would then no longer be opposed to each other but at one in all the different aspects of our lives. Schiller said (again as quoted by Jung), "Man is only fully human when he is at play."

We may begin to intuit the nature of true play if we listen and listen again to the words of Sophia, the holy wisdom of the feminine in the Godhead. They are written in the Book of Wisdom (8: 22-25) (and they are also in the epistle for the celebration of the birth of Mary the mother of God, in the Roman Catholic liturgy). Without this wisdom of Sophia there can be no Mary within us, women or men, to give birth to the divine, incarnate Child. The translation is from the Douai Bible:

> The Lord possessed me from the beginning of his ways, before he made anything from the beginning. I was set up from eternity, and of old, before the earth was made. . . . I was with him forming all things and was delighted every day, playing before him at all times, playing in the world; and my delight is to be with the children of men. Now, therefore, ye children, hear me. Blessed are they that keep my ways. Hear instruction and be wise and refuse it not. Blessed is the man that heareth me, and that watcheth daily at my gates and waiteth at the posts of my doors. He that shall find me shall find life, and shall have salvation from the Lord.

When Christ said, "Whosoever shall not receive the kingdom of God as a little child, he shall not enter therein" (Mark 10: 15) he was speaking out of this feminine divine wisdom, affirming that beyond the essential "ethical phase," to use Jung's phrase, and beyond all the splendor and beauty of theology, of philosophy, of psychology and scientific research, beyond all the efforts of mankind to understand good and evil, matter and spirit, there still remains a gate through which we must pass if we are to find the ultimate freedom of "the Kingdom of Heaven." It is the gateway to the spontaneous play, not childish but child-like, of the feminine spirit. Without it there never could have been and cannot ever be any creation that knows eternity again after the long journey of Return in the dimension of time. She is and always has been "playing in the world" in the sheer delight of the Fool and the Child hidden in every one of us. As we wait "at the posts of her doors" she may reveal herself to us: then indeed all work is transformed into play and play becomes the work that is contemplation, and we know the delight of being with the sons (and daughters) of men.

I was in the process of writing the above when, synchronistically, I received notice of a seminar to be given by Adolf Guggenbuhl-Craig in New York on "Aging." In the summary of his theme it is said that he suggests it is time to see aging as a process of becoming free . . ."the real archetypal image, the stimulating symbol for the aging would be, not the wise old man or woman, but the 'foolish' old man or woman," then they would find freedom from all conventions and will not care if they show their deficiencies. They would be able to let go of all need to be wise and to do the right thing; they could admit now that they don't understand the world anymore. The archetype would be more accurately described as the Fool and the Child within us rather than as "foolish." The freedom of the Fool and the Child is never silly: it is Sophia "playing in the world."

English literature offers a number of characters who awaken in us that kind of laughter which is beyond all analysis. Through these images we experience the wonder of that sense of humor which, breaking through the bonds of cause and effect thinking and superficial morality, touches the innocence of the Fool and the Child in us and brings with it compassion and love.

In Dickens' novel *Dombey and Son*, who can ever forget Mr. Toots? In our day he would have been labelled with some of those empty collective words—"handicapped," "retarded," "brain-damaged," etc.—and treated accordingly, but even today one feels he would have transcended all that. There are many comic characters in Dickens—some great like Toots; others, like Captain Cuttle in the same novel, are mildly funny, though somewhat boring, and do not awaken that fundamental laughter at all. Why? Because Mr. Toots and his peers are wholly themselves, as a small child is wholly him or herself, and have at the same time a strange kind of natural wisdom that cannot be defined. Mr. Toots, as G.K. Chesterton so beautifully said of him, "always got all the outside things wrong, but all the inside things right." His natural emotions were wholly involved in what he did and felt, but he always assured everyone that it was "of no consequence," as indeed he knew in the humility of his extraordinarily accurate sense of proportion. Susan Nipper, whom he eventually married, said of him, "Immediately I see that innocent in the hall I burst out laughing first and then I choked."

The second immortal image whom one hardly dares approach is Shakespeare's Sir John Falstaff. How can one speak of the essential innocence of the Fool in that fat, drunken, cowardly thief and deceiver? Yet it is there, miraculously there; and he inspires so much true laughter, so much love and delight—both among those who have been most injured by him in the play and in all those blessed with a true sense of humor who read and re-read his story—that again we are left with a vision of wonder and delight beyond that final gateway into freedom. This miracle is of course absent from the Falstaff of *The Merry Wives of Windsor*, who is primarily a figure of farce: we may laugh at this Falstaff but we cannot love him. In *Henry IV* and *Henry V*, however, that kind of laughter disappears. To judge his deplorable qualities would be to miss the point absolutely: he is as he is and retains that extraordinary divine quality through it all. He truly loves "sack," as he truly loves life: "If I had a thousand sons, the first humane principle I would teach them should be to forswear thin potations and to addict themselves to sack." On the rational level, his long paean of praise to "sack" is indeed nonsense, but on Falstaff's lips it is a gorgeous celebration of joy in life. Let us indeed forswear the thin potations that we so often give our souls to drink with dreary solemnity. Falstaff creates laughter of the deepest kind all around him and there is no "why" about it. Even the Chief Justice, most reasonably rebuking him for his outrageous behavior, is unconsciously won over.

We feel the tragedy of his rejection, harsh, however necessary, by the Prince, now king, and in *Henry V* we are deeply moved by the account of his illness and death when he was nursed by Mistress Quickly—the woman whom he had almost ruined financially and who loved him nevertheless. "Nay, sure, he's not in hell: he's in Arthur's bosom, if ever man went to Arthur's bosom. A' made a finer end and went away an it had been any christom child . . ." (Act 2, Sc. 3). And Bardolph, his much abused servant, says, "Would I were with him whether in heaven or in hell!" (Act 2, Sc. 3) How splendid a tribute! Laughter and tears come together as we read this scene if we hear it with the same sense of humor in which these two realities are always present.

Early in *Henry IV, Part 2* Falstaff seems to recognize for a moment his extraordinary vocation as a kind of divine Fool. "The learning of this foolish and compounded clay, man, is not able to invent anything that tends to laughter, more than I invent or is invented on me: I am not only witty in myself, but the cause that wit is in other men." And later he surely has his values straight when, after the young sober Duke John of Lancaster has said pompously, "I, in my condition, shall better speak of you than you deserve," Falstaff says to himself, "I would you had but the wit: 'twere better than your dukedom. Good faith, this same young sober-blooded boy doth not love me, nor a man cannot make him laugh." (Act 4, Sc. 3).

In our own time the voice of Christopher Alexander is being heard by more and more seekers. He has written and is writing of architecture, of building as a way to the creation of wholeness in the individual and in the community; and he speaks the same truths as do all the other contemplatives through the ages. In a seminar of his on tape one can hear his belly-laugh and recognize it as of the same nature as that of Jung and of Charles Williams as described here — of the same nature as that which bubbles up with our tears as we meet and experience characters such as Toots and Falstaff. In *The Timeless Way of Building*, Alexander writes about the long discipline (the ethical phase of the search for self knowledge) which teaches us "the true relationship between ourselves and our surroundings." We come then at last to the perception which he calls "egoless" and then we may pass through

> the gate which leads you to the state of mind, in which you live so close to your own heart that you no longer need a language (the old discipline). It is utterly ordinary. It is what is in you already. . . . There is no skill required. It is only a question of whether you will allow yourself to be ordinary, and do what comes naturally to you, and what seems most sensible to your heart . . . not to the images which false learning has coated on your mind.[8]

When we will consent to be "utterly ordinary," to be simple instead of wise, then the "humors" will transform into that *sense* of humor which brings sheer delight in that ordinariness, in the joy of what *is*. Then our instinctive emotions, our moods, the "melancholic, choleric, sanguine or phlegmatic humors" will no longer possess us and project themselves around us in the unconscious. These projections always add to the weight that breeds a desperate need to create drama and excitement in the environment through the hidden greed which is a kind of "anti-play." Instead, in that perception of wonder that is the sense of humor, we can begin to play in the freedom and simplicity of the child. No longer will there be any need to strive after anything—especially not after the spiritual—because the spirit itself would be present in each moment. As the old monk, who was the author of *The Cloud of Unknowing* in the fourteenth century, wrote in his other little treatise, *The Book of Privy Counselling*: [After the long work of learning to know your sinfulness] "Stop thinking about what you are! Know only that you are what you are. . . . Remember that you possess an innate ability to know *that you are.*"

At this level the East and West with their different languages are at one. Sri Ramana Maharshi, that most simple and direct of Hindu sages (1890-1950) whose laughter and compassion reach us through his words and his silences, once in answering a question, said: "There is no greater mystery than this—that *being* the reality, we seek to gain reality. We think there is something hiding our reality and that it must be destroyed before the reality is gained. It is ridiculous. A day will dawn when you will yourself laugh at your past efforts. That which will be on the day you laugh is also here and now."[9] This is "the laughter at the heart of things": this is the Divine Comedy of Being.

NOTES

1. Barbara Hannah, *Jung, His Life and Work: A Biographical Memoir* (New York: G. P. Putnam's and Sons, 1976), p. 40.
2. Charles Williams, *All Hallows Eve* (New York: Farrar, Strauss and Giroux, 1948), p. xviii.
3. *Ibid.*, p. ix.
4. Laurens van der Post, *Jung and the Story of Our Time* (New York: Pantheon Books, 1975).
5. C.G. Jung, *Letters*, Vol. 1 (Princeton: Princeton University Press, 1973) p. 375.
6. Van der Post, *Jung and the Story of Our Time*, p. 45.
7. Etty Hillesum, *An Interrupted Life* (New York: Washington Square Press Pocketbooks, 1985).
8. Christopher Alexander, *The Timeless Way of Building* (New York: Oxford University Press, 1979), p. 547.
9. Edited by David Godman, *Be As You Are: The Teachings of Sri Ramana Maharshi* (London: Arkana Books Paperback, Routledge, Kegan and Paul, 1985).

Chapter   Eleven

The Joy of the Fool

I REMEMBER THAT, during a discussion of Charles Williams' novel *The Greater Trumps* some time ago, someone asked for a definition of "the Fool." It was, of course, not forthcoming, for the Fool of the Tarot eludes all analysis. If he could be rationally defined, he would cease to be the Fool. This is true, in fact, of any numinous symbol. When we perceive an image in the immediacy of imaginative vision, it glows with an undying vitality and changes our lives, but as soon as we insist on a rational understanding of it, the symbol is dead.

The always dreary occultist definitions of the symbolism of the Greater Trumps are worse than boring in the case of the Fool; they deprive him of all his meaning. Only the poet, inarticulate in most of us, can reveal to us the Fool, and our perception is sharpened, our vision intensified by response to those moments when the Fool is incarnate.

Charles Williams has written about the actual image of the Fool of the Tarot, and nothing can awaken us more surely to the difference between head knowledge and vision than to go straight from a perusal of the usual "explanations" of the cards to a reading of the scene in *The Greater Trumps* where Sybil is first shown the tiny golden images of the Tarot moving unceasingly on the round table.

The image of the Fool, in the version of the cards used by nineteenth-century and modern occultists, is a picture of a young man stepping gaily and fearlessly, without looking where he is going, to the edge of a precipice. Over his right shoulder he holds a wand with a bag on the end of it; in his left hand is a white rose and at his feet a little dog stands on his hind legs. The signs of the Zodiac are on his belt and other symbolic designs are on his tunic. In the French Marseilles version, the figure is much simpler and there are many fewer symbols. We see the Fool from behind and he looks back over his right shoulder; the dog, if it is a dog, is tearing a rent in his trouser leg. There is evidence that the animal was originally a white lynx (Williams calls it a tiger) biting the Fool's left calf; so we may think of it as an animal both wild and domestic. The card is unnumbered, marked 0. It has been variously placed, by those who failed to understand, at the beginning, at the end, or between cards 20 and 21, but it is plain that it does not belong in the series at all—that it is quite separate from the numbered trumps and yet, we may add, essential to each. It is nowhere and everywhere.

A sample of the usual kind of interpretation is found in a little book published by the School of Ageless Wisdom, of Los Angeles. "The wreath around the Fool's head symbolizes the vegetable kingdom; also Victory. The wand is Will, the Wallet memory. The white rose represents purified desire. . . ." and so on.[1]

The Fool has also been described as the Cosmic Life Breath about to descend into the Abyss of Manifestation. There is nothing inaccurate in these pompous statements; there is simply no imaginative truth in them. They "darken counsel by words without knowledge" and the Fool remains motionless, a dead picture in our minds. So in Charles Williams' story the little golden figure of the Fool with the tiger leaping beside him remained, for all but one of the watchers, unmoving in the center of the table, while the other images moved in a kind of patternless dance around him. Mr. Coningsby (the narrow-minded, self-centered extravert) says:

> "Why doesn't the one in the middle dance?"
> "We imagine that its weight and position must make it a kind of counterpoise," Henry answered. . . .
> "Has he a tiger by him for any particular reason?" Mr. Coningsby inquired. "Fools and tigers seem a funny conjunction."
> "Nobody knows about the Fool," Aaron burst in. . . .
> Mr. Coningsby was about to speak again when Sybil forestalled him.
> "I can't see this central figure," she said. "Where is it exactly, Mr. Lee? . . ."
> Henry leant forward suddenly. . . . "Miss Coningsby . . . can you see the Fool and his tiger at all?"
> She surveyed the table carefully. "Yes," she said at last, "There—no, there—no—it's moving so quickly I can hardly see it—there—ah, it's gone again. Surely that's it, dancing with the rest; it

seems as if it were always arranging itself in some place which was empty for it. . . it certainly seems to me to be dancing everywhere."[2]

He is dancing everywhere, always dancing in the place which is empty for him, and the tiger, the dog, dances with him; and where they dance there is order and peace of a kind that the world calls folly or idiocy or sheer madness; but only those who, like Sybil, have come to live from that center of order and peace can see him dance at all times and in all places—the dance which is the joy of the universe. "Never forget," says R.H. Blyth, "all joy is idiot joy—all love is idiot love."[3] And he quotes from Shakespeare: "The lunatic, the lover and the poet are of imagination all compact."[4] The lover or the poet who does not know the apparent lunacy of the dance of the Fool is never in truth a lover or a poet at all.

Sybil Coningsby in Williams' novel is a woman who, through years of interior suffering, living a most ordinary outer life without any dramatic experiences visible to the world, has come in full consciousness to that state of "complete simplicity, costing not less than everything," as T.S. Eliot describes it.[5] She does nothing *for* anyone anymore; she does not teach or plan; yet her every word or action spontaneously and inevitably transforms each situation in which she is involved from chaotic movement into an ordered dance—a dance of "idiotic" joy, even when, as in the great magical storm of the book, the destruction of the world is threatened. For she moves in unison with, in Williams' words, "that which has no number and is called the Fool, because man finds it folly til it is known. It is sovereign or it is nothing, and if it is nothing, then man was born dead."[6]

Teilhard de Chardin once wrote, "Joy is the most infallible sign of the presence of God." Teilhard did not, of course, mean the kind of happiness, as interpreted by most, which we have a right to "pursue" as is stated in our Declaration of Independence—for to *pursue* happiness is to lose joy. He meant the joy that flows into the lives, conscious and unconscious, of men and women whenever there is a true *meeting*, personal and impersonal, between friends, or even momentarily between one individual and another, or between a human being and any fact of his life and environment—a meeting which springs from an instant recognition of the innocence of the Self at the center of all life. The innocence of any small child is obvious. The innocents are those who are incapable of deliberately hurting anyone or anything (*in-nocens* = not, plus the present participle of *nocere*, to hurt.) So innocence that is conscious is the rare fruit of wholeness.

As Jung very often said, so much depends on the few who have begun to know, to glimpse, the unity beyond the opposites in time and space. Surely the great and certain hope of our time is in this — in the obviously growing, gloriously growing signs of the spirit of the innocent child within, seen in individuals, each returning to his or her roots in nature and in spirit, consciously seeking global, not national solutions, and in their daily lives evading nothing of the essential suffering which is true compassion.

NOTES

1. *Highlights of Tarot* (Los Angeles: BOTA, 1931), p. 17.
2. Charles Williams, *The Greater Trumps* (Grand Rapids, Michigan: Wm. B. Eerdmans, 1976), pp. 73-75.
3. R.H. Blyth, *Zen in English Literature and the Oriental Classics* (Tokyo: Hokuseido Press, 1948), p. 369.
4. William Shakespeare, *A Midsummer Night's Dream*, Act 5, Sc. 1.
5. T.S. Eliot, *Four Quartets*, part 5, ll. 40-41.
6. Williams, *The Greater Trumps*, p. 196.

Chapter Twelve

Pride

IN THE CHRISTIAN tradition, pride has always been regarded as the first and most deadly of the seven deadly sins. In the myth of the Creation, it was the awakening of pride in Eve and Adam when they heard the serpent say, "Ye shall be as gods knowing good and evil" that led to their eating of the apple from the forbidden Tree of Knowledge. The Greek work *hubris* conveys the full meaning of this sin — it carried the specific meaning of a pride so overweening that it arrogated to itself the power of the immortal gods, and those who were possessed by it inevitably suffered a fall which destroyed them utterly, as in the story of Icarus and his attempt to fly to the sun.

Psychologically these myths are entirely accurate. This kind of pride, once it invades and possesses the ego in a man or woman, becomes the root of all the other six, the root of our envy, anger, sloth, covetousness, gluttony, and lust. We can have no hope of redeeming these evils while the arrogant pride of the ego remains. All these six are distortions of instinctual drives for power or perversions of love; but *hubris* is an identification of the ego with the divine totality itself. *My* skill, *my* opinion, *my* comfort, *my* need, *my* safety, etc., are to be served as the essentials of life. I want something and I must have it because it is obviously my *"right."*

I have listed the seven sins in the order given to them in Dante's *Purgatorio*, which is symbolically the place, or the condition of the soul, in which the ego slowly purges itself and is freed from each of them. The proud are met by Dante and Virgil on the lowest cornice, where they walk around the holy mountain weighed down by enormous stones carried on their backs, unable to look up, to look anywhere but down at the ground — the *humus*, the earth of humility.

Dante's symbolism of the sufferings each sin engenders speaks with wonderful clarity to our understanding of the unconscious today. Always the suffering is precisely the sin itself known in the perception of its true effect on the individual (or collective) psyche.

The envious, for example, sit with sealed eyes unable to see anything, for envy kills all true discrimination of values; the wrathful are choked and blinded by the smoke from their burning fires of resentment; the slothful never stop running—and this is particularly obvious in the driven busyness which is the bane of our society and which is, fundamentally, a slothful escape from the hard work of the journey within. Once a man or woman has said "yes" to the inner process of purgation, these things are experienced willingly and gladly as the essential conflicts on the way to wholeness, to the marriage of the opposites. He or she has set foot on the spiral way of Dante's Mount Purgatory. If we do not so choose, however, we remain in the infernal state in which we shall suffer the opposite aspect of our hidden sin neurotically and unconsciously, until the day when the neurosis itself may drive us to the journey and be known as a blessing.

The image of the proud, bent over under the weight of huge stones, is especially powerful, for from primitive times in all religions and cultures, the stone has been a symbol of divinity and immortality here on earth—a symbol of the Self, to use C. G. Jung's term. For Moslems the black stone in Mecca is the center; for the alchemists for centuries the "lapis" was the image of the goal of their quest for the transcendent unity of the Self. In some versions of the Grail legend, the Holy Grail itself is called the stone; for Christians, Christ is the "stone which the builders rejected," "the headstone of the corner"; and in the Apocalypse the true name of a man or woman which "no man knoweth but he that receiveth it" is written on a white stone.

We can perceive in those figures bearing the weight of the stones what it is that pride does to us. The *hubris* of the ego identifying with the Self, usurping the divine power and wisdom, demanding always to be first and right, looking down on others from above with a contempt well hidden, perhaps, but nevertheless "deadly"—this soaring pride will inevitably constellate in the unconscious a growing weight—a weight often felt in the atmosphere which such an ego spreads in the environment, and which inevitably at last pulls down, crushes, and destroys that ego itself. An inferiority complex is as dangerous a manifestation of pride as is its opposite.

Moreover, pride is the first and most sinister of all the seven because, unless it has been faced and purified in the ground of our psyche, successful efforts towards purging of the other sins will only lead to the worst and most poisonous threat of all—the hidden pride of spirit which rejoices in its own "goodness," its own wonderful insights, its own martyrdom even, its own saintliness, even its own imagined humility.

"Pride goeth before destruction, and an haughty spirit before a fall." So it has been since Lucifer fell from heaven. The proud reject and refuse to carry the weight of the stone consciously; the other kind of suffering is so much easier because the ego can still feel proud of its nobility or can project its cause onto someone or something outside itself. Lucifer, nevertheless, is also the light bringer. There is no one who does not seek to become a god, for that is the original sin. But having fallen, we may begin to see the light, to be aware of objective good and evil in the ego with its shadow, no longer as the center but as the servant of the Self. We then begin to understand the words of Julian of Norwich, "Oh happy fault that wert the occasion of so great a redemption. For when Adam fell Christ fell into Mary's womb." The original sin is also the original opportunity whereby we may come to conscious oneness with God. Dante shows us that the redemptive process for the individual is the lifting and the carrying with joy the weight of the Stone—the weight of the human condition exactly as it is in the pattern of the totality in each one's particular life. This chosen carrying will force us to keep our eyes on the earth at our feet, on every smallest happening, the little things of every day, the often disregarded images that come to us.

There is no doubt at all about the initial "weight" of the Self when we consent to life and carry our suffering and the agonies of fact. We are exposed to the constant temptation of self-pity and complaint about the nature of our particular weight of suffering. But the moment in which we consent to it without any conditions on every level of our being, the miracle happens and the weight disappears. Most wonderful of all, we realize that the neurotic suffering which had for so long oppressed us has become a valid carrying of the burden and that it now reveals meaning in our lives and has finally forced us to abandon the ego as the center and glimpse the circle whose "center is everywhere and circumference nowhere." In Dante's imagery, as the poet with Virgil comes to the stair by which he will emerge from the state of pride, the angel of humility brushes his forehead with his wing; he hears joyful voices singing "Blessed are the poor in spirit," and as he climbs he asks in wonder:

> Master, what heavy load
> Has slipped from me,
> So that I walk with ease,
> And scarcely feel fatigue upon the road?[1]

He has begun to experience the meaning of Christ's words, "My yoke is easy, my burden is light."

In a lifetime's journey such moments may come and recede again many times, but even once truly experienced they are known forever as truth, however emotionally remote they may usually seem. Dante has still a long and arduous climb ahead of him and a purging of all his lesser distortions of love. All those efforts to gain the heights are a lie unless we have recognized the lurking shadow of pride as it serves the ego and begin to be aware of the true nature of humility.

Like all the "sins," pride is not in itself a sin or an evil. Nothing in the instinctual nature of human beings is a sin unless it is used by the ego with some kind of profit motive—even if that profit motive is seemingly justified, respectable, "good" in a collective sense. As so often, the dictionary may open our eyes startlingly to the root meaning of words we so frequently use without discrimination. The root of the word "proud" is the Latin *prodesse*, which means "to be beneficial," and our word "prod" is a variant of *pro* (for) and *esse* (to be). The old French root is *prod, prud*, meaning "good," "gallant," "brave." The first meanings of the English word given in *The American Heritage Dictionary* are all concerned with self-respect. Only meaning number 4 is equivalent to the sin of pride, synonymous with arrogance—the arrogating to oneself, to the ego, of that which belongs to the Self. It is easy to recognize in the root "to be for" the paramount importance of the first and most fundamental of the sins. To be for—what or whom?

It is therefore as vital for the inner journey in each of us to look as deeply into the meaning of the positive nature of pride as to recognize the deadly nature of its distortion. I once heard a dream in which there was an image of a man who had lived fully and deeply through much suffering and had come to a turning point in his life. A voice spoke in the dream and said of him, "He has learned the pride of the lion; he must now learn the pride of the unicorn." This dream led me to a long reflection on these two images of pride and their meaning.

It is not by chance that we speak of a "pride of lions," for those old collective words often expressed a salient quality in the beasts or birds they described. The lion is felt by man to be a king among beasts. His pride is very different from the human sin of usurping a merit not his own; it is a natural pride which is the quality of being absolutely true to oneself. A lion who turns man-eating when unable through injury to catch his natural prey becomes a pariah, cast out of his pride, for he is untrue to his lion nature, no longer a proud king among beasts. It is interesting to remember how Laurens van der Post writes in *The Heart of the Hunter* of the Bushman's feeling for the lion, and of his own observations. He says the lion is by far the most individual of the wild animals in Africa. Every lion you encounter will act in a different way and you can never predict his behavior as you can with almost all the other species. This is reflected in the beautiful Bushman story of how the lion singled out a man and forced him finally into coming out from behind the protection of his tribe, into taking responsibility for his own decisions.

This, then, is how a man learns the pride of the lion. He must emerge from dependence on collective authority and enter into life with the courage both to kill and be killed, as it were, a thousand times, as a lion must kill to eat and risk the guns of the hunters. For, once we have experienced the Fall and innocence is lost, we are plunged into the battle of the opposites, and we can never be involved in this battle as anything but unconscious pawns until we have learned that we must, symbolically speaking, kill in order to eat, and be killed that others may eat. "The pride of the lion" in this context is that which comes to the man who consciously accepts this symbolic truth, and the suffering it brings. Thus he emerges from the meaningless state of tearing others to pieces and being torn in the *unconscious*, which is so often the condition of those who preach universal good will and a bloodless kind of psychic pacifism. We have only to think of what would happen if all fighting and killing were to be expunged from the great myths of the world to realize that life would be meaningless without fighting. The long journey towards consciousness involves constant and ruthless fighting and killing; primitive man would have starved without it, and a man in any age who tries to evade it on all levels is still sucking milk from his mother's breast in a state of arrested development. Any kind of pacif-*ism*, as opposed to the true understanding of peace, is not only doomed to failure, since it denies validity to one of the basic facts of the unconscious, but it actually breeds more and more violence, violence of an unconscious kind which kills in order to feed those hideous distortions of human nature, the pride of the ego, its power and its greed. To be released from this kind of violence, we have to accept the necessity of fighting with every ounce of our strength, but *on an inner not an outer battlefield*.

I believe that as long as men are unable to fight and to kill and to expose themselves to be killed in their inner world, then it is a great deal better that they find the meaning of courage and self-sacrifice on an outer battlefield than that they live out their lives in a simulation of peace under which they spread destruction through the unconscious into the lives of their neighbors. Increasingly through the centuries, man's urge to stir up war has been generated by his boredom. He has an absolute need to fight obstacles, to "kill the dragon," to know in himself the heroic devotion which proves him a man — and the fewer natural obstacles he has in life, the greater is his need for either an outer or inner battlefield. That is the choice. Until there are enough individuals who find and fight their inner battles, wars must continue and the horrible thing is that war today, even without the atomic bomb, has become largely a matter of long-distance destruction of targets, stripped of all individuality. It is the coldness of hell itself.

So it becomes more and more imperative that we dare to fight in our own personal lives; and it is a great deal better that we fight openly and outwardly the people around us when it is a matter of standing by our *essential* values, however immature these values may be, than that we hide behind a pacifistic pseudoharmony and then go about spreading hostility and bad feeling in an indirect manner. As long as we are split and the opposites hold sway we will do as much harm to others in our lives as good. We may, however, think of the immense debt we owe to those who have dealt us mortal blows in the course of our lives, thus revealing to us our own truth, and while it does not relieve us of our guilt for our own unconscious killing, we still may know that perhaps our darkness has brought light to others.

Some pacifists hold that a man is almost as guilty for killing another man in war as he is if he kills for some personal end. But the practically universal judgment of mankind on this issue does not err, and the distinction is valid in the personal world. If a man fights out of his devotion to something—a value, a feeling beyond his ego's pride and desire—if he kills out of *need*, whether it be the killing of animals for food, or of men when an essential value is threatened, he is not guilty as he is guilty if he kills out of greed and hatred. It is here that the natural "kill and be killed" of the animal world brings us a basic lesson. In a Hindu story, a lion who is brought up with sheep who then refuses to eat meat is shown to be an offense against nature—a shocking, ugly thing. We are not animals, and for us to live out the animal side of our nature without conscious choice and ethical judgment is equally an offense against the nature of man. Jung repeated many times that a man—if he is to be true to his humanity—must live by an ethic which every person who seeks individuation must find for him or herself. When we have accepted both these things, the animal and the ethical, and we are willing to kill and be killed, if necessary, in the service of our deeply held values, then we have learned "the pride of the lion." "I am come not to bring peace but a sword."

The pride of the lion, however, is far from being the end. There comes a time when this pride must in its turn be abandoned, transmuted into the pride of the unicorn; and if a man refuses this sacrifice and the quest of the "unicorn" when the time is ripe, he will surely fall back again into a worse and more deadly state of personal pride.

When the pride of the unicorn is born in a man, he has no more need to fight, for he has begun to find his nourishment through that love which is beyond the love-hate opposites. The unicorn does not kill; he harms nothing. His horn is uplifted in a remote and lovely pride as we glimpse him now and then on his swift course. Yet like all true pride it is humble. The power of his horn comes to rest, in the myth, on the lap of the virgin (the ancient meaning of the word "virgin" was "she who is one-in-herself"), and here he gives himself willingly to the knife of the hunter. The sage, the holy one, the Bodhisattva, who *chooses* to remain in this world, as it is said in the East, has reached the stage where no hurt of any kind goes out from him or her. Nevertheless, being here in the world of opposites he is not freed from their effects. Consciously, willingly, he exposes himself to the hatred of the world, not in a weak and watery pacifism but having fought the bitter and bloody battle entirely within himself through repeated sacrifice.

Frodo, at the end of J. R. R. Tolkien's *The Lord of the Rings*, is an image of this. At their return to the Shire after the defeat of the Dark Lord, the Hobbits had to fight to clear the land of the evil that had crept in in their absence. For Merry and Pippin and Sam this was an inevitable duty, "lions" as they were, in spite of the killing it involved. But Frodo had become a "unicorn." He could never draw sword again, though he accepted with sorrow that it must be so for others. No hurt went out from him, though, for the brief time that remained before he "went into the West," he suffered still from the wounds that he had taken in the days of his fight with the dark powers.

Surely we glimpse and faintly experience this "pride of the unicorn" every time we succeed in detaching for a moment from the battle of the opposites, repressing neither the one side nor the other, accepting both—a thing which can be done through the intense imaginative experience of a uniting symbol. When our feelings are hurt, or we are angry or depressed, if we make the effort to objectify the emotion, not rationally but through imagination in some form or other, and so give it validity as separate from the ego, we are able to accept conscious responsibility for it as part of the suffering of all humanity. Thus a little bit of our ego's pride is laid at the feet of the "virgin," and for that instant no harm goes out from us into the world as we touch the final innocence.

Only by entering through imaginative vision into the sacrificial death can we come to the transition from the pride of the lion to the pride of the unicorn. Man has known this intuitively from the very beginning, as all the great myths show. An angel with a flaming sword guarded the backward way into Eden. So every adolescent must learn to fight for his life, must find the ego and its pride, then the pride of the lion, until, if his courage holds, he may come finally to know the pride of the unicorn, laying down his strength in the virgin's lap.

NOTES

1. Dante, *Purgatory*, translated by Dorothy L. Sayers (London: Penguin Classics, 1974), p. 161.

C h a p t e r   T h i r t e e n

Exchange

IN THREE OF his works, Charles Williams wrote explicitly of that which he called "the practice of substituted love," which was, in his thought and in his life, the conscious and active manifestation of the "co-inherence," or "exchange," at the heart of the universe. In the novel *Descent into Hell*, two of the characters consciously practice this substitution, and in the poem "The Founding of the Company" (which is part of his Arthurian cycle), the king's poet Taliessin becomes the leader of a company of those who are linked together, not by any rule or outer form, but simply by "a certain pointing," a free choice of the way of exchange that is conscious love. (C.S. Lewis says of this poem that it is autobiographical as well as mythological, for "something like Taliessin's company probably came into being wherever Charles Williams had lived and worked."[1]) The third and theoretical definition of this concept comes in one of the chapters of Williams' essay *He Came Down from Heaven*. By summarizing the ideas in this chapter, we can perhaps see the ways in which they may operate in our lives.

There are three degrees of consciousness, Williams says: (1) the old self on the old way, (2) the old self on the new way, (3) the new self on the new way. Williams writes:

> The second group is the largest at all times and in all places . . . it forms . . . at most moments practically all of oneself that one can know, for the new self does not know itself. It consists of the existence of the self, unselfish perhaps, but not yet denied. This self often applies itself unselfishly. It transfers its activities, from itself unselfishly as a centre to its belief as a centre. It uses its angers on behalf of its religion or its morals, and its greed and its fear and its pride. It operates on behalf of its notion of God as it originally operated on behalf of itself. It aims honestly at better behaviour, but it does not usually aim at change.[2]

147

This change Williams now defines as the birth of a new kind of love: "To love is to die and to live again; to live from a new root. . . . We are to love each other . . . by acts of substitution." "'He saved others; Himself he cannot save,'" is, Williams says, an "exact definition of the Kingdom of Heaven in operation and of the great discovery of substitution then made by earth."[3]

The maxims of unselfishness are universally preached and, as long as "the old self on the new way" remains, they are perhaps a necessary stage; but the difference between unselfishness and self-denial is very rarely understood. In Jung's language, as long as we are trying to improve the ego by inducing "good" feelings in it or urging it to the performance of "good" works, then we merely succeed in nourishing an equivalent amount of "bad" feeling in the unconscious, which will have negative effects somewhere in our environment. Only when the center of our feeling and action is rooted in the Self instead of the self (ego) can our love and goodness reach beyond this pendulum swing of the opposites.

The word *self-denial* as used by Williams means exactly this. The denial of the ego does not imply that we are rid of it; it means that it acts only as the agent, so to speak, of the Self, or the "new self on the new way," which has transcended both selfishness and unselfishness by the acceptance of substituted love. "Neither Jew nor Greek, but a new creature." Neither self-sacrifice nor self-gratification as such; both may be sacraments of love at any moment, but neither is covenanted. The denial of the self affects both. "It is no more I that live, but Christ that liveth in me" is the definition of the pure life that is substituted for both.

Williams, who is never content with mere words, now proceeds to a practical definition of how this new love is to be lived. He takes the hackneyed text "Bear ye one another's burdens" and gives it a new dimension, interpreting it as a law of interior self-denial instead of the usual exterior exhortation to unselfishness. How can we literally carry the anxiety, fear, or misery of another? At this point we should be warned that the actual person-to-person exchange of burdens described so vividly, especially in *Descent into Hell*, would be a dangerous and unreal thing for most of us if we self-consciously copied the technique. Nevertheless, something like it does actually come about in those who have chosen to follow the way of individuation, of "self-denial" as defined above. To understand another's technique can lead either to literal copying, which is worse than useless, or to more light on our own way.

In the poem, Taliessin's company has three degrees. In the first degree are those who live by "a frankness of honorable exchange" on the outer level.[4] C.S. Lewis, speaking of these, calls them "those . . . who willingly and honorably and happily maintain the complex system of exchanged services on which society depends. There is nothing to distinguish them from people outside the Company except the fact that they do consciously and joyously, and therefore excellently what everyone save parasites has to do in some fashion."[5]

In the second degree are those who practice substitution, as Williams defined it, by bearing consciously a particular interior burden for another person. To do this there are three necessities. The burden must first be fully known; secondly, it must be freely given up by the one; and thirdly, it must be consciously taken up by the other. In *Descent into Hell* these three points are seen in action. Pauline has first to find the courage to tell Stanhope of her fear, which sounds ridiculous and of which she is ashamed; she then has to consent to his carrying it and to letting go of it herself. Stanhope must offer to carry it, opening himself in imagination to all that she is experiencing but without personal, emotional involvement. The result is not the release of Pauline from the necessity of facing her problem but the lifting from her of the personal terror that had literally forced her into a continual running away. The "new self," however, is not fully born in her until she, in her turn, is willing to carry the suffering of another. Sometimes, Williams says, it is a reciprocal exchange between two individuals; more often it is a chain—you carry my burden, I carry someone else's.

We may try now to translate these three points into terms of our own experience. Substitution is a fact of the psyche and will take place either through the mechanism of projections, forcing others to carry bits of ourselves, or by sucking strength from them via the unconscious; or it can become a conscious exchange of love in the way that Williams describes. First, then, there is the necessity for an absolutely honest speaking out of our problem, our misery, to another person whose offer of himself we recognize and accept. This is no easy thing, but we all know that without it no change of any kind, let alone exchange and substitution, can even begin. It is simple to go to someone and complain of our problems, leaving out the essential facts, but that is an entirely sterile proceeding. In fact, the second necessity, the willingness to give up the fear or the grief or the anxiety, is easily recognizable in the manner in which the suffering is expressed. As long as there is any trace of self-pity, there is no hope at all that the burden can be lifted by another, nor if there is any dramatization or implication of "hard luck" or of throwing the blame upon another. "Self-denial" is as necessary for the sufferer as for the one who offers to help. Williams says, "It is habitual with us to prefer to be miserable rather than to give and to believe that we can give our miseries up."[6]

To give up a pleasure is not so difficult, because it is easy simply to replace it with a still more pleasurable feeling of being noble and self-sacrificing; but to give up a misery (truly to let go of it, not just replace it temporarily with an evasion) is to deprive the ego of one of its major sources of nourishment. The ego, taking its problem to another, is merely making a bid for attention, trying to involve the other emotionally; and to build up a sense of significance that covers the inner bankruptcy of the "old self." In order to feel meaningful, the old self must always be either dramatically weak and miserable, or dramatically strong and unselfish, busily helping the weak and miserable and deciding what is right for them. The two attitudes are often there together, compensating each other in a futile waste of energy. The "new self," on the other hand, will, when in misery, ask for help with simple acceptance and willingness to let go no matter how empty he may feel; or, if he is the taker of the burden, he will give of himself without any sense of being thereby increased in significance. The "old self" can only be thrust into another swing of the pendulum. There is no real healing. It must be emphasized again that the relief of the sufferer in no way implies that he is saved from the necessity to meet his problem, to face the facts, but only that the terror or anxiety that has sapped his strength is lifted from him.

The taker of the burden must consciously take it up, says Williams, by imagining, feeling himself into the fear or pain of the other. For us to say, even to ourselves, "Now I am going to carry this person's burden for him" would be very dangerous because almost certainly we would find ourselves on the wrong level, caught by the old self and unconsciously building up a sense of power and importance. Only he who is completely rooted in the Self, the new "self," can use this language safely. We have to be constantly on the watch for emotional dramas in the unconscious that feed our greed for giving (a specifically feminine trait), just as easily as they nourish our greed for taking. The former is the more dangerous because it looks good. The conscious taking of the burden is for us rather the meeting of any request for help on any level, outer or inner, with a high degree of awareness, both of feeling and intelligence. It is very difficult indeed not to respond to either with a rush of identifying emotion—"I can't stand to see this person suffer. I must make him feel better"—or else with some kind of evasion based on a fear of our own. We have to open ourselves to the impact of another's suffering, *not* on the level of emotional involvement but through real feeling, which always involves intelligent discrimination. So there must be the clear refusal to accept a mere bid for attention, or to respond to self-pity or false emotionalism in the other, and only then may we use all the powers of the imagination to understand and the strength of our perception of the "new self" to relieve the suffering of another. In this kind of meeting between two people, there may superficially seem to be one who helps and another who is helped, but in the moment of truth between them there is no such distinction—each is helper and helped in the same moment and in each there is a new birth of consciousness.

Any other kind of "helping others" is psychic trespassing. Surely "Forgive us our trespasses" may be said to apply with especial intensity to this urge to solve the problems of others who have not asked in any real way for help, or who, having asked, are only looking for a bolstering up of the "old self." If we become aware of such an urge or drive in ourselves, so different from a simple openness to any real need that is brought to us (and this is a highly active state of consciousness, not just a passive drifting), then we may be sure that we are evading some fear of insignificance, some misery of our own that we are not willing to know and to give up. Indeed, the only safe and sure way for us is to concentrate on the exceedingly difficult task of knowing our own misery and letting it go, because only to the extent that we attain to this shall we be in the state of consciousness that bears another's burden. It will come to us inevitably without any seeking, as a necessity of the way.

There is likewise a need for intelligence in the meeting even of real requests for help of any kind. Williams insists on this at some length. Before offering our help, outer or inner, we are obligated to weigh the extent of our available energy and whether the taking of a new burden would be to the detriment of other values or other people in our lives. This kind of discrimination can be very difficult, as we well know. There is a beautiful passage toward the end of *He Came Down from Heaven*: "The new earth and the new heaven come like the two modes of knowledge, knowledge being the chief art of love, as love is the chief art of knowledge."[7] Love without intelligence is formless emotion, and intelligence without love an empty sterility.

The third degree in the Arthurian Company is something, as C.S. Lewis says, much harder to understand except for those few who have achieved it. It can come only when the "new self" is fully realized — in Jung's language, when the Self has finally replaced the ego at the center of life — or, in the words of St. Paul, "I live, yet not I, but Christ liveth in me." We may conclude that these few experience, beyond all individual substitution, the total coherence of all things at all times and in all places.

NOTES
1. Charles Williams and C.S. Lewis, *Arthurian Torso* (Oxford: Oxford University Press, 1969), p. 141.
2. Charles Williams, *He Came Down from Heaven* (London: Faber and Faber, 1950), p. 85.
3. *Ibid.*, p. 96.
4. Charles Williams, "The Founding of the Company," in *Region of the Summer Stars* (Oxford: Oxford University Press, 1950), p. 37.
5. Williams and Lewis, *Arthurian Torso*, p. 142.
6. Williams, *He Came Down from Heaven*, p. 90.
7. *Ibid.*, p. 97.

Chapter Fourteen

Levels

A VITAL NECESSITY for any association between persons is the discrimination of the levels of relatedness. In any context, as we know, there can be no true meeting or harmony where there is an unconscious mingling—a fuzzy mixture—instead of a conscious separation between the people, things, or functions which seek to unite. This mingling is equally damaging when it involves a confusion of the various *levels*, whether of our activities or of our relationships.

For a woman especially, since she is so close to nature, there is danger that she may mistake this kind of diffuse mingling for a warm connectedness, and the more she falls into this mistake the stronger becomes the compensating divisive factor in the unconscious, erupting into cutting and destructive opinions, vehemently affirmed by the animus, or into gossip and talk with hidden barbs. It may also breed a rigid adherence to rules or to critical and exclusive judgments. Let not the man, however, think it is easier for him! His refusal to "mingle" in the feminine manner, his immunity from what he deems female nonsensical concern over details, may very easily become a kind of superior isolation which of course sets up an extremely "fuzzy mixture" in his unconscious, so that he spreads a fog of moody imprecision around him. Thus in him, too, the awareness of the relative importance of the different levels of life may be distorted, and the true meaning between them precluded.

What are these different levels of which we need to be particularly aware? First and foremost there is the level of the Self, of the Christ within, by whatever name we call it. Our contact with this reality can only be maintained through our efforts to live the symbolic life. It is the responsibility of each one of us to ensure that in the hours of discussion, whether individually or in a group, we keep this truth in our minds and our hearts so that we do not fall into a mere search for outer or comfortable solutions or into disconnected talk. It takes immense vigilance to see that our meetings, one-to-one or in groups, do not become a kind of field-day for losing touch with the Self.

We come now to another level—the personal contact between individuals. A true friendship doesn't just happen; it must be built and maintained by constant hard work. The mutual attraction on which it is built is merely the promise, not the fulfillment. The work to which a person is committed may limit not only the amount of time, but the *kind* of energy which he is at liberty to spend in personal contacts; or the development of his inner life may require of him a greater or lesser degree of involvement, as the case may be.

We must be clear, too, about the levels of friendship itself. In its essence, friendship is the capacity for absolute trust in another *as person*, involving a complete honesty with oneself which is extremely hard to attain. At this level it has nothing to do with like or dislike of another's qualities, with agreement or disagreement, or with frequency of contact. It dies if one covers over the qualities in another which one dislikes or exaggerates the things one likes in him. It is killed by any kind of demand, or by such thoughts as "she will be hurt if I don't do what she wants, so I must consent no matter what other values are involved"; equally damaging is the opposite point of view, "my own values are always more important than his or her feelings." In relationship there are no rules, only basic guiding lines, and each tiny situation must be met as something unknown in which we must seek reality and love through a new effort of discrimination.

To the extent, however, that we have grown into the state of basic trust and integrity which is friendship, the other levels of personal relationship will become real and nourishing—a sharing in varying degrees of ideas, feelings, pain, happiness, sheer fun, with those individuals to whom we feel personally akin. Best of all, in contacts between true friends the most hidden tendencies to projection may be uncovered, as well as our subtle demands to be mothered, and our refusals of responsibility. Thus we may grow from unconscious attraction into love.

A third level of relationship involves a whole group of people. At this level, the relationship will be real and nourishing only to the extent that the individuals concerned are connected with the fundamental spontaneity and gaiety of heart which is an essential element in the symbolic life. It is a quality that has nothing to do with the frivolity or escaping which are the polar opposites of too great a restraint. Humour and gaiety are an integral part of *real* seriousness.

We may now begin to see that the discrimination of levels is the very reverse of living our lives in compartments. It is indeed our one hope of wholeness. For what is it in fact to live the symbolic life? It is most definitely not to spend certain hours of the week on the study of symbols and images and then to live the rest of our lives on a non-symbolic level. This is compartment living. On the contrary, the study will be arid and sterile if we do not very quickly realize that there is no smallest detail of our lives that is not symbolic. This does *not* mean that while we are cooking the dinner or dancing with our friends, we solemnly think to ourselves, "Now what is the meaning of this?" This is to miss the point entirely. We live symbolically when each thing that we do or say, think or feel is *whole* — not split into the "fact" and the "meaning," not marred by ulterior motives however lofty, when it simply is in itself, not done or said *because* it is useful or good or whatever. When we are caught in this kind of split attitude, we act always out of one opposite or the other, or worse still, out of the two inextricably mixed, and nothing we do is symbolic or has any real meaning.

We return once more to the paradoxical truth that the symbols which unite the opposites and bring us to the beginnings of this kind of wholeness in our day-to-day lives cannot possibly be born in us until we have learned to separate, to discriminate the different levels of being. The meeting between them which we experience through the uniting power of the symbol is entirely different from the kind of half-way house attitude — a little bit of this and a little bit of that. If we find ourselves thinking some such thing as "a relationship ought to be both personal and impersonal; therefore I won't let myself love so-and-so personally too much, and I will watch that I don't withdraw too far," we are indeed far from the symbol. But it is possible to glimpse for a moment that love which is personal involvement *and* impersonal detachment, each discriminated with the utmost exactitude and at the same time indissolubly one.

There are also the levels of our most secret individual inner lives at one end of the scale and of the ordinary practical tasks and day-to-day responsibilities at the other. These, too, need to be consciously contained and separated so that there may be a unity between them. If we do not set apart a time for the former, it will spread itself all over the place in an inferior and meaningless way, turning into pointless daydreams which go on all the time, either consciously or unconsciously, and steal away energy from our conscious tasks.

There is also the very difficult matter of the shifts we must continually make from one level to another, which is something we too seldom attend to consciously. The *rite d'entrée* and the *rite de sortie* were essential needs in primitive societies — a dance to whip up the mood of war, another to end the war fever and make the transition to peaceful pursuits, a time alone before initiation, and so on. Every individual still needs to find his own "rites," so that he may clearly emerge from one level and enter another. A cup of coffee, listening to music, a brief walk, or, best of all, a few minutes of complete relaxation, are some of the ways we may find. The important thing is to do them consciously; even a few seconds of objective awareness that we are passing from one kind of activity to another is often enough. A great many of our mixed up approaches to whatever we may be doing, resulting, as they often do, in misunderstandings and resentments, are due in large measure to the fact that we jump from one level to another without so much as drawing breath, so that we never completely let go of one level and never completely enter the other — or are already jumping over the present into concern about future tasks, a condition producing exhaustion, if nothing worse. I do not think the importance of such pauses can be exaggerated. I am reminded of a beautiful sentence from an Indian Tantra which is thought to be as much as 5000 years old. It says, "When in worldly activity, keep attentive between the two breaths (the in breath and the out breath), and so practicing, in a few days be born anew." Well! We can perhaps make a start by attending for a moment between two levels of our multifarious activities.

To the extent, then, that we achieve this discrimination, this attention, our lives are freed from a sense of rush, and begin to resemble the pattern of a dance instead of a wild plunging about, each movement clear and whole in itself yet related to all the others in the totality of the great pattern. This is the symbolic life. As Irene de Castillejo has said, in her book *Knowing Woman*, this end may seem very remote but all that matters is that we move towards it. Somehow in each tiny effort the whole is already there if we could but recognize it. Julian of Norwich in her *Revelations of Divine Love* affirmed that no one can seek God who has not already found Him.

C h a p t e r   F i f t e e n

Inner Relationship
and Community

THE WISDOM OF the *I Ching*, the Book of Changes, speaks to us across the three thousand years of its life in a language that, though strange to us at first, has an extraordinarily modern accent.[1] This is not the occasion for a detailed explanation of the structure of the book, and for our purpose it is enough to say that it contains sixty-four so-called "signs" or "hexagrams," representing different combinations of the masculine and feminine principles, the "yang" and the "yin" aspects of life, each hexagram giving wisdom for a particular situation of human life in time.

A hexagram is composed of six lines, unbroken masculine and broken feminine lines, and each of these lines refers to a special aspect of the time situation symbolized by the particular sign. Each hexagram begins with a "judgment" and an "image," the first describing the basic meaning of the whole sign, the second expressing another aspect of it in imagery. Thus the clarity of conscious judgment and the symbolism of the unconscious meet and illuminate each other throughout the book.

There are a number of hexagrams that deal specifically with different kinds of relatedness. They include: The Family, Fellowship with Men, The Marrying Maiden, Holding Together, Gathering Together, Influence, Inner Truth. It is particularly interesting to examine some of the wisdom they contain.

We begin with the natural group of The Family (Hexagram 37). The basic teaching of this sign lays down at once an unchanging essential for any kind of real relatedness between people at any level. There must be boundaries, separateness; each individual must be distinct, and there must be discrimination of function. In the Judgment it is said, "If the father is really a father and the son a son . . . if

157

the husband is really a husband and the wife a wife, then the family is in order." How well we know in our day that the breakdown of the family comes from the loss of this wisdom! We see on all sides the woman behaving unconsciously like a man, the man a prey to feminine moods and softness, the child treated like an adult, or parents descending to childish behavior, and all the resulting misery and disorder of the indiscriminate mixture of function.

Of the six lines of the hexagram, one speaks of the child, one of woman and child, two of woman, and two of man. For the child the essential is that there should be rules of order that he may recognize from the very beginning and within which he may be entirely free. Freedom without such basic rules is a terrible burden to lay on a child. "When tempers flare up in the family, too great severity brings remorse, good fortune nonetheless. When woman and child dally and laugh, it leads in the end to humiliation." Even if we make occasional mistakes, it is better to have too much discipline than to descend to the child's level. We need to "build strong dikes" within which each individual (not only the child) can move freely, but one small hole in a dike can let in a flood.

To the woman the *I Ching* speaks in this sign with special force. "It is upon the woman of the house that the well-being of the family depends." "The atmosphere that holds the family together" depends on the woman, for she is the heart of the house, the one who nourishes it both outwardly and inwardly. "She should not follow her whims. She must attend within to the food." "She must attend to the nourishment of her family and to the food for the sacrifice. In this way she becomes the center of the social and religious life of the family. . . ." In Jung's language, it is the feminine principle that binds people together, the "cement" in all relationships, and this binding force of the heart may either bring people together in a true meeting or turn into the destructive and imprisoning possessiveness of the woman who follows her whims; that is to say, whose feeling consists of unconscious emotional drives instead of conscious discrimination and warmth. It is the woman, or the *anima* in man, who maintains the link with the depths of the unconscious, the springs of the religious instinct in man. Hence, she provides "the food for the sacrifice."

On the father of the family, the *I Ching* urges the cultivation of his own personality so that he may carry his responsibility freely and willingly and exercise authority through trustworthiness and love, never through fear. If his character is centered on inner truth, his influence in the family will operate for its well-being without conscious contriving.

"The family is society in embryo," says the *I Ching*. In every sign there are different levels of interpretation—the personal, the social and political, the cosmic; and we today may add another, the interpretation of these signs as inner situations of the individual psyche. In this particular hexagram, the advice as to discrimination of function, for instance, is profoundly valid as applied to the different aspects of a single personality. We need to be aware of the child in us, to give him or her discipline and freedom; the feminine parts of our nature, whether we be men or women, must attend to the "food" and beware of "whims"; the masculine authority must be realized through objective love and not through fear; and so on. We have not evolved any better advice in 3,000 years.

We move out from containment in the family to seek Fellowship with Men (Hexagram 13). Here the necessity for discrimination, for "distinction between things" is again stressed. "Fellowship should not be a mere mingling of individuals or of things—that would be chaos, not fellowship." The lines speak of the most dangerous pitfalls. "Fellowship with men in the clan. Humiliation. There is danger here of formation of a separate faction on the basis of personal and egotistic interests." Any kind of exclusive feeling must wreck real fellowship, and is something entirely different from separateness and observance of boundaries between men.

The next line warns against mistrust and suspicion. If we have mental reservations, if there is a conscious or unconscious holding back, or refusal to give of ourselves, then we will always be suspecting the same wiles in others and "the result is that one departs further and further from true fellowship." Interpreting this inwardly we know that mistrust of ourselves is the root of all suspicion. We "condemn one group in order to unite the others;" that is, we want to accept the parts of ourselves that we like and esteem, and to reject those impulses and weaknesses which make us feel small or guilty. This rejection we project outward into condemnation of other people, feelings of superiority, or into protestations of our inferiority and worthlessness. We are thus incapable of fellowship.

The Marrying Maiden (Hexagram 54) speaks of close personal relationships based on affection:

> Affection as the essential principle of relatedness is of the greatest importance in all relationships in the world. . . . Affection is the all-inclusive principle of union. . . . But every relationship between individuals bears within it the danger that wrong turns may be taken, leading to endless misunderstandings and disagreements. Therefore, it is necessary constantly to remain mindful of the end. If we permit ourselves to drift along, we come together and are parted again as the day may determine.

We must "understand the transitory in the light of the eternity of the end." In other words, if our love for another person becomes an end in itself, shutting out all other loves, breeding jealousy and exclusiveness, it is not real love at all. It is by no means easy to remain "mindful of the end," of that which is beyond the personal, when we are seized by an overmastering longing for another person's love. The top line of the hexagram stresses the absolute necessity for "sacrifice" in the real sense of the word, if love is to endure. If "the woman holds the basket but there are no fruits in it," or "the man stabs the sheep, but no blood flows," then affection and love will turn in the long run to hate. The meaning of this image is that in the Chinese rite of sacrifice to the ancestors the woman presented harvest offerings, while the man slaughtered the sacrificial animal. We should say that the woman must sacrifice her possessiveness, must offer her "fruits," let go of her children, her *demand* to be loved, while a man must sacrifice his aggressive instincts, his sensuality in its blind, unfeeling form.

We come now to the hexagram that deals specifically with the coming together of men in communities or groups. The *I Ching* points out that there is in man a need for relationship in groups as well as between individuals. In our day, owing to the breakdown of the traditional family, social, and religious values, and still more because of the split between intellect and instinct, between conscious and unconscious, in the collective psyche, this need has become almost frenzied. "Togetherness," that frightening word, has replaced relationship, and has become a cultural idea. Study groups, conferences, camps, "workshops," human "laboratories," spring up on every side to meet a very real human need, but they have also their danger. Often designed to help people toward self-knowledge, they become for many a protection against that very thing, a running away from the essentially lonely tasks of facing the dark sides of the individual soul. Therefore, very great care and awareness is needed before one joins any kind of group. Will this mean running away for me, one must ask, or will it bring real support and new consciousness? The essential inner journey must be made alone, but all of us need support and relatedness with others of like mind; and it is fatally easy to mistake dependence, a blind acceptance of the opinions of others, for real mutual support, for the humility that respects another's view but never swallows it whole. We all long to fly from loneliness to "togetherness," but the only real cure for loneliness is to accept the "aloneness" of the spirit, and then, to our astonishment, real relatedness, real friendship, will come to our doorstep, wherever we may be.

The *I Ching* says of itself that it speaks only to the "superior" man, which in Jung's language means the "conscious" man, and the wisdom of Holding Together (Hexagram 8) and Gathering Together (Hexagram 45) would mean little to those who seek community for escapist reasons. It speaks to those who seek a holding together with others of like mind as free individuals, to those who are striving for the wholeness that Jung has called "individuation."

Both hexagrams begin by emphasizing the necessity for a leader, a person around whom others unite. The ancient Chinese culture was feudal, but the validity of the principle remains. The elected representative in a democracy must take up and carry the responsibility of leadership for his term of office, but he is protected as far as is collectively possible from identifying personally with his power. In every kind of group, even that which is a gathering of free and conscious individuals, there must be leadership—the kind about which Charles Williams wrote so beautifully when he described the "excellent absurdity" of one man acting as a center for others. He must at all times be aware of his ultimate unimportance and dispensability, must be wholly aware that he is not the center, but merely a focal point through which, if this task has been laid upon him, others may recognize *the* center within themselves. In expressing this, Charles Williams shows himself entirely at one with the ancient teaching of the *I Ching*.

In the commentary on one of the lines in the sign Holding Together, it is said of the leader:

> Those who come to him he accepts, those who do not come are
> allowed to go their own way. He invites none, flatters none — all come
> of their own free will. In this way there develops a voluntary depen-
> dence among those who hold to him. They do not have to be con-
> stantly on their guard but may express their opinions openly. Police
> measures are not necessary. . . . The same principle of freedom is
> valid for life in general. We should not woo favor from people. If a
> man cultivates within himself the purity and strength that are neces-
> sary for one who is the center of a fellowship, those who are meant for
> him come of their own accord.

If there is this kind of freedom in a community, then each member of
it will begin to find real leadership within himself, the impersonal
purity and strength, the center, the "Self" displacing the ego's leadership. Around this center first of all his own personality will
"gather," and it will then be felt by all those who are "meant for
him." "This leader must first of all be collected within himself."

In another hexagram called Following (Hexagram 17), it is said
that all those who are followed must themselves know how to follow.
When the situation requires any one of us to lead, we must have the
courage and humility to do so, and when it is time to be led, this also
we accept in freedom and true independence. The one requires the
other; indeed, they beget each other.

The first line in the sign Holding Together (Hexagram 8) speaks of
the fundamental sincerity that is the essential for all relationship:
"This attitude, symbolized by a full earthen bowl, in which the
content is everything and the empty form nothing, show itself not in
clever words but through the strength of what lies within the
speaker." The second line points out that if we are seeking any kind
of personal advantage from our association with a group, then we
"lose" ourselves. In other words, we are merely bolstering up unconscious demands; we are not individuals anymore.

The third line reads, "You hold together with the wrong people."
This is a warning against false intimacy with people who do not meet
us on our own deepest level. This does not mean that we may not
enjoy the company of such people, but the commentary insists with
surprising force on the danger of *intimacy* in the wrong place. "We
must beware of being drawn into false intimacy through force of

habit. . . . Maintaining sociability without intimacy is the only right attitude . . . because otherwise we should not be free to enter into relationship with people of our own kind." In our terms, to reveal ourselves, our thoughts and feelings to someone who does not understand our basic values is not only pointless—it exposes us to invasion by superficial attitudes and literally corrupts or steals away our energy, dissipating it, or imprisoning it, so that we have nothing left to give to the true relationship.

Another line warns against too long a delay in giving "complete and full devotion" to the group that we have recognized to be the carrier of our real values. The hexagram is concerned with groups, but we may interpret this line as also warning of those moments when we are capable of a new and more complete commitment to the way of individuation, moments when we have to make a vital choice. "If we have missed the right moment for union and go on hesitating to give complete and full devotion, we shall regret the error when it is too late." A dream will often bring to consciousness this necessity for a choice and if we refuse it, it may be a long time before the opportunity returns.

The hexagram of Gathering Together (Hexagram 45) is very similar to that of Holding Together, but it deals with one other aspect of the subject—the danger of strife and conflict within a group and of "robbery" from without. The *I Ching* says that there is one strong defense against these splitting attacks from within and from without—a constant watchfulness and foresight. We must *expect* these things. "Human woes usually come as a result of unexpected events against which we are not forearmed." We are continually thrown by our own moods and weaknesses into destructive attitudes, because, when things are going well, we cease to expect any setback, and when it comes, we fall into discouragement and seek for scapegoats. In the first line we are told what to do in such a case. "If you are sincere but not to the end, there will sometimes be confusion, sometimes gathering together. If you call out, then after one grasp of the hand you can laugh again. Regret not."

A beautiful passage from the commentary on another line may end our study of these two signs.

> In the time of gathering together, we should make no arbitrary choice of the way. There are secret forces at work, leading together those

who belong together. We must yield to this attraction; then we make no mistakes. Where inner relationships exist, no great preparations and formalities are necessary. People understand one another forthwith, just as the Divinity graciously accepts a small offering if it comes from the heart.

There is a passage in *Man and His Symbols* in the section by Marie-Louise von Franz that sums up this wisdom in modern terms:

> It is ultimately the Self that orders and regulates one's human relationships, so long as the conscious ego takes the trouble to detect the delusive projections and deals with these inside himself instead of outside. It is in this way that spiritually attuned and similarly oriented people find their way to one another, to create a group that cuts across all the usual social and organizational affiliations. Such a group is not in conflict with others; it is merely different and independent. The consciously realized process of individuation thus changes a person's relationships. The familiar bonds such as kinship or common interests are replaced by a different type of unity—a bond through the Self.[2]

In the sign Dispersion or Dissolution (Hexagram 59), the necessity for dissolving these old familiar bonds to collective groups is stressed, so that the new and free type of union may be born. "He dissolves his bond with his group. Supreme good fortune. Dispersion leads in turn to accumulation. This is something that ordinary men do not think of." In another sign (Decrease, Hexagram 41) there is a line, "When three people journey together, their number decreases by one. When one man journeys alone, he finds a companion." Only when a man can stand alone does he find the real unity with others.

Influence (Hexagram 31) is concerned with the ways in which one may safely influence others or be influenced by them. The image for this sign is a mountain with a sunken peak holding the water of a lake. The mountain in the *I Ching* is the symbol of keeping still; the lake stands for joy. If we know how to keep still inwardly, others may be nourished by our joy and we will be receptive to any true influence from without. The lines point out some of the pitfalls: if a man should run "precipitately after all the persons whom he would like to influence" or "yield immediately to every whim of those in whose service he stands," then the result is inevitably humiliation. The most superficial of all ways of trying to influence others is through talk with nothing real behind it, mere tonguewagging. However:

> When the quiet power of a man's own character is at work, the effects produced are right. All those who are receptive to the vibrations of such a spirit will then be influenced. Influence over others should not express itself as a conscious and willed effort to manipulate them. Through practicing such conscious incitement, one becomes wrought up and is exhausted by the eternal stress and strain. Moreover, the effects produced are then limited to those on whom one's thoughts are consciously fixed.

Finally in the hexagram of Inner Truth (Hexagram 61) there is a line that most beautifully expresses this deepest level of all in the relationship of one man with another. The text is "A crane calling in the shade. Its young answers it. I have a good goblet. I will share it with you."

And the commentary:

> This refers to the involuntary influence of a man's inner being upon persons of kindred spirit. . . . The crane may be quite hidden when it sounds its call. . . . Where there is a joyous mood, there a comrade will appear to share a glass of wine. . . . Whenever a feeling is voiced with truth and frankness, whenever a deed is the clear expression of sentiment, a mysterious and far-reaching influence is exerted. At first it acts on those who are inwardly receptive. But the circle grows larger and larger. The root of all influence lies in one's inner being. . . . Any deliberate intention of an effect would only destroy the possibility of producing it.

Confucius said about this line:

> The superior man abides in his room. If his words are well spoken, he meets with assent at a distance of more than a thousand miles. How much more then from near by! If the superior man abides in his room and his words are not well spoken, he meets with contradiction at a distance of more than a thousand miles. How much more then from near by! . . . Through words and deeds the superior man moves heaven and earth. Must one not, then, be cautious?

NOTES

1. All quotes are from *The I Ching, or Book of Changes*, the Richard Wilhelm translation rendered into English by Cary F. Baynes (Princeton: Princeton University Press, 1950). Copyright by the Bollingen Foundation, New York, NY.
2. C.G. Jung, *Man and His Symbols*, (New York: Doubleday, 1964), p. 221.

Chapter Sixteen

The Marriage Vow

"I TAKE THEE . . . to have and to hold from this day forward, for better or worse, for richer or poorer, in sickness and in health, to love and to cherish, till death us do part . . . and thereto I plight thee my troth." There are few more lovely words in the English language. The man who speaks them with all his heart, standing in the holy place, is pledging himself to more than the personal marriage between himself and his beloved. She carries for him in that moment, consciously or unconsciously, the image of all womanhood—of that which nourishes and gives birth, not only to physical children but to all the values of true relatedness and to the tender understanding of the heart. To the woman in her turn, her man is the symbol, however obscurely felt, of the sword of the Spirit—of the clear shining of the Word in the darkness. So they take this most solemn vow to love this innermost beauty and cherish it, no matter what the cost, as long as life shall last. Many who have no use for the Church and its rituals will find themselves moved at a wedding as their unconscious responds to the deeply buried image. For the two before the altar are more in that moment than simply the "John" or "Mary" whom we know; they are the symbols of the marriage for which all men yearn in their hearts—the I-Thou meeting, the marriage of Heaven and Earth.

The fact of this commitment in a dimension far beyond their ego consciousness does not, of course, mean that their promise to each other in this world is in any way weakened or devalued. On the contrary, they are now pledged to the daily attempt to live as truly as they are able the meaning of the symbol in all their dealings with each other. They have chosen a partner in their search with whom to bring forth children, both human and spiritual. There is no hope that they will be able "to love and to cherish" each other unless each is prepared to accept his or her own darkness and weakness and to strive for the "holy marriage" within, thus setting the other free to

166

find his or her individual reality. If there is a continual growth of consciousness through the daily abrasions and delights, and through the hard work of maintaining contact with a sense of the symbolic, then indeed they will together grow into maturity of love. Those who do not marry are equally committed to find partners on their way if they are to know love, bringing the symbol to incarnation in all their relationships with others of whatever kind — with their friends, lovers, enemies, or casual acquaintances.

Married people, however, have made a particular choice, and I am not suggesting that they are not bound to stay with that choice in the face of even repeated failure, as long as there is even a small chance that by staying together they may grow into love. If we break vows for any other reason than out of obedience to a more compelling loyalty, then the situation from which we have tried to escape will simply repeat itself in another form. Nevertheless, for thousands of men and women who take the marriage vow in sincerity, the test of daily life through the years makes it plain that the choice they made was conditioned by projections, which, as they fade, leave exposed the fact that the two personalities are, or have become, destructive of each other; or perhaps their levels of consciousness are so far apart that their bond is the cause of their drifting further and further away from the true meaning of their vows. These thoughts, of course, have no validity for those couples who never had any motive in their mating except the satisfaction of their immediate desires and ambitions. For them the vow is in any case devoid of significance and whether they keep it conventionally or not is of no ultimate importance except insofar as children are affected.

Divorce does not always mean that a marriage has been a failure. There are some marriages in which, though both partners have been true to their vows, and have grown through the years into a more adult love, a time may yet come when unlived parts of their personalities are striving to become conscious. A situation may then arise in which it becomes obvious that if they remain together, these two, who basically love and will always love each other, will regress into sterility and bitterness if they do not have the courage to accept the suffering of parting. Their quest for wholeness may then demand that they ignore the outer laws of church and society in order to be true to the absolutely binding inner vow "to love and to cherish from this time forward." One does not have to be living with a person — or even to see him or her ever again—in order to love and cherish through everything. A conscious acknowledgment of failures, an unshaken devotion to the love that sets free, can turn a divorce into a thing of positive beauty, an experience through which a man or woman may bring out of the suffering a purer love to all future meetings. The divorce is then a sacrificial, not a destructive act, and the original marriage may remain in the deepest sense procreative to the end of life.

It will be said that the promise at the altar includes the words "and forsaking all others keep thee only unto her as long as ye both shall live." The essence of this vow is a commitment to the utmost loyalty and integrity of which a human being is capable. It is a statement that a man's physical actions are as much a symbol of the singleness of the holy marriage within as any other part of him. In our state of partial consciousness, however, it may and does come about that the man or woman chosen no longer carries the symbol for the partner in any way at all, so that all love, all creation, is dead between them. Surely then the greater loyalties lie in the conscious acceptance of failure and separation. Thus each is set free to seek once more the realization of inner singleness of heart through new experiences of relationship and sex, through a new marriage, perhaps. "Until death us do part." When the symbol is dead between two people, when there is no communication left except on the level of the ego swinging between the opposites, then, if they cling to the letter of the law, a horrible betrayal of the marriage vow results in the unconscious, where animus and anima struggle to destroy each other. Death has parted them in the most real sense of the word.

Yet the Church still clings to its undifferentiated attitude to these things, she refuses to her children the opportunity of growth through a second marriage, and clings to the rules without regard for individual truth. I read the other day of the simple and beautiful ritual of divorce in the Orkney Islands long ago before the coming of the courts of law. The couple who had decided to part had to go into a certain church together and then quietly go out of it, one by the north door and one by the south. That was all. It was surely the perfect symbol of a true divorce—a hint of its potentially holy character. The couple returns to the altar before which they made their vow as though to renew it in the moment of their parting. One does not stand before the altar in order to announce that one is deliberately about to commit a sin. That simple ritual is an image through which we can feel the humble acceptance of failure, respect for individual responsibility, and the seeking of a blessing on a new attempt.

One of the great arguments against recognizing divorce is always the damage that the broken home brings to the child. If it were possible to assess this kind of damage, it would almost certainly be found that the hurt that is done to a child through the unconscious, when he or she is forced to live with parents in whom love for each other has turned to bitterness, is far worse than that caused by a physical breach. However successful the parents may be at covering up the fight between them, the child will suffer the terrifying consequences through the unconscious and will often carry the unsolved conflicts of his father and mother all his life. Insofar as a divorce really means a new chance for the parents to learn to love and is not just a running away, it can be a great gift to a child. Outer-seeming which is not true to the inner condition is a deadly thing—far worse in its impact on others than forthright, passionate sin.

Chapter Seventeen

The Voice Within

THE "VOICE WITHIN" speaks to us from the unconscious (to use the terminology of C. G. Jung) and, whether or not we hear it consciously, it is an all-pervading influence in our lives. Those of us who attend to our dreams will certainly have experienced moments when an actual voice speaks with such authority that we know immediately that its words cannot be set aside, however little we may yet understand them, whereas other voices may make suggestions that are highly suspect. In the face of these it behooves us, as the First Epistle of John urged, to "question the spirits whether they be of God" (4:1).

Anyone who seeks for meaning in his inner life must therefore learn to listen with all the discrimination of which he or she is capable for that which he or she recognizes, however dimly, as the ultimately single voice with a thousand names. It comes to us from the ground of our being and brings in a unique way to each individual an intuition of the unchanging oneness of life. It speaks through word or though image and the looking and the listening are ultimately one experience when we have ears to hear and eyes to see.

It is our task to "test the spirits," or voices, through the effort of expressing them, perhaps in an audible or visual form of our own, and certainly through the realization of their meaning in our actual lives. We are inspired and carried a long way by the "seers" who have gone before, by great poetry, art and music, and by the creative spirit of all whose lives have touched our own, but ultimately no one of us can hear the voice more than partially without his or her own unique re-creation, whatever its form, and quite irrespective of its merit or importance in the eyes of the many. All our efforts will seem inadequate: we fall again and again into mistakes, inertia or *hubris*, but it is the perseverance itself that will sharpen our hearing — not success or failure.

The word *voice* has a meaning in grammar defined by *The American Heritage Dictionary* as "a verb form indicating the relation between the subject and the action expressed by the verb (active and passive voices)." This is a beautiful hint about the meaning of the voice within. It is a voice that reveals to us the relationship between the subjective and objective truths of our lives. It brings into consciousness the acceptance of the human condition in which we must suffer the tension between active and passive, inner and outer realities, between all the opposites of life, and it leads us ultimately to an intuition of the whole in which subject and object are one.

This voice is speaking less and less in the language of collective institutions or through external rules of morality, and more and more in the individual soul. Man can, indeed must in this age, seek *individually* his interpretation of the voice within. First Freud and then Jung were the great pioneers, and the "way of individuation" that Jung both lived and charted for us with such depth of poetic vision, is the same "way" that the dogmas of the Church define, interpreted anew for our age. The new approach, however, has brought with it a great danger. The outgrowing of all collective answers exposes men and women to the equal and opposite blindness of "individualism." Everywhere we see a woolly-minded tolerance, or else rebellion for its own sake breeding again its opposite — a complete disregard of the values of the individual and a new kind of total authority. However unconscious of it one may be, everyone's need is to find the totality — the wholeness — that is God. The more we are cut off from the symbolic life, through which alone we may approach and reconcile the opposites, the greater the danger of our projection of this reality onto totalitarianism of one kind or another. The total authority of the Church is replaced by the total authority of unbridled instinct and we have the spectacle of the grandeur of the free spirit of the individual reduced again to a conformity, this time devoid of all meaning.

In the midst of these growing dangers, it is alarming to see the failure of the Church to respond with vision and guidance. It will be said that all the churches are vibrating with new voices, and this is true; but what are they saying? Instead of reasserting the eternal values of the interior and the symbolic life in the individual, they appear to be joining in the flight from these truths which it is the whole function of a church to maintain. They seek to put in their place a well-meaning assertion of *relative* human values, social action, etc., as though these things could make up for the decline of worship. There are even those who openly advocate the "de-mythologizing" of religion, which means, of course, the destruction of the religious function itself.

The storm over Pope Paul VI's encyclical *Humanae vitae* on birth control is an example of how the whole point is missed—not only by the Pope himself and the hierarchy, striving pitifully to answer the great question in the old outgrown way, but by most of those who protest against this blindness. If the sanctity of the commitments that express the fundamentals of Christian faith (or of any faith in life and love as having meaning beyond the desires of the ego and the concepts of the intellect) is not to be lost and sink into a matter of social good intentions or meaningless license, then indeed it is time for a new assessment of their meaning and application to outer life. What is needed is not a loosening of the binding quality of these vows, but, on the contrary, a tremendous assertion of their validity and permanence, not as promises to be kept in a fixed and unchanging frame of reference in this world, but as absolutely binding *inwardly*, informing all the constantly changing circumstances of one's outer life with meaning. We can no longer disregard the split between the conscious and unconscious and cling to the illusion that by following the old rules we can still be protected from the dark things below and from the individual responsibility to find one's own way in which to be true to one's basic commitment.

What, for instance, could the Pope have said on the issue of birth control that would have resolved this dilemma without watering down the Church's age-old teaching, and that would have challenged bewildered men and women to a new and deeper understanding of the meaning behind this ancient prohibition? It is an eternal truth that where there is an act of generation, it is a sin against all the values of life, divine, human, or natural, to take steps to ensure that no new life is born from that act. The meeting of male and female, of seed and egg, of divine and human, is quite meaningless if all possibility of creation is eliminated beforehand. Archetypally it is as though the Holy Spirit, as he descended into the womb of the Virgin had said, "I have made sure that no child shall be born. All that will happen is that you will feel special." But when the Church, at the present stage of human growth, holds to this as meaning that no man or woman may have intercourse without intending a physical child, it is surely interpreting this truth of the inner world in so blind and cruel a fashion as to be totally *untrue* to the real meaning of the eternal law.

At the primitive stage of consciousness this literal interpretation was, of course, valid. In the final return to unity it would again be valid but unnecessary—matter and spirit being one thing. But we are cast out of Eden, and there are two levels of truth—the truth of fact and the truth of meaning. It is our task to look through the outer fact to the inner meaning, and we can experience their final unity only through living contact with image and symbol. All our problems come from confusion between these two levels of reality, from their unconscious identification on the one hand, or their complete separation on the other. Only after the long effort of discrimination can we make the leap beyond fact and meaning to the truth which simply "is."

Men and women whose love is expressed in the sexual act may be creating a new value between them in their relationship, each in his or her own inner world, which is in very truth a "child." The constant fear that a physical child may be born, rejected and unwanted in the moment of conception, adding perhaps an intolerable burden, may in fact destroy the creative meaning of the act on all levels but the physical. "Marriage," says the encyclical, "has two aspects, unitive and procreative," and it goes on to assert that the unitive function is permissible without the procreative only when there is some physical or medical reason for the prevention of birth. There is likewise no sin, it continues, in sexual intercourse when the time is carefully chosen to avoid the likelihood of conception.

This statement appears to be mere quibbling. Either there is no choice whatever—everything is divinely appointed and the processes of nature must never be interfered with, or, if choice is allowed to the individual at all, it becomes his responsibility on all levels. There is no word in the encyclical of the real sin in this matter—which is the sin of intercourse without creation of *any* kind—sexual indulgence without love, without tenderness, without responsibility, from which no new and lovely thing can possibly be born except physically. The unitive and procreative aspects of marriage, of all sexual activity, can never be separated, and a reading of the encyclical in fact leaves one with the feeling that the Church is exalting physical values far above the truths of heart and spirit.

It is not surprising that the way of the East appeals to many who, realizing their danger, seek new disciplines of an inner kind; but the Westerner who goes this way is exposed to another threat. With his highly differentiated ego he strives upward in meditation so that the split between the conscious and unconscious becomes greater and wider, and he loses contact with his shadow and the values of humanity; or else, as in the case of Zen, true freedom is confused with the immediate satisfaction of desire. Great wisdom the East can teach us, but to copy the way of another culture is as unreal as any other kind of imitation. It is from within our own tradition that the new way must be born.

Eight hundred years ago a Christian mystic foresaw the essential spirit of the age that is now dawning. The Abbot Joachim de Fiore was the first to say that the age of the Son (New Testament) would be followed by the age of the Spirit. In that age, he said, there would be no more need for the hierarchy of the Church, for all men would then be contemplatives. He imagined it as a millennium in which every individual would have achieved the freedom of the Spirit that needs no law, but his vision was entirely accurate as to the meaning of our age. If their lives are not to dissolve into the meaningless, individuals in ever-increasing numbers will be forced by the breakdown of laws and by the rationalization of collective myth to seek, each within himself or herself, the contemplative vision.

Young Catholics who remain deeply faithful to the truth that they know to be alive at the heart of the Church try to restore meaning to their religion by such things as the alteration of ritual—whereupon, of course, it ceases to be ritual, the essence of which lies in unchanging, time-hallowed words and forms. A ritual is *born* from the unconscious and will certainly not be revivified by deliberate turning of poetry into prose, often bad prose at that, which is too often the result of these changes. In the attempt to make the great poetry of the Mass "intelligible" to all, the power of the old imagery is lost and replaced by something that, though it may be very fine and full of meaning on its own level, is simply not religion, and therefore no answer to the overwhelming need of the psyche for the *mysterium* within.

The young throw out the traditional words and rituals because of their yearning for individual spontaneity of feeling, speech, and action, and for community based on personal relationship instead of conventional structures. The taking of the Mass into peoples' homes is a beautiful expression of the "bringing home" to the individual of the inner mystery, but too often it may result in the banishment of *all* mystery. The silence and "secrecy" and the beauty of vestment and gesture in the old rite were an evocation of the sense of the numinous. The Mass is a drama, a dance of images, and in the old ceremonies the emphasis was on *looking*—for, as the mystics have always known, we become that which we look at, not that which we think about. The new experiments in the liturgy will stand or fall by their power to give life to the images in the unconscious and not by any appeal to conscious understanding. This is not to decry the value of conscious understanding—far from it. It is essential that we think—each one with all the clarity of which he or she is capable, but not *while* we are looking at the image, for the analyzing intellect will immediately destroy the numinosity. The whole point of a symbol is that it is an entirely different thing from an allegorical metaphor. It takes us immediately into the region beyond the definitions of the thinking mind.

The hierarchy of the Church has not yet made any attempt to interpret clearly for the faithful that for which they truly search and of which the changes in the Mass are the outer symptoms. Meaning, it would seem, is to be restored to the churches by banishing the inner silence—in which alone the voice of God may be heard, and by turning the attention more and more exclusively to action and good works. The new Masses reflect this attitude. It is now rare indeed to find anywhere an almost silent, contemplative Mass in the quiet of the early morning. One almost feels that no one can stand a moment of silence. Sermons have been introduced into all of them, and the involvement of the people has shifted from inner intensity to outer speech and action. Yet our need is precisely the opposite in this age of appalling secular busyness and collective thinking. The sense of the numinous then, in Christian ritual is fast dying, and while we grieve at the passing of so much beauty, it is a fact to be accepted and understood in its positive meaning, for in an accepted death lies the seed of birth.

The Church of Christ has preserved through two thousand years the message of God incarnate. It has also rightly protected men in their weakness from the full impact of that message, as Dostoyevsky's Grand Inquisitor so clearly saw. The vast majority have been too weak to bear it alone. The ego, paradoxically, has to grow immensely strong before a man, alone and unprotected, can challenge its leading role. In the past men found salvation from the devouring greed of the ego by obedience to the wisdom of the Church and by response to the great symbols preserved in her rituals. It will be said that there is still a great majority who need this protection, and this is surely true. The Church must still fulfil her ancient task, but the help and guidance needed is of a different kind. The old language, the old emphasis, is becoming useless not only to the stronger souls but to the many. To bolster it up with a "social gospel" or a changing liturgy is like building a wall of sand to stop a flood.

The Church is ordained not to give specific answers on external issues, but to listen to the voice of the Holy Spirit and to interpret it with humility for all those individuals whose imaginative consciousness is not yet strong enough to enable them to find their own symbolic life. But of course an institution is incapable of listening to anything—only an individual can do that. If all those "chosen" ones from the Pope downward who choose a religious vocation were to listen individually to that voice like a breath of wind within, resolutely refusing to be distracted by any of the interpretations of the past, they would hear again the pure essence of the Faith in this new age of the Spirit. Then indeed the Church in her great wisdom and with all her symbolic power might speak to her children the *positive* truth of that urge to overthrow all authority, all discipline, all checks on the individual. She might say, "Yes, you are right in what you seek. This is the true voice of the Spirit. No outer law, no conformity of any kind can bring you to the meaning of life, to the vision of God. But if you have grown to this point, then the form and discipline and the moral laws against which you rebel outwardly must be found inwardly, and the challenge of this quest is a great and exciting thing, far more exciting than an easy grabbing at 'experience' through the short cuts of drugs and indiscriminate sexual indulgence. It is a quest of the individual imagination, which is both contemplative thought and active love, whereby man finds in and beyond the fact the symbol that gives it reality."

Jung wrote:

By becoming conscious the individual is threatened more and more with isolation, which is nevertheless the *sine qua non* of conscious differentiation. The greater this threat, the more it is compensated by the production of collective and archetypal symbols that are common to all men and women. This fact is expressed in a general way by the religions, where the relationship of the individual to God or the gods ensures that the vital link with the regulating images and instinctual powers of the unconscious is not broken. Naturally this is true only so long as they have not lost their numinosity; that is, their thrilling power. Once this loss has occurred, it can never be replaced by anything rational.[1]

As has already been said, it appears that the Church and the religious orders often try to do just this—hoping to compensate for the loss of the numinous with all kinds of rationalizations, instead of proclaiming the profoundly moving and thrilling truth that the Holy Spirit no longer speaks through outer structures and rules but in the living imagery arising from the unconscious "poet" in every individual man and woman. "The Spirit bloweth where it listest and no man knoweth whence it cometh or whither it goeth." (John 3:8) R.H. Blyth, in the preface to his book, *Zen in English Literature and the Oriental Classics*, now out of print, quoted Confucius' definition of a teacher: "A true teacher is one who knows and makes known the New by revitalizing the Old."[2]

NOTES
1. C. G. Jung, *Alchemical Studies*, vol. 13 of *The Collected Works*, The Bollingen Series (Princeton: Princeton University Press, 1968), para. 395.
2. R.H. Blyth, *Zen in English Literature and the Oriental Classics* (Tokyo: Hokuseido Press, published in occupied Japan in 1948).

Chapter Nineteen

The Vows of
the Interior Life

To ALL RELIGIOUS who have a sense of the interior life, the vows of poverty, chastity, and obedience mean far more than the renunciation of material possessions, celibacy, and obedience to the rule and to their superiors. Nevertheless, few voices have yet been clearly heard within the Church, breaking through the present ferment of change, to proclaim the eternal meaning within every individual soul of these vows and the temporal and changing nature of all outer structures by which men and women seek to live them. The result of this silence is that large numbers of sincere people, aware of an increasing meaninglessness in the rules they have promised to follow, seek to restore life to the old kind of structure by tinkering with its forms. They change or abolish the habit; they try to form small groups within their order and undertake new kinds of work; they reduce the number of offices, alter timetables, demand the right to engage in social action, and so on. Others leave their communities altogether, and among these many perhaps carry unconscious guilt for the rest of their lives, in spite of the formal release that may be given to them.

The use of the phrase "release from *vows*" is in itself a revelation of the lack of discrimination in the Church between the deep commitment of the vows and the varying disciplines to which a woman or a man submits in the attempt to keep them. Surely there should be no talk at all about "release." Not only monks and nuns but no human beings anywhere are ever "released" from allegiance to these three commitments if they would come to the company of the Blessed. If a man has promised to follow the monastic way of life outwardly, he is pledged to seek and live the realities of poverty, chastity, and obedience, in the context of that way, through doubt and suffering, aridity and discouragement, for just so long as the symbol behind this way remains alive for him. The moment it is dead and he knows it, without question, then *because* of his vows, not in spite of them, he must dare to break with the safe conformity of the known, the support of law and habit, and must seek a new symbolic life in which to devote himself to those deep commitments. The vows must now be lived more profoundly with less support and the new inner discipline will be far more difficult than the old.

There are certainly very many individuals among those who leave the orders and among those granting release who understand this. Indeed there are signs that large numbers of religious have seen this essential truth. Nevertheless, is it not time for a clear and unequivocal statement of these values by the authorities of the Church? So very many bewildered and less conscious souls, caught in half measures, driven to neurosis by guilt, would be supported and set free to find inner reality according to their capacity by such a positive call to turn their gaze from the letter to the spirit of their vows. Definite encouragement to leave, as an act of devotion, not of failure, is the need of those who obviously cling to the monastic way for infantile reasons that stifle for them any possibility of growth, any chance they may have of understanding the real meaning of their commitment.

The wind of the Spirit is blowing, sweeping away the old law, but many religious of goodwill are bound to the old by their sincere acceptance of the facts that they have made a vow that binds them to the structure itself. A wise mother superior said recently that if the Holy Spirit wishes to destroy the religious life as we know it, then so be it. If an old thing is destroyed, however, it may disappear in one of two ways — either by slow disintegration with the authorities fighting a losing battle, a way that brings meaningless suffering to who knows how many; or by a conscious sacrifice whereby the values of the old are transmuted and reborn on a new level of meaning.

In childhood, rules are an absolute essential, even when misunderstood and resented. A child is in misery when there are no fixed boundaries and he is asked to make his own decisions too soon, as witness the very many unhappy "little adults" whose parents have no notion of the difference between discipline and repression. So it was entirely right in the childhood of our civilization that the vows of the interior life, consciously taken, should include the imposition of unbreakable rules for outer behavior. This is no longer tenable. A true resurrection may await the religious life if Christians can pass through the present adolescent stage of rebellion to the freedom of full individual responsibility. The meaning of poverty, chastity, and obedience in the Kingdom of Heaven which is within can no longer in our time be bound for life to an unbreakable outer rule of any kind whatsoever. Conversely, we cannot without disaster dispense with outer rules until the true meaning of the inner reality begins to dawn in us, until we are aware of that which we seek.

What, then, are those three great visions that are the foundation of the interior life? In all religions, east and west, they are the same. "Blessed are the poor in spirit, for theirs is the Kingdom of Heaven." "Blessed are the pure in heart, for they shall see God." "Blessed are the meek for they shall inherit the earth."

"Blessed are the poor in spirit, for theirs is the Kingdom of Heaven." (Matthew 5:3)

The "poverty" of the religious orders and communities, that is, the renunciation of all personal possessions, is a symbol before the world of that inner poverty of spirit that is the Way for every man and woman. The outer fact of possession or lack of material goods is beside the point. The poor man demanding his "rights" and the rich man clinging to his wealth are in like case. A vow whereby a man or woman renounces material possessions, and, incidentally, is relieved of the responsibility of earning a living, is not only meaningless but actively harmful the moment it loses its inner meaning—the moment it is clear that freedom from outer concerns has become an escape for any given individual, and therefore a hindrance to his or her quest for spiritual poverty. Such a person will then be hiding behind a religious habit, identifying ego with clothing, instead of wearing it with a humble consciousness of its beauty as a symbol.

The changing attitudes of religious toward the habit, particularly in the women's communities, are the clearest possible proof of the loss of a sense of the symbolic. For the habit was the image that declared to the world that the man or woman who wore it had renounced not only material possessions but the *claims of the ego to any kind of specialness.* This is why the habit used to be held in such reverence both by its wearers and by the world outside. It awoke in its beholder a response, an effect, whether positive or negative, springing from the unconscious desire in every man and woman for that very poverty of spirit whereby alone we possess the Kingdom of Heaven. To give up specialness is the very reverse of giving up uniqueness. Poverty of spirit is richness in the Spirit, which can be known only by the man or woman who has found his or her unique individual meaning and accepted anonymity in the context of society.

The habit is now increasingly looked upon merely as an uncomfortable and impractical uniform, to be abolished or approximated to ordinary dress. If the numinous meaning has gone from it, of course there is no sense in maintaining it; the halfway measures, the rationalizations are the damaging thing. For we cannot go back. Once the *mana* has departed from something, we must let go of it; but unless it is a conscious sacrifice out of which the symbol is resurrected on another level, then the old imagery will simply disappear into the unconscious and turn negative. The symbolism of the habit is losing its numinosity because the collective way of institutional religion is no longer for most people anything but a social activity—often of great value on that level but unconnected with the interior religious life of the soul. It cannot be too often repeated that, as Jung said, it is impossible to replace a symbolic with a rational truth. Those who see the habit as a uniform to be abandoned are moved by their urge toward outer individual differentiation, but, if at the same time they lose contact with the numinous image altogether, then the change defeats its end. It is an illuminating fact that the conservative, contemplative orders are losing fewer of their numbers than the progressive, active communities.

Meister Eckhart defines poverty as that state of being in which a man is wholly detached from "things," and to the extent that he empties himself, just so much does God enter into him and fill his emptiness. In our own time, Jung has defined the same reality as that wholeness that a man may know when the ego, through experience of the great symbols in the unconscious, is purged of all demand and concupiscence and is replaced at the center of the psyche by consciousness of the Self in which the opposites unite. Those religious who feel that they are called to activity in the world are still bound by their vow to the immensely difficult task of holding inwardly, in the midst of all action, to the poverty of spirit in which there can be no demand for results of whatever kind, no matter how "good" they may deem their goals. It is obvious that, as Jung said, only the transcendent and numinous symbol in which the two realities of matter and spirit, of conscious and unconscious are united in a single image can take a man "beyond himself and beyond his entanglement in the ego" to the resolution of this paradox, to the blessedness of the poor in spirit.

"Blessed are the pure in heart, for they shall see God." (Matthew 5:8)

This is the reality of the vow of chastity. The renunciation of the instinctive life breeds dark and ugly things as soon as it loses its symbolic meaning and becomes mere evasion. If the instinctual urges have been experienced without repression, emotionally and physically, and the agony of no fulfillment of those levels consciously endured, then to those few who are capable of this way will come a great transformation of love through suffering. They will create and give birth in the realm of the spirit where there is no marrying or giving in marriage. But as a way of life unbreakably imposed from without on adolescent souls who so often are not able to realize the evasive motives underlying the promises they made in good faith, it may lead over the years to an impurity of heart more dangerous than the open concupiscence of the prostitute.

Purity of heart has nothing whatsoever to do with sexual inter-course as such; it is a matter of the quality of love. There is plenty of adultery between very respectable married couples, for every mating is adulterous where there is no love and no creation. The purity of heart that brings the vision of God, like poverty of spirit, will come to us only when our love, our desire is free from every *demand* for fruition.

We must be clear about the distinction between the demand and the desire itself, for these two things are very generally confused, with deadly effect. It is essential that we allow our desires absolute freedom if ever we are to be free from unconscious demand. I cannot do better than quote here from Max Plowman's book, *Introduction to the Study of Blake*, in which he comments on one of Blake's poems. There are two verses in the poem, one of which begins, "Love seeketh not itself to please," and the second, "Love seeketh only self to please." Plowman writes:

Here are contraries that are true and must remain coexistent. . . .
Without self-pleasing there can be no love. . . . Invertebrate sentimental self-negation is the destiny of those who think love can be
comprehended by the love that seeketh not itself to please. . . . Self-
assertion is essential to individuality, and until we have achieved
individuality through self-assertion, imagination cannot function.
Love without desire is sterile; but love is redeemed from greed by
imagination. That is the miracle.[1]

The word *imagination* is, of course, used in Blake's sense. For
Blake it meant the only power in man through which he might come
to the vision of God, the one way out of absorption in the ego; and
when he spoke of the life of the imagination he meant exactly the
same thing as Jung meant by the symbolic life.

We may come, then, to the love that is pure only through setting
free the imagination in the world of symbol, and by rejecting nothing
of ourselves, dark or light. The way is overwhelmingly hard and
beset with dangers, for imagination can very easily degenerate into
daydreaming fantasy if it is undisciplined. No wonder, then, that
there are rules to protect and help us on the road; without them we
should have no hope of growth. But it is fatally easy for us to turn
these rules into ends in themselves, and the churches, whose whole
vocation it is to protect us against just this betrayal, are too often the
worst offenders of all.

True celibacy, then, is not the outer state of remaining unmarried;
it is the inner condition that every man or woman, married or unmarried, must seek if he or she is to "see God." It is the state of being
whole, one-in-himself, so that he no longer seeks unconscious parts
of himself in his relationships, whether with wife, friends, or enemies. Then he may come at the last to awareness of the marriage of
Heaven and Earth that is God incarnate. For this reason the Roman
Catholic priest is bound to celibacy, for he is symbolically the representative of Christ.

The ego in our time is so far from the unconscious, the onesided
development is so powerful, that the imposition of a rule from
without easily becomes a positive incitement to the priest either to
identify his ego with his symbolic function or else to live his life
comfortably in two rationalized compartments, and this amounts to
a real betrayal of his vow. The priest in all of us is forever celibate, but
the ego struggling along the way must pass through the fullest expe-

rience of personal relationship on all levels, physical, emotional, and spiritual, before it can find the purity of heart that is the vision of God. If we are to avoid both identification and compartment living, it is again clear that only the experience that comes through the uniting symbol can save us. This is the profound meaning carried by the Mass, and by all the sacraments, to those for whom they retain their numinous power.

"Blessed are the meek, for they shall inherit the earth." (Matthew 5:5)

The third vow, of obedience, is a commitment to total response at whatever cost to the voice of the Holy Spirit within. The enormous difficulty of recognizing "the still small voice," as we listen to the confused clamor of voices in the psyche, in no way excuses in any adult soul the comfortable acceptance of an unchanging lifelong substitute for the dangers of the individual search.

The word *meek* has nowadays an almost entirely pejorative meaning. Meekness has come to mean a tame kind of submission, and the nineteenth-century image of a "gentle Jesus meek and mild" is about as far away as one could get from what Christ must have meant when he said, "Blessed are the meek." Ronald Knox uses the word *patient* in his translation, and that is nearer the mark in our ears. A patient man is one who suffers without protest but *not* submissively. He consciously *chooses* obedience. The kind of obedience that submits without discrimination, out of fear or weakness, certainly "inherits" nothing; but that rare quality of unconditional obedience, each man or woman to his or her own deepest vision of truth, does inherit the earth, for nothing can shake the one who has it out of the calm which is born of a fundamental acceptance of all the phenomena of existence. This is not at all the same thing as fatalism or a passive state of noninvolvement. On the contrary, such a man will be profoundly involved in all the changes and chances of his life, content to live with his doubts, to risk mistakes and failure as wholeheartedly as he embraces his certainties.

The question is immediately asked, "How can a man know that his supposed vision of truth is in fact anything but a subjective delusion?" The answer is that of course he cannot know, but that is not the point. There is an unconscious assumption in most people that "subjective" and "deluded" are synonymous, whereas a subjective reality is every bit as true as a so-called objective fact. The vital discrimination is rather between the different levels of our desires. We betray our most real intuitions of truth by running after superficial opinions or longing. Nevertheless, the one necessity is that we be wholehearted in our obedience on *whatever* level: "Unless devotion is given to the thing which must prove false in the end, that which is true in the end cannot enter."[2]

Even Christ himself could not answer Pilate's question, "What is truth?" The only answer to that question was Christ himself. For this cause, he said, was he born . . . that he might bear witness to the truth that was in him. For this cause is every human being born—not to live out his or her life in blind conformity to this code or that but to suffer unto death for his or her own truth. To the discovery of this truth beyond both the desires of the ego and of intellectual concepts, everyone must bring the devotion of a whole heart and mind.

It should not be assumed that intensity of imagination does away with facts. No indeed! True imagination is born only out of the clearest possible discrimination of facts exactly as they are, and the penetration through them to the symbol beyond them. This is why the man or woman who is obedient to his or her imaginative vision inherits the *earth*. The down-to-earth facts of everyday life are filled with meaning, and transformed by the image, they too become truth. Blake said of himself, "I question not my corporeal eye, any more than I would question a window concerning a sight. I look through it, not with it."[3]

People laugh nowadays at the story of St. Teresa telling her nuns that their vow meant unquestioning obedience even if a superior told them to go and plant a cabbage upside down. In our enlightened times such supine obedience would be idiotic. But the story has a beautiful symbolic truth. St. Teresa is in fact saying that the essence of obedience is imaginative, and that it has no meaning whatever if it is merely a matter of following a rational judgment. The man or woman who has entered a religious order and promised to obey its rule out of an intense imaginative experience of the truth it symbolizes will not be troubled by the minutiae of that way of life, or by the often mistaken and meaningless interpretations of the rule on which superiors may insist. He is obedient to his inner vision, and the way of his order with all its faults may remain for him to the end of this life the outer form through which the symbol becomes incarnate. But the moment the form becomes for him an empty conformity cut off from the symbol—the moment his life regresses into a matter of good works only and obedience to facts alone instead of truth, then he is no longer among the meek who inherit the earth; he becomes a tame cipher dominated by the "letter which killeth." The window has become opaque.

So it is for all of us, accepting this or that discipline, whether of work or relationship. To run from one opaque window to the next because its shape or color is different and pleases us better is quite pointless. The saint or sage, the great poet, can see through all windows, but he, too, has sought and found, through many choices and changes, that way of life through which the light pours for him most clearly, so that at the last he becomes himself a clear window for others. We see "through a glass darkly," as St. Paul says, but always *through* it if we would know truth.

When the chosen way of life has become something that obscures the living image, then, if a person begins to see the light shining through another window, he or she not only may, but *must* break every law, even the laws of the outer Church, in order to be true to the solemn and binding vow of lifelong obedience. The Church through her priests has only one unchanging function—to keep alive the numinous image behind every fact and every law, so that our choices may be made in obedience to the symbolic truth of the moment and not to the thousand and one conformities that are its substitute.

The simple people of goodwill, of whom there are so many in the religious communities, are in great need of this kind of positive help from their priests. They need to be freed from guilt and helped to the knowledge that there is no sin involved if they have found the rule to be something that stifles their growth, but equally that there is no substitute to be found simply by plunging into all sorts of other activities. It is a matter of putting the emphasis where it belongs—on the inner commitment. As Thomas Merton once said, even one monk or nun in a community who is there for the wrong reasons, and whose personality is stifled, will inject poison into the life of the whole. If this attitude resulted in the emptying of the monasteries and convents in a wholesale manner, what of that? The Spirit is not served by large numbers of people conforming to a rule but by the intensity of imaginative devotion in individual men and women, and society itself can be transformed by this kind of obedience alone. All other panaceas or crusades simply turn into their opposites.

NOTES
1. Max Plowman, *An Introduction to the Study of Blake* (New York: Barnes and Noble, 1967), pp. 128-29.
2. Charles Williams, *He Came Down from Heaven* (London: Faber and Faber, 1950), p. 25.
3. Plowman, pp. 79-81.

Chapter Twenty

Courtesy

ORIGINALLY COURTESY WAS the standard of behavior demanded at the court of a king, the outward sign of the true aristocrat. The courteous knight of King Arthur's court, for instance, had to practice an unfailing gentleness and forbearance toward women; he had to be always true to his word at no matter what the cost, and he had to be ready to meet any danger arising from his task of protecting the weak and oppressed; he had to show mercy to the defeated and be devoted to the principle of "fair play."

All these qualities, though they have remained to this day as the hallmark of the true gentleman, have also degenerated, as do all collective ideals, into a rigid outer code of manners, and so courtesy has often become identified with mere politeness and conformity with the collectively "right" way to behave in given circumstances. True courtesy, however, is a kind of behavior that expresses a quality of the soul, an essential attitude of the whole person, and it is not by chance that the word takes us back to the court of a king; for, no matter if every king should disappear from the earth, the psyche remains, as Jung said, aristocratic in its fundamental nature. In our dreams, as in fairy story and legend, it is the image of the king that carries the symbol of ruling value, the ultimate authority beyond the law. Aristocracy means government by the "best," the most noble, and in the mature psyche it means the preeminence of the objective, impersonal values over the little personal demands of the ego. So the royal quality, the aristocratic principle, is that which brings courtesy, is that which annihilates at once all feeling of superiority or inferiority between person and person. Only a true inner hierarchy of values can bring true equality of persons; also, this equality—another paradox—can only exist where there is accurate discrimination of *factual* differences of ability and knowledge. In the counterfeit gentleman, high birth and breeding, or any outstanding quality, become not merely superior in their proper sphere, in their factual aspect, but are believed to constitute a superiority as person, and no degree of polished manners or correct behavior can turn that man into a real gentleman, a courteous person.

How do we distinguish courtesy in a man from mere politeness? We may start by translating the knightly code into psychological terms. First the gentleness and forbearance toward women would be, in that language, an unfailing sensitivity to the claims of feeling value. Secondly, the knight's fidelity to his word implies for us a searching honesty with ourselves of which is born both trust and trustworthiness. Protection of the weak is the quality of acceptance and respect for the failures and inferiorities we meet within ourselves as well as in others, and the willingness to expose ourselves to any threat or to any labor rather than take refuge in contempt or repression or unawareness. Mercy to the defeated is that essential element of courtesy, the absence of personal resentment when wronged—again it is respect for every human being no matter how hostile he or she may be. There is a most rare and beautiful example of this in Julia de Beausobre's account of her terrible experiences when she was a prisoner in Communist Russia.[1] She tells the usual story of the attempt to break down her human dignity, and says that one thing alone was finally left to her—the intense determination not to allow her tormentors to succeed, because, if she yielded, she would commit a terrible sin *against the questioners* themselves, monsters as they appeared. In other words, her simple, universal, unshakable courtesy kept her related to the human persons hidden under the inhuman cruelties of her tormentors, and so both saved her own integrity and released them from a small portion of their guilt.

The final knightly quality, devotion to "fair play," is emphatically not the whining cry so often heard, "That's not fair—life is unfair to me!" It is rather devotion to the quest for freedom to be oneself, to make one's own choices, however mistaken, and the refusal to weight the scales in any conflict by using weapons that the opponent does not possess. For instance, a man may defeat another in argument by a parade of specialized knowledge or wit designed to make his opponent feel his inferiority or ignorance. A knight would throw away his sword if his enemy did not have one.

All these things are contained in that little word *courtesy*, and yet it is an immediately recognizable quality, and there is no need to know much about a man or woman to sense its presence or absence. A courteous person will always make everyone around him feel at his best and most alive. No matter how superior his knowledge, his breeding, and so on, he will bring to his meeting with another person an absolutely genuine interest, respect, and concern for that person; and above all, he will give him his whole *attention* without curiosity or demand, and so immediately communicate to the other a freedom and sureness of which, perhaps, he did not know himself to be capable.

Courtesy is not to be equated with "kindness" in the sense of never hurting anyone or their feelings, any more than it can be confused with politeness, though if we think of the basic meaning of the word *kindness*, they are indeed practically synonymous. The word is derived from the same root as *kin* and implies the standard of behavior required between primitive people of the same kin. This idea lived again in the debased external gentleman's code, which enforced courteous behavior to a man's own class and to no one else. The courtesy of the soul is lived only when every man as an individual person has been recognized as *kin*—and indeed when every animal and thing too is given the rights of kin in the oneness of creation. The courteous man is sensitively aware of the nature and need of the animal; recognizes with love and respect the infinitely varying functions of the different levels of life, animal, plant, and inanimate thing, and treats all with courtesy even when the demands of real values make unkindness in the ordinary sense a necessity.

Courtesy most emphatically does *not* mean covering up one's feelings in order to be superficially "kind." It does mean that these feelings are to be spoken out forthrightly and courageously in the appropriate place and to the appropriate people. If, however, the personal negative feelings that seize us all from time to time are allowed to swamp us in such a mood, and to permeate the atmosphere, then obviously we must lose all respect and concern for the individuals around us and, even if we do not speak a word, we are guilty of discourtesy. We are then enclosed in a private world, and for the moment people don't exist except in the mass or as a projection point for our bad feeling. Thus we evade the pain of fact, in a family or any household group. The existence of such a mood, uncontained, in one individual, or an unresolved conflict between two members of a household can invade the atmosphere and disturb the free flow of courtesy and attention between each and all. One does not need to be talking to someone in order to maintain the offer of full attention.

These thoughts bring to light another paradox at the heart of courtesy. It is born of the union of austere discipline and complete spontaneity. A spontaneous, joyful feeling is engendered by the mere presence of a courteous person, but someone who is simply impulsive, at the mercy of thoughtless, undisciplined moods, can never bring forth the free spontaneity of real courtesy.

Another kind of courtesy that is valid is the respect due to a person's function or rank. This can of course become hypocritical and distasteful if it is not joined to the deeper person-to-person courtesy of which we have spoken. Where there is discrimination of the individual value, there will be true respect for the function, no matter how much the person carrying it may be disliked. Courtesy is good taste in human behavior.

In Tolstoy's *War and Peace* there are some beautiful passages describing what is essentially the transformation of a truly good, kind man, into a courteous man. Pierre in his early life was invariably kind and polite, full of plans to free his serfs, intent on his search for the meaning of life, but nevertheless he makes everyone he meets uneasy and his good schemes always go awry through his lack of discrimination. He goes through a time of great suffering as a prisoner of the French, and meets, in conditions of terrible hardship, an ignorant peasant who is nevertheless a completely whole man, simple and selfless, living each moment in its fullness. Pierre emerges from this experience transformed. Now whomever he meets—whether an embittered spinster, an avid intellectual, his servants, or his pompous doctor—each one of them begins to reveal his best side, instead of his worst. Each one, not knowing why, loves to be with Pierre, who talks very little himself (whereas before he was forever making speeches about his ideals) but draws out the other with understanding and genuine interest. Of the new attitude Tolstoy writes:

> This was his acknowledgment of the impossibility of changing a man's convictions by words, and his recognition of the possibility of everyone thinking, feeling, and seeing things each from his own point of view. This legitimate peculiarity of each individual, which used to excite and irritate Pierre, now became a basis of the sympathy he felt for, and the interest he took in, other people.[2]

This kind of mature courtesy can surely only be reached through deep suffering.

Those who knew the late Charles Williams spoke always of the beauty and power of his courtesy. As C. S. Lewis wrote:

> The highest compliment I ever heard paid to them [Williams' manners] was by a nun. She said that Mr. Williams' manners implied a complete *offer* of intimacy without the slightest *imposition* of intimacy. He threw down all his barriers without ever implying that you should lower yours. . . . He gave to every circle the whole man: all his attention, knowledge, courtesy, charity, were placed at your disposal. . . . This total offer of himself but without that tacit claim which so often accompanies such offers, made his friendship the least exacting in the world, and explains the surprising width of his contacts. One kept on discovering that the most unlikely people loved him as well as we did.[3]

NOTES
1. Julia de Beausobre, *The Woman Who Couldn't Die* (London: Victor Gollanz, 1948).
2. Leo Tolstoy, *War and Peace*, Book XV, Chapter 13.
3. C. S. Lewis, *Essays Presented to Charles Williams* (Oxford: Oxford University Press, 1947), p. x.

Chapter Twenty-One

The Stranger Within

WE LEARN FROM *The American Heritage Dictionary* that the Indo-European root of the words "host," "hospice," "hospitality," and "hospital" is *ghosti*; it is, surprisingly, also the root of the word "guest." Moreover, in the Indo-European Appendix the meaning of this root includes another word: *ghosti* meant "stranger" as well as "guest" and "host," properly, "someone with whom one has reciprocal duties of hospitality." There follows yet another meaning: from this root word also came the English "hostile," via the second meaning of "host" as a multitude—often of enemies. This, again, is connected to the fear of the unknown, which leads to the frequent projection of suspicion and hostility onto anything or any person that is strange to us.

Russell Lockhart, in his splendid book *Words as Eggs*,[1] has said that behind every word that we use—for the most part so casually—there lies a story to be found, if we are willing to attend to its inner meaning. There is a level on which the essential story will be the same for all seekers, but also a level where it will be unique for every one of us. As the pattern of every snowflake is unique, so also are the stories that nourish every single human life.

Most men and women who seek wholeness, or in Dante's words, "the love that moves the sun and the other stars," will easily recognize consciously the outer duties of hospitality whether as host or guest (I hope that throughout this bit of writing, readers will know that in this context "host" includes both genders, so that they will not accuse me of ignoring the hostess! The word "host" transcends gender). However, the degree to which we live the beauty and courtesy of the exchanges between hosts and guests, particularly when we are strangers to one another, will surely depend on our attitude to those inner images which are either the guiding truths of our lives, or, especially while they remain wholly unconscious or repressed, the controlling addictions or hidden goals of the psyche.

Imagination in its fundamental meaning, as defined by Shakespeare or Blake, and known to all great creative artists, is the making and the responding to images of all kinds in the outer and the inner worlds. We don't have to be great artists to do this; every one of us has the ability to respond by at least beginning to say "yes" or "no" to the strangers who knock on the doors of our souls. Even if our clear and honest response is "I am too weak to confront this threatening, hostile stranger. I am as I am." That too may be the saving humility that admits the divine and transforming guest; but to shut one's ears and eyes and ignore the knocking within delivers the ego over to possession by the demand for security or power, from which is born anger, violence, and hardness of heart. How easy it then is to be blind to the needs of those we meet—especially if they are personalities who irritate or bore us—because only a truly imaginative response can keep us aware of the effect on the other of an insensitive lack of warmth in our welcome.

I have had considerable experience with the messages that come to us through dreams. The voice of the dream will either warn of dangers in our attitudes to the journey of life or else give us courage as it points the way to new awareness. Thus we are enabled to take up the responsibilities of joy and so to find the kind of imaginative exchange which heals and unites. A very common theme in the dreams of someone who is unconsciously resisting a new awareness of such a responsibility, evading some hidden creative ability in him or herself, is that of a burglar or terrifying unknown person, or even a monster, who has broken into the house or is trying to get in to steal or perhaps to kill. The dreamer is often terrified and trying desperately in the dream to call the police, or find some means of evasion or escape from the intruder and so banish the threat to his or her inner security. Sometimes, as Marie-Louise von Franz has written in one of her fairy tale books, it is *necessary* for the one threatened to run away. Much discrimination is needed to recognize these occasions.

However, more often when the stranger takes this form, it becomes clear that the unknown, or as yet rejected, new attitude has turned dangerously negative and threatening, determined to make itself felt. If the dreamer is able in imagination to turn the dream into a story, into which he or she actively enters, opening the door perhaps and confronting the intruder, asking what his need is, inviting him in as one would a guest, then a conversation may ensue, a recognition, a lessening of fear. Gradually if the dreamer truly attends and does not just forget it all after a day or two, the changed attitude begins to alter behavior, and even leads to a long resisted major change in the way of life. Thus do one's personal images bring to mind the great stories in the myths.

We remember that among so-called primitive people a stranger who came to the door of tent or home, seeking shelter and food, was to be welcomed as an honored guest, especially because so easily he might be a god in disguise, even if he could also be a disguised enemy. We may also remember those saints or sages in all the great religious traditions who would invite an obvious thief to take any of his possessions and make no effort to oppose him—and, more delightful still, the many hermits, and indeed the great naturalists of our own time, who realize they are guests, as it were, of the wild animals into whose land they intrude, and who treat them with respect and love and so are not threatened by them. As an example, I saw a program on PBS recently in which the white wolf mother of a pack on Ellesmere Island (in the Arctic, north of Canada) positively invited the man (whose name, I regret, I have forgotten) who had been living there in a tent for many months, to enter her den and see her new cubs. The exchanges of true hospitality were between them.

It is sad when we compare this to the almost universal collective behavior of civilized man as he explored new lands in search of power or wealth. Any thought of being a guest of those races who had lived there for thousands of years came only to the very few, and it may be that the worst damage of all was done by those who, with excellent intentions, tried to "rescue" their hosts from their ancient traditions and ways of life. Nevertheless, as always, there are the shining stories of great individuals—travellers and explorers—in whom the respect and courtesy of the true guest and host stand out and the patient interest of "reciprocal hospitality" has brought about a final trust even after centuries of hostility. To mention one example among many in our own time, Laurens van der Post's books about his search for the remnants of the Bushmen—the first men of Africa—are a constant joy, recreating in the reader glimpses of the power and beauty of this latent spirit of hospitality in all the true meetings of our inner or outer lives.[2]

More than fifty years ago, I myself had the great good fortune to experience with my husband the extraordinarily gracious and spon-

taneous hospitality of a small group of Bedouin in the desert beyond
Aman in Jordan when our car broke down. It was near sunset and we
were welcomed into the young sheik's tent, given water to wash with,
fed with specially prepared food, and entertained in every way they
could devise without a shared language, as we waited for a mechanic,
fetched by one of their young men who was sent on foot to the nearest
village. Night fell and the stars shone out in the clear desert air while
camels sat around resting. We were even offered a night's shelter.
The experience left a living memory of the essential courtesy to the
stranger in a strange land—a welcome with no hidden demand for
any return, no questions asked—a free giving and taking of the
simplest kind.

Perhaps it is because of this memory that the great story in our
own tradition that stands out for me as of a particular power when we
turn to the very difficult task of creating this kind of simple guest
and host exchange with the unknown aspects of ourselves, is the
story of the coming of three men to Abraham in his old age (he was
99) as he sat at the entrance to his desert tent. After he had welcomed
them and brought them water and food, the strangers asked him
where his wife Sarah was, and then told them both that she would
conceive and bear him a child. But Sarah laughed to herself, thinking
them foolish, knowing that it was impossible at her age. And the
guest (who had become one it seems, instead of three, and was
indeed Yahweh himself) asked, "Why did Sarah laugh . . . is anything too wonderful for Yahweh?" "I did not laugh," said Sarah,
lying because she was afraid. But he replied, "Oh, yes, you did
laugh."

However, "Yahweh dealt kindly with Sarah . . . and did what he
had promised her"—in spite of her somewhat contemptuous laughter at such nonsense. So Sarah conceived and bore a son to Abraham
in his old age. And then comes the altogether delightful ending to
the story. Then Sarah said, "God has given me cause to laugh; all
those who hear of it will laugh with me."[3] From the laughter of
rejection she has brought to birth the child and found the laughter at
the heart of life in which all with ears to hear may join.

So it can be with all those strange and seemingly hostile or meaningless images that knock at our doors, either in dreams or in irrational moods, in emotions or cravings, in unnoticed use of words or
habits of movement, both physical and psychic. If we dream, we may

experience all these habits and unconscious patterns already personified (though of course one needs a guide). If that is not our way, we can allow our imagination to do the same for them, and we may recognize them perhaps in our projections onto others, and then we may treat them all as the strange and unknown guests within who may have been wandering without food or water—that is, starving or withering from lack of acceptance, growing hostile and angry, and so shaking us awake. Then indeed we discover that they bring us a message from the Spirit within, from the Self, the God of innumerable names, the "I am that I am." The message is a birth in us—even a rebirth of the inner child—a newness of life and laughter, no matter how impossible that may seem, as the stranger brought the child to Sarah in her old age.

In all the stories the emphasis is on food and drink—always symbols of the kind of attention and concern which is the essence of hospitality. The guest is to be offered nourishment on every level—nourishment of the kind we all need—the best we can offer—emphatically not our own concept of what is "good for" the other, including the other within. It is easy to forget that only to the extent that we listen and attend to these figures who express our own weaknesses and potential strengths have we any hope of recognizing, in all those we meet in the outer world, either their needs as guests to be honored by us whether we like them or not, or their dues as hosts as they offer to us their acceptance and trust. We may find it hard to personify these unconscious denizens of the psyche; but mere "good" resolutions never change anything fundamentally. Shakespeare tells us that "the lunatic, the lover and the poet are of imagination all compact."[4] Within us these strangers bring the divine guest who transforms us, often through simple and unnoticed actions. That doesn't mean that we must necessarily write poetry or paint pictures, but simply allow the "poet" within us to give "a local habitation and a name"[5] to our strange inner guests. When the reciprocal rules of hospitality have become a spontaneous and joyful reality in the soul, then the divine spark will live between the individual and the other in all her or his meetings with every form of life.

Although it is so well known, I want to end with some brief quotations from that story, beloved among all the Greek myths—the tale of Baucis and Philemon, as told by the Roman poet Ovid in his *Metamorphoses*, and translated by the American poet Rolfe Humphries. Humphries' translation conveys to us in our own language, with sheer delight, the spontaneous essence of true hospitality, as Ovid describes the actions of two souls who have grown into the simplicity of that love which no abstract words can describe—the love in which mind and heart and instinct are at one in the web of life, in time and in eternity.

Ovid describes how Jupiter and Mercury, disguised as mortals, travelled the earth looking for rest.

> . . . They found a thousand houses
> Shut in their face. But one at last received them
> A humble cottage thatched with straw and reeds,
> A good old woman, Baucis, and her husband
> A good old man, Philemon, used to live there.
> They had married young, they had grown old together
> In the same cottage; they were very poor,
> But faced their poverty with cheerful spirit
> And made its burden light by not complaining.
> It would do you little good to ask for servants
> Or masters in that household, for the couple
> Were all the house; *both* gave and followed orders.
> So, when the gods came to this little cottage,
> Ducking their heads to enter, the old man
> Pulled out a rustic bench for them to sit on,
> And Baucis spread a homespun cover for it.

There is no male superiority in this house! Ovid goes on to describe the kindling of the fire, blown on by Baucis, who hadn't much breath to spare in her old age; the cooking in a copper kettle of the cabbage brought in from their well-watered garden by Philemon, and a chunk of their precious side of bacon. And they made conversation:

> To keep the time from being too long. . .
> Baucis, her skirts tucked up, was setting the table
> With trembling hands. One table leg was wobbly,
> A piece of shell fixed that.

The food is described, cottage cheese and eggs. The earthenware and the wine "of no particular vintage"

> . . . and apples in wide baskets—
> Remember how apples smell?—and purple grapes

Fresh from the vines, and a white honeycomb
As centerpiece, and all around the table,
Shone kindly faces, nothing mean or poor
Or skimpy in good will.

Then they noticed that the mixing bowl kept filling up all by itself
and that scared them, and they thought anxiously that their food
wasn't good enough for such guests and wanted to kill their precious
goose who was a sort of watchdog for them. But the goose ran to the
gods and they revealed themselves, preventing the killing, and took
the old couple up the mountain from which they saw that the houses
in the valley whose doors had been closed to strangers were now
flooded with water—all except their cottage. "And while they wondered they wept a little for their neighbors' troubles." Their cottage
was now turning into a temple, and Jupiter asked them what they
would like for themselves.

. . . And they hesitated,
Asked, could we talk it over just a little?
And talked together apart.

Then Philemon spoke for both and asked that they might be priests
having care of the temple and that they might die in the same hour.

And one day as they stood before the temple
Both very old, talking the old days over
Each saw the other put forth leaves, Philemon
Watched Baucis changing, Baucis watched Philemon
And as the foliage spread, they still had time
To say "Farewell, my dear". . .

The peasants in that district still show the stranger
The two trees close together, and the union
Of oak and linden in one.

The beautiful ending of this story is a simple, natural image of the
hierosgamos, the final unity, the marriage of the opposites in which
duality is transcended yet each partner remains unique—the oak
and the linden remain themselves as their roots and branches inter-
twine in a single tree of life. The two old people had become hosts
and guests to each other in their daily lives, and so to all life—to the
gods and to all the unknown who came to their temple to honor and
worship the divine images in their own hearts.

Ovid ends his poem by telling how he himself had seen this tree—
one and yet still two—and brought a garland and said a verse:

The gods look after good people still, and cherishers are cherished.

NOTES
1. Russell Lockhart, *Words As Eggs* (Dallas: Spring Publications, 1963).
2. Sir Laurens van der Post, *The Lost World of the Kalahari,* and *The Heart of the Hunter,* both
   published by Harcourt Brace Jovanovich.
3. Translations are from the Jerusalem Bible.
4. Shakespeare, *A Midsummer Night's Dream*, Act IV, Scene 1.
5. *Ibid.*

The Way
of
Story

Chapter Twenty-Two

The Inner Story

THE ESSENCE OF all religions, from the most primitive to the most highly developed, has always been expressed by the human soul in stories. The Mass itself is a story—a symbolic drama telling the great story of the death and resurrection of Christ. We can say, "I believe in this or that," and assert the truth of many doctrines, but these things will not affect the soul of any one of us unless in some way we experience their meaning through intense response to the images conveyed in story. Innumerable tales in all ages have expressed the changing relationships of human beings to their gods and have told of their search for the divine meaning behind their lives.

Before the invention of writing all human knowledge was conveyed from generation to generation by storytellers who were the sacred minstrels and medicine men of the people; and, even after the growth of consciousness had brought about the formulation of doctrines and the definitions of dogma, the great storytellers kept alive into our own day the imaginative response to the numinous, which alone gives life to conceptual dogma.

Many theologians and psychologists nowadays are joining poets in affirming anew the tremendous importance of story. A friend who is a theologian was saying to me the other day that, valuable as conceptual theory is, it can only speak to the intellectual faculties in men and women; whereas in a story the living confrontation of the opposites and the transcendent symbol that resolves conflict speak directly to the listener's mind, heart and imagination in the same images.

C.G. Jung has told us how he found, after his own lonely confrontation with the powers of the unconscious, the life-giving wonder of the inner myth, or story, behind his life; and it is in part by our response to the great stories of the world that we too can begin to find, each of us, this individual story, expressing the symbolic meaning behind the facts of our fate and behind the motives that determine the day-to-day choices of our lives. If we are not aware of the need for this imaginative search, and continue to base our attitudes purely on the kind of thinking that is bounded by the laws of materialistic cause and effect and statistical data, then sooner or later we shall be forced to see how the springs of life dry up, and how nature, physical as well as psychic, is gradually polluted and sterilized, so that we look forward to a time when there will be no pure water left for us to drink. Yet there is a steadily growing hope in the increasing number of people who drink from the life-giving springs of the images within. Many of my writings are simply a collection of studies made with small groups over the years, as we looked at some of the great stories, ancient and modern, and sought to realize their meaning in our lives.

The experience of darkness, of evil, is essential to redemption and there is no inner story that does not contain this truth. As Judas and the Pharisees were essential to Christ's death and resurrection, so in every story of the soul, the tiny flame of love and awareness is threatened with extinction, and saved only through the humility and sacrifice of an individual human being.

At the end of his life, C.G. Jung (as we can see in his later letters) continually stressed that *only* if enough individuals would commit themselves totally to this search, each for his or her own inner truth, could the world avoid disaster. The inner story, though the same in essence for all, is always single and unique in each human being, never before lived and never to be repeated.

Chapter Twenty-Three

An African Tale

A REAL STORY touches not only the mind, but also the imagination and the unconscious depths in a person, and it may remain with
him or her through many years, coming to the surface of consciousness now and then to yield new insights. A great teacher of English at
Swarthmore College, the late Harold Goddard, wrote in his book
The Meaning of Shakespeare, "The destiny of the world is determined
less by the battles that are lost and won than by the stories it loves and
believes in."[1] This love and belief begins and ends, of course, in
individuals and their responses to such stories in their own lives. I
heard the following story a number of years ago told by Laurens van
der Post at a conference.[2] He had heard it from a Zulu wise man in
Africa, and he was retelling it as an offering of gratitude and respect
to the women of the world.

All those stories that deal with basic human themes draw their
power from the archetypal world that is common to people of all
cultures and of all times, but the images in each culture will, of
course, differ greatly, and it is for us to penetrate through these
varying pictures to the universal wisdom that underlies them. I
propose to tell the story first, simply, as it is told in its African
context; and afterwards I will go through it again with a few indica-
tions as to how it may yield its wisdom in terms of our own lives. It is a
story about young women on the threshold of their adult lives — and
that is a rare thing to find. There is no hero in it at all — only one
somewhat devastating male figure!

In an African village a group of young women had banded together to humiliate one of their number of whom they were jealous
and whom they had rejected because she was "different," and especially because it seemed to them that she had a necklace of beads that
was more beautiful than their necklaces.

These jealous young women ran down to the banks of the river and
there they planned a trap for the envied one. When she joined them,

207

they told her that they had all thrown their necklaces into the river as an offering to the river god. The young woman was a person of generous heart, so she at once took off her own necklace and threw it into the river; whereupon the others dug up their necklaces, which they had buried in the sand, and went off laughing and sneering.

The young woman, left alone, was very sad. She had been duped into a well-meant but foolish act, and she wandered along the river-bank, praying to the god to restore the necklace. There was no answer until at last she heard a voice, bidding her plunge into a deep pool nearby. She did not hesitate, for she knew it was the voice of the god. She plunged down into the unknown and found herself on the riverbed, where an old woman sat waiting. This old one was exceedingly ugly, even repulsive, for she was covered with open sores, and she spoke to the girl, saying, "Lick my sores!" At once the girl obeyed out of her compassionate heart, and licked the repulsive sores as she had been asked to do. Then the old woman said to her, "Because you have not held back and have licked my sores, I will hide and protect you when the demon comes who devours the flesh of young women." At that she heard a roar and a huge male monster came, calling out that he smelled a maiden there. But the old woman had hidden her away, and soon he went off cursing.

Then the old woman said to the girl, "Here is your necklace"— and she put around her neck beads of far greater beauty than any she had had before. "Go back now," the old woman said, "to your village, but when you have gone a few yards from the pool, you will see a stone in the path. Pick up this rock and throw it back into the pool. Then go on without looking back and take up your ordinary life in your village."

The young woman obeyed. She found the stone and threw it back and came to the village without a backward look. There the other girls quickly noticed her beautiful new necklace and clamored to know where she had found it—to which she replied that it had been given to her by the old woman at the bottom of the pool in the river. Not waiting for more, they all rushed off in a body and jumped into the pool. And the old woman said to each of them as she had said before, "Lick my sores!" but these girls all laughed at her and said they wouldn't dream of doing anything so repulsive—and useless, too—and they demanded to be given necklaces at once. In the midst of all this there came the roar of the giant demon, who seized upon those girls, one after the other, and made a mighty meal of them. And with that the story comes to an end.

I shall now look briefly at the images in the story as symbols of certain attitudes, conscious or unconscious, that are alive in each one of us and influence us in often unrealized and subtle ways. Stories like this are not manufactured by the intellect; they are the symbolic dreams of humanity.

The necklace in Africa is a highly prized symbol of a woman's identity and worth as a person. The group of girls in the story play a particularly unkind trick since it concerns devotion to a divine, transpersonal value. It is the product of group mentality, mass thinking, which so often covers and excuses hatred and cruelty. This is perhaps the worst menace in our society, requiring great effort and integrity to resist.

Notice the ease with which the simple girl falls into the trap. This is surely a warning of the dangers that lie in wait for the generous-hearted, who are so quickly induced by the slogans of some cause or crusade, fine in itself perhaps, and sponsored by people we long to please. We lose sight of our individual responsibility to reflect and to *choose*, and thus, as it were, we throw away our identity. Nevertheless, the story goes on to show us that such naive enthusiasms, *if* they truly involve the intention of a personal sacrifice to that which is greater than our egos, to the river of life itself, may indeed bring about the shock that leads us out of group thinking to the discovery of our meaning as individuals on a much deeper level.

The young woman in the story had a rude awakening from her identification with her peers. We may notice that she did not waste energy on resentment or remorse. She stayed alone beside the river of life, praying that she might rediscover her value as a person, waiting for an inner voice to bring her wisdom. And it came. She was to look for her necklace down under the water. Only by going *down*, not by striving upwards, would she find herself. She must plunge into the river of life *unconditionally*, risking mistakes or failure, not just throwing things, however valuable, into the river. Only by trusting herself to the unknown, both in her outer life and in her own hidden depths, would she find her unique way.

This young woman was now obedient, not to convention or opinions or slogans, but to that voice from within that may be heard by us all at the crucial moments of life, if we will truly listen.

She plunged down into the pool and there she found—not a radiant woman, symbolizing her potential beauty and power, but an old, ugly, repulsive thing with open sores. How shall we read this image for ourselves? When we enter with open eyes into the river of life, we find ourselves face to face with the ugliness, the suffering from which we have perhaps been protected hitherto in many different ways. And it is now that the story yields to us its specifically *feminine* wisdom.

We may take this image of the old woman on two levels. She may stand for the suffering that contempt for the feminine values has brought to all women through the ages—a contempt of which not only many men have been guilty, but also large numbers of women themselves, especially in our time. And secondly, the old woman is an image on the personal level of the most despised and repellent things in our own psyches that we refuse to acknowledge and from which we turn often in disgust.

The old woman's invitation is clear. "You can't bring help to me by any kind of technical, scientific, impersonal and collective panacea, or by *talk about* justice and freedom. Only with your own saliva can you bring healing to these sores in yourself and in the world." Saliva is symbolically a healing water that we are all born with. The licking of an animal is its one means of healing wounds, and we may remember Christ's saliva on the blind man's eyes. So the girl is asked to give of her own unique essence—to bring healing to the sores, not by words out of her mouth but by water from her mouth. Because she is on the threshold of true womanhood the girl at once responds out of that essential core of the feminine being—the compassionate heart. Here I would emphasize that true compassion bears *no* resemblance to a vague and sentimental pity. Compassion is not just an emotion; it is an austere thing and a highly differentiated quality of soul.

And now comes that universal threat—the demon of inferior masculinity that can so easily devour our womanhood. When this happens, we simply lose ourselves in an imitation of men, which kills the truly creative masculine spirit in a woman, and, however outwardly successful she may be, all hope of equality of *value* in the world of men disappears.

Had there been a male "hero" present, we might imagine the old woman telling him to take up his sword and fight the monster of greed and aggression. But to every woman she will always say, "Because of your compassion you will be freed from him."

So it came about that the devouring ambition and greed had no power over the woman who had the courage and humility to lick the repellent sores. It is at this moment that she receives her own individual and unique necklace—she does not just recover the old one that had come from her family before her initiation into life. This necklace is hers and hers alone.

It is time to return to her life in the world, to the daily, ordinary tasks and relationships. In her case, marriage and children awaited her and the building of a home; in our time and place, a career most probably awaits her, with or without the ancient way of woman in the home. But whether she marries and bears children or not, this ancient responsibility of woman remains. She is the guardian of the values of feeling in her environment, and if she remains aware of that compassion, that quiet, hidden nurturing that is the center of her feminine nature, then her skills in any kind of work whatsoever will grow in the manner of trees, well rooted and strong, and her creative spirit will be free. The woman who has received the necklace from the old woman in the pool does not seek compulsively to achieve success after success, collecting necklace after necklace, so to speak. Always she will remember to "lick the sores" and to remain still and hidden when the demon of greedy ambition threatens, whether at home or in the public arena.

Now as to the stone that the girl was to find and throw back, I'll give you one hint and leave you to work it out. The stone in all cultures is the symbol of the immortal Self, and this is the true offering to the divinity in the river. Don't pick it up and put it in your pocket!

The last bit of the story speaks for itself. All those greedy girls who did not bother to reflect on the meaning of life went rushing off in a mob, all wanting more and better necklaces, which in our day would be more and more demands for wealth, or success, or men, or publicity, or security, or even for spiritual experiences. They refused with contempt the essential task of a woman, the compassionate "licking of the sores" in themselves and in their immediate environment. They were therefore devoured by the demon that rages around, assimilating such women to itself.

I believe it was Charles Williams, the English poet and novelist who died in 1945, who once defined the art of living as the ability to live the ordinary in an extraordinary way and to live the extraordinary in an ordinary way. The story iluminates this beautiful saying. Dame Janet Baker, a great singer and a great woman, said once in an interview, "I've found that the ordinary things are the important things. . . . We all—in life and music—have our backs up against the wall trying to preserve order and quality. . . . My gift is God-given and it must be given back. We all have a gift to give, and if you give it with sense of holy obligation everything clicks into place."

Each of us, as we journey through life, has the opportunity to find and to give his or her unique gift. Whether that gift is great or small in the eyes of the world does not matter at all—not at all; it is through the finding and the giving that we may come to know the joy that lies at the center of both the dark times and the light.[3]

NOTES
1. Harold Goddard, *The Meaning of Shakespeare*, Vol. 2 (Chicago: University of Chicago Press, 1965), p. 208.
2. Story told by Laurens van der Post at the Notre Dame Jung Conference, Notre Dame, Indiana, 1973. He has warmly approved Helen Luke's use of it.
3. This essay was part of a commencement address by Helen Luke at St. Mary's College, Notre Dame, Indiana, in 1981.

Chapter Twenty-Four

The Hunter and the Hunted

THE HUNTER STOOD still—still without the tiniest movement, his bow in hand, gazing into the mist ahead of him. "Gazelle," he thought, and his heart lifted. He was upwind, the herd was moving slowly toward him as it grazed, and the mist would soon be gone under the morning sun. The hunter was not young. His hair was grizzled and his face lined with the mark of years, but his body remained strong and supple and his eyes keen. Few other hunters of the tribe could match his skill. Now, as he stood like a stone and waited, he saw that one of the herd was ahead of the others, that he grazed alone, and the hunter caught his breath. "A chief among gazelle," he murmured as the mist lifted and he saw the size and beauty and grace of the noble animal, the long tapering horns, the slender neck, the graceful strength of the legs, and the body built for speed. Almost he wished to shoot an arrow harmlessly into the air for the utter delight it always gave him to see gazelle in motion, flying as it were over the rolling plain. But he knew that he must take home food.

He concentrated now on his task as hunter—judging the distance, marking with his eye the spot over the heart that he would hope to hit so that the animal might die quickly and with little pain. Slowly, very slowly, he had begun to move his hand up to take an arrow from his quiver when a sound from behind him turned him rigid. Only his perfect discipline kept him from a quick turn, which would have sent the gazelle in a few swift bounds to safety—his discipline and also his recognition of the sound. He had heard it before, that sound of a twanging bowstring like no other bowstring—not often, but on all the great days of his hunting life, and always it carried with it a strange feeling, compounded of fear and excitement, that behind

213

him was one who hunted *him* as he hunted his game. When young he had turned quickly and angrily as the sound reached him, ready to meet and fight this enemy who pursued him. But always behind him was emptiness and silence. He remembered now the first time it had happened. When hunting with his father as a boy, he had made his first kill and his heart was high with pride. As they moved toward the dead quarry, he had heard the twanging bow and had jumped round in fear, feeling for the first time the terror of the hunted beating down the pride of the hunter. His father had questioned him, "What ails you, boy?" And stumblingly he had told of his strange feeling of the sound he had heard. His father had looked long and deeply into his eyes, saying no word. At last he spoke. "My son," he said, "Tell no one of this thing. If it should come again, ask no questions either of others or of yourself—and the day may dawn when you will have no need to ask." He had obeyed, but, from that time on, the exhilaration of the hunt, and the joyful pride of the kill had carried with them an undercurrent of sadness and pain, for he knew within himself the panic fear of the hunted as the bowstring twanged and the arrow flew to its mark.

He had schooled himself through the years not even to turn his head when he heard the bow of the Great Hunter (as he had named the unseen), but the moment of terror could not be schooled and he had learned to accept it together with the hidden pain it left behind in his heart.

This time, he thought, it seemed nearer than ever before—he had even imagined for an instant a sharp pain in his back—but his eyes never left his quarry, and his hand, checked for that brief moment, moved on toward the quiver. Now as his fingers touched an arrow his stillness vanished and in one incredibly swift movement he had strung it, bent his bow, and shot. The beautiful creature, realizing his peril too late, fell as he gathered himself for flight, the arrow striking deep into his side but not to the heart. The hunter ran now, drawing out his knife to end quickly the pain of the gazelle, but as he reached the dying animal he stumbled and fell and the knife flew from his hand. He raised himself to his knees and found that he was gazing straight into the eye of his kill, the soft brown antelope eyes, the unfathomable mysterious eyes of the animal. Then, without warning, he felt a pair of very strong, yet gentle, hands covering his eyes and bearing him backward and sideways until he lay with his head on the body of the gazelle. Wondering at himself, the hunter did not resist. He lay still and waited, for he knew with absolute certainty that he, the hunter and the hunted, had finally been brought to bay by that other unknown and he waited for death quietly, as his gazelle also waited with the life blood pouring from its side. The hands were withdrawn from his eyes and, as he had looked now from below into the eyes of the hunter, and he smiled as he knew and recognized the unknown who bent over him, holding his own fallen knife poised above his heart. "Strike now," he said and closed his eyes. A searing pain shot through him as the knife cut the flesh between his breast bones and a mist came down and he lay as though dead.

The afternoon sun was slanting toward the West as he opened his eyes in wonder that he lived. He looked down at his breast — a deep cut was there — the knife had drawn a perfect circular furrow and the blood had flowed, and falling had mingled with the blood of the gazelle, now dead. The wound was not deep — already the bleeding had stopped, but the circle of the scar would remain to the end of his days. His knife lay beside him and he picked it up to begin the skinning of his kill. Then he stayed his hand, his heart beating fast. The gazelle lay with its head thrown back, its white throat and chest exposed, and in the center of that whiteness was a clear circle of dark hair. "The King Gazelle! He is the King!"

The hunter sheathed his knife. He knew now the meaning — the meaning of the unknown hunter, of his lying under the knife, of the circle on his own breast. He had killed the King gazelle and he would hunt no more. For once, once in a generation perhaps, a hunter would bring home the King gazelle — bring him intact, unskinned, to the elders, and then that hunter must give up his beloved bow, his knife, his home and his wife, and go to live in the house of the "Hunter and the Hunted" as it was called (he had never understood before the true meaning of the house for no one ever spoke of it). He would join the wise old ones of the tribe, who killed no more but who tended the dark and the light, the fire and the water, the dance and the dreams of them all. He lifted the gazelle and carried it over his shoulders like a yoke as he walked steadily back to the tents away to the East.

A woman stood alone beside the steam to the West of the encampment. Small, grey-haired but erect, she was very still, waiting, watch-

ing for her man as the shadows lengthened. He came at last, weary
and sweating, bent almost double by the weight of the animal.
Pausing by the stepping stones across the stream, he put down his
burden to rest and his eyes lit up to see her cross swiftly to meet him.
They did not speak but the hunter pointed silently to the dark circle
on the chest of the dead gazelle. She gave it a brief quiet glance. "I
knew," she said, "Indeed I have known the day would come, for your
mother told me before I came to your tent that you were a hunted
one." She bent down to the clear running water and filled an earthenware bowl she carried. "Drink," she said. He took it in both hands
and drank deeply, then bathed his face and hands and washed the
blood from the circle on his breast. But now his face was drawn with
suffering and he turned again to her with tears in his eyes, reaching
for her hands. "My husband and my love," she said, "the knife cuts
deep in both our hearts, but the parting is clean and whole and holds
no bitterness, as when death rends a pattern half complete. Go now
and fear not for me. Our stream divides, but all water flows forever
to the sea. The news of your coming has spread and all are gathered at
the place of council to greet you, and my joy in you is great." Her
voice trembled slightly on the words. He kissed her gravely on the
brow and lifting his kill again onto his shoulders, he passed over the
stream and out of her human life.

She sat long beside the stream as the twilight darkened and the sun
sank behind the hill—and the sound of the water entered into her
and brought peace. Then she rose and walked slowly back toward
her tent. All the others, men, women, and children would be at the
great ceremony, watching the skinning of the King gazelle, the clothing of her man in its royal skin. And then they would feast and dance,
dance all through the night the greatest and rarest of the dances—
the dance of the hunter and the hunted. But she must sit alone in her
tent tonight. Her heart failed her for a moment as she braced herself
to face the emptiness of that long-shared place, where they had lain
in the joy of their youth, where she had borne her sons and daughters,
where she and he had loved and laughed together in the perfect
companionship of later years. She reached the threshold and paused,
hearing a rustle. Then merry laughter greeted her as out of the dark
tent rushed two small vigorous figures, one clutching at each of her
hands. "Grandmother," they said, jumping up and down. "Grandmother, they have all gone to some big meeting and we hate crowds,

so we ran away here to you. Tell us a story, Grandmother dear, tell us a story—please, please do!"

The woman smiled and hugged them both—the boy and the girl, her youngest twin six-year-old grandchildren. "Very well," she said, "but first we must build a campfire. Come, little ones, gather sticks and I will kindle it." The children obeyed eagerly and soon the flames were leaping, the three were squatting round the fire, and the children gazed raptly and expectantly at the old woman. "Once upon a time," she began, "once upon a time . . . ." And at those timeless words all gaps were closed. Together the old and the young, the wise and the innocent, entered the gate and passed into that country where yesterday and today and tomorrow meet. "Once upon a time there was a hunter whose name was 'Swift Gazelle' . . . "

Chapter Twenty-Five

Salmon-Fisher Boy

HE WAS KNOWN to the few who lived on the mountain as Salmon-Fisher Boy. He had no other name. He lived with the old grandmother in the woods and wandered, free and happy, through the days, returning in the evening to the old woman's fireside to eat freshly baked bread with the rich soup from her big round pot hanging over the flames. On most days he could be seen lying flat on his stomach on the bank of the small river that ran through the woods, at a place in a small, hidden valley where the rocks contained a deep, clear pool of the flowing river water. He would lie gazing into the pool, very still, and often he would gently plunge his arm down through the water reaching out to the dark shape of the old fish that lay at the base of the rock. Little fishes flicked past his arm, unafraid and indifferent, but he paid no heed to them. The great salmon that lived in the pool, gliding, sliding through the clear water, dark with a glint of silver where the sun struck down at midday—this was his concern.

Sometimes when the boy was still enough, quiet enough, Old Fish, Wise Fish, would, with a slight powerful movement of his fins, rise swiftly through the water and briefly touch the boy's fingers with his head before turning in a perfection of grace to pour his great length down again to the bottom, where he lay again a dark shadow beside the dark rock, swaying with the gentle movement of the water. When this happened, Salmon-Fisher Boy knew perfect content. Old Fish, Wise Fish, had spoken to him and he had heard, though the speech had no words; and as he ran happily back through the wood he felt, could he have spoken it, that Old Fish, Wise Fish, went with him in the clear air, and that yet together they were gliding, sliding through the dark water of the pool, and that nothing could break the joy of this secret.

On such a day in the autumn of the year the boy had been lying still and happy for a long time beside the pool. It was time to go when something compelled him to strip off his shirt and plunge both his arms to the shoulders down into the water. Then suddenly to his astonishment and joy he saw the great fish rising. He came higher than ever before to the level of the boy's elbows, and then swam slowly in a figure of eight between and around his arms. The boy did not move as the fish swam free into the center of the pool and then leaped out of the water in a great arc of silver, touched by gold by the setting sun, and plunged down again to disappear completely under the rock. Now he rose and in a daze of wonder and happiness turned homewards. Soon he was running with eager thoughts of supper and the long evening ahead with the old grandmother, when they would sit together by the fire and she would tell him stories of the birds and beasts and fishes and, most fascinating of all, of the ways of the salmon and of their journey to and from the great sea. He had never spoken of Old Fish, Wise Fish, but somehow he was sure that she knew him too. He was one of those few who had stayed long in the sea, and, bringing its stored wisdom with him, had now come up the river to the pool and would not return.

This evening, as the boy came to the open door of the cottage, he stood still and felt the brush of fear. The sound of a man's voice came to him from inside, and instinctively, though he heard no words, he knew that the man was talking about him. Slowly the boy moved forward through the doorway. "Here you are, boy!" said the voice. It was a kind voice yet somehow stern and cold in the boy's ears. "I have come to take you away now to school, for you are no longer a child, and it is time for you to learn many things and to see the great world and meet the people in it, so that you may grow to be a man of learning and be able to do some worthy work and earn your bread."

Slowly the boy raised his head and looked the man in the eyes. "Yes," he whispered. It was as though he had always known that someday this must come. "Good boy," said the man. "Now what is your name?" "My name is S-s-almon-Fisher B-b," he stuttered. He had never spoken this name, the only name he knew, before, and it now sounded all wrong, whereas unspoken, it had seemed to fit him like a glove. But the man interrupted, "Oh yes, 'Sam Fisher,' a good name. Well, Sam, be ready in the morning. I will come for you early." He bowed to the old grandmother and was gone. Stunned, the boy turned to the old woman. Her usually merry twinkling eyes were sad, but she came to him and took his hands in hers. "It has to be," she said, "but do not ever forget, dear boy, whatever may come to you, your true unalterable name. You are the Salmon-Fisher Boy. Remember this in your heart as I will remember it in mine, and you will not lose Old Fish, Wise Fish, who, I know as I look at you, has laid upon you this day the sign of the wisdom of the fish. Now go to bed and sleep and tomorrow go to meet the new without fear!"

The journey to the south was long, and the boy's spirits rose as he eagerly absorbed the sights and sounds that were so new to him. His companion was gentle and told him many stories of the countryside and of the cities through which the train passed. Arrived at the school, the boy suffered much at first from homesickness and the strange confined life, but his longing to learn was strong and some of his classes were good, which his growing mind happily absorbed. So the time passed and his memories of the old life began to fade. Yet he remained always, in some way that he did not understand, an alien among his fellows. The other children liked him. He joined in their games and their interests, but from everything in the school life a part of him remained aloof. Perhaps the others felt this, for he was never teased or bullied—he was respected and perhaps unconsciously a little feared, for children shun the strange and the different. As he grew older this alien feeling began to grow stronger. The boy hated and rejected this thing in himself and tried to throw himself into the life more wholeheartedly, but the effort merely increased his trouble. He found himself losing interest in both work and play. Worst of all, the teachers whom he most respected, alarmed at his listlessness, began to press him, to reproach him, to urge him to greater effort, holding out to him pictures of the future, of worldly and intellectual success which, they said, he had the ability to achieve. He was bewildered, not understanding why he could not respond, and sank into a sullen hopelessness.

One day he lay out on the playing fields, alone, lethargic and without hope. Suddenly he heard a woman's voice. He looked up and saw a stranger on whose face was a deep concern. "What is the matter with you?" she asked. "Do you need a holiday? I'll ask if you may come away for awhile and stay with me." Then he heard another voice answer. It was an older boy whom he knew only slightly, but who, alone of all the people at the school, had often looked at him as though he understood. This boy spoke to the woman and said, "A holiday would do him no good at all. He is being badgered here to become something which will kill him." "What does he really want to do?" she asked. "He wants to fish for salmon," replied the tall boy, "though he has almost forgotten it himself." The woman bent down and took the boy's hands, pulling him to his feet. "Come with me," she said, "we will go to the authorities and you shall leave this place, and I will take you to those who will teach you to be a fisherman."

And so it came about that the boy travelled north once more. The woman took him to a tiny village where the mountains rose on three sides, and on the fourth side was the sea. Only one small road, too steep for motor traffic, led down to this village and all their supplies came to the little bay by boat. The woman and boy came in the evening to a stone-built cottage, where lived a tall, strong fisherman with graying hair and his quiet wife. Their children were all grown up and had left the village, and the woman knew they would take the boy in as though he were their own son. Fish fresh from the sea was frying in the pan as they walked through the door, the peat fire glowed on the hearth; the fisherman's wife smiled a true welcome. The boy's lethargy dropped from him in that moment, never to return. Tomorrow he would go out and begin to learn the ways of boats, the lore of the nets and the fishing lines, of winds and tides. He turned, radiant, to thank the woman who had brought him, but she was gone.

So began his new life. He was eager, fearless, happy, intelligent, and so he learned fast and his skill was a delight to his foster parents. Years passed and he was now a tall, strong young fisherman whose fame began to spread up and down that coast of fishermen. For added to his skill he had, it was said, the most extraordinary luck. Whenever he was out with a trawler, the nets were always full; if he went out alone with a line he came home with a catch large enough to feed almost the whole of his tiny village. He moved now from his beloved foster home into a small cottage of his own nearby and all expected him to seek a wife and settle down to family life. Everywhere he had friends, both men and women, but always there remained that strange core of aloofness and none could say they shared his inmost thoughts. He did not marry; not that he was cold—far from it—and he himself did not know why he felt it impossible. It was as though the sea itself were his beloved, and coming back from a night of encounter with wind and storm, or the quiet of calm, dark water under the moon he was fulfilled. He became known affection-ately as Fisher Sam, instead of Sam Fisher, and few men begrudged his luck.

There was one silent, almost morose old man with whom he constantly sailed. They exchanged no thoughts, but with him Fisher Sam felt a closeness and an understanding that no one else shared. One day as they sat mending their nets the old man said, "You have caught every kind of sea fish, Sam, but you have never been up the river with a rod to fish for salmon. Let's take a holiday and go inland." Sam felt his heart leap with excitement, but also a strange reluctance. He was silent for several minutes, then answered, "Yes, it is time I went up the river. There is grey in my hair already."

So they sailed up the coast to the mouth of the river, moored their boat, and started on foot up into the mountains. They camped overnight beside the river and in the early dawn went to cast their lines. Fisher Sam watched the old man, who was an expert angler, as he made the first cast. Almost at once a salmon bit and as the old man landed it, Sam, that fisherman of long experience, had a strange and violent reaction. His whole being revolted at the sight of the dying fish—faint memories stirred in his heart—and he turned and plunged in among the trees bewildered and ashamed at the violence of his feeling. He wandered restlessly for hours and then lay down under a tree and fell immediately into a deep sleep. He dreamed, and in his dream he saw himself lying beside a clear, deep pool of the river and staring down into the water where a great salmon lay near the bottom. The fish was slowly rising toward him and as his head broke the surface, he spoke.

"I am Old Fish, Wise Fish," he said. "You have forgotten me in your head but never in your heart and soul. Years ago I, or my grandfather, no matter, set upon you the sign of the fish, and one day when you are old, you will come back to this pool. But you still have work to do. Do not hesitate to cast your line and catch the salmon. Men need fish to eat, need it desperately. They are surfeited with the red meat of animals. Food from the rivers, food from the sea, this is the nourishment their souls crave. And most of all, they need salmon, for we are kings among fishes. Do you not know that what men call your 'luck' is no such thing? You carry the 'sign of the fish' and all our kind will offer themselves to your net or your line, for you fish for love not for greed. You were the Salmon-Fisher Boy."

Sam woke and lay very still. His lifelong feeling that a part of himself was shut away had disappeared. All things fell into place with an intensity of meaning that flooded his whole being. He rose and saw that it was evening. Beside the river the old man had returned to fish again and Sam now joined him quietly and spoke. "We will go home now," he said. "I am going to move from the sea and live up here beside the river to catch salmon for the villages." The old man asked no questions, simply nodded in understanding. Sam knew now that he, too, had been marked with the sign of the fish.

And so for many more years Sam lived beside the river and people far and wide ate of the salmon he caught. There came a day in his old age when he knew it was time to leave—to fish no more. He packed his few necessities in a bundle, walked out of his house, leaving behind his beloved rods, and set off up river. For three days he climbed higher into the mountains, led by an instinct that he trusted but could not explain. On the third day he stood on a flat rock and looked down on the pool of his dream—and not only of his dream, he now knew. Memory flooded back, the little boy, Salmon-Fisher Boy, lying there on the rock with his arms in the water and Old Fish, Wise Fish, swimming around them in the figure of eight. He saw, too, his grandmother in her cottage, and turning, he strode unerringly along the path through the forest and stopped. A very thin but clear, calm voice called to him. "Come in, Salmon-Fisher Boy. I have been waiting for you." He entered and there lay old grandmother on her bed, very old now, frail, almost transparent, but with the same twinkle in her eyes and a peace surrounding her that soothed all unrest. "Now I can go, dear boy," she said. "This is your home and here you will live, not fishing anymore, but passing onto those few who will come to you the wisdom of the fish."

He knelt beside her and took her hand as she closed her eyes. So they stayed as the sun sank slowly, and when the fisherman rose to light the lamp, he saw that she had quietly died. He covered her gently and stood in the doorway, his eyes on the crescent moon in the fading glow of the sunset. An end and a beginning. He had come home.

C h a p t e r   T w e n t y - S i x

The Story of Jacob

IN THE BOOK of Genesis the theme of the two brothers at enmity begins with Cain and Abel, continues with Isaac and Ishmael, and culminates in the much more complicated story of Jacob and Esau. With the Fall and the knowledge of good and evil began the inevitable split between person and person and between ego and shadow within a person. The life of Jacob is a turning point in the Old Testament accounts of this struggle with the dark brother, which every human being must encounter on the long road to the healing of the split.

Abel took the first step towards consciousness by realizing that the offering to God involved the shedding of blood, which in Jung's language would mean that the approach to the divine must involve the death of an old attitude that costs our life blood, not just a giving up of something we can well spare. Otherwise Cain would have killed Abel simply out of envy. How often do we remain at the Cain stage, wiping out immediately any glimmering of a new way? The next fraternal conflict was resolved by the banishment of Ishmael, the son of the bondwoman, so that Isaac, the son of the freewoman, might carry the torch of consciousness and civilization forward unmolested by the wild, regressive brother who would resist free growth. In the infancy of consciousness this separation is necessary, but if maturity is to come it must not endure. If the unacceptable, regressive tendencies are thrust completely out of sight, out of mind, they do not therefore cease to exist. Either we hand them on to our wives, our husbands, our children, and our enemies or friends, or we are eventually swallowed by them ourselves. We shall see how Isaac both hands on his conflict and suffers it himself in physical blindness.

Jacob and Esau were twins, and according to the legend, they started fighting even before they were born, in the womb of their mother, Rebecca. Esau emerged first, with Jacob close behind, holding onto his heel. From birth Esau was red-skinned and red-haired; in fact, he was hairy all over. Later he was known as Edon, the red one: red is the color so often associated with evil. Set, the brother and enemy of the god Osiris in Egypt, was also the red one, and Mephistopheles by tradition wears red. Red is the color of the impulsive, emotional, instinctive nature, which, if in control, can swallow all civilizing tendencies and so become evil. If, on the other hand, it is repressed and denied, it will leave the conscious personality dry and unreal, and finally more completely at the mercy of its fiery power. The story of Jacob can bring much insight into the way that every person must follow if he or she is to avoid either falling under the domination of the red one or banishing all instinctive wisdom from the conscious personality.

Esau was hairy and red, the cunning hunter, full of rude strength. Jacob was smooth and white-skinned, a man of the "tents," his mother's favorite, cunning of mind but not strong of body, sensitive, fearful even, and, we may imagine, with a love of beauty, hearing already the inner voice to which his brother's ear was closed. Jacob's first recorded act is the trick whereby he persuades Esau to sell his birthright. He knows that his brother is stupid and greedy, unable to resist his immediate desires or to see the relative importance of the different values of life: so he prepares a red pottage and offers it to Esau at a moment when the latter is extremely hungry after a day's hunting. The insistence on "red" hints at the symbolic nature of the story. Esau is offered food that will nourish his already dominant quality, his desirousness, and his hunger for this food is so great that he parts with his birthright in order to satisfy it immediately. For him this meant that he held the right of the first born in contempt, the right that brought in those days not only the material, but the spiritual leadership of the tribe. For us our birthright means the high dignity of our free will and capacity for consciousness. Every time we sell out on our essential values, driven by fear or by the desire of the moment, we relinquish our freedom, our birthright, and so become the "child of the bondwoman," dominated, for the moment anyway, by the red one within. It is easy to see why Rebecca, the mother, with her sure intuition, knew that Esau must never receive the blessing.

Most people react to the story of Jacob with a bewildered feeling that by our standards it is all wrong. Why does Jacob, who behaves throughout in the most reprehensible manner, tricking and deceiving first his brother, then his father, then his uncle, get all the rewards? To answer this we must look more deeply at the meaning of "the blessing." The birthright involved leadership and power, but the blessing of the old father, given to the chosen son, was much more than this for the people of God. It was the handing on of the light, the spark whereby a man became aware of God's voice, of the divine within himself. Now, as then, it is essentially the same. A true blessing may pass from one person to another insofar as the one who blesses has become a channel for it. (Never, of course, can it be given through the ego, the personal will.) Or it may come collectively through a true ritual. In either case, its effectiveness must depend on the state of receptivity in the one who receives it.

The father's blessing bestowed on his son was, in those days, a ritual act. As we have said, beyond the outer gift of riches and leadership, it laid on the son a great spiritual responsibility, for Yahweh spoke directly to the bearer of the blessing. In later times the blessing passed from anointed king to anointed king, from prophet to prophet, and the beautiful story of the taking up into heaven of Elijah illustrates the immense care that must be taken not to allow the blessing to fall on the wrong person. Elisha was told that he would receive a double portion of Elijah's spirit *only* if he were present and saw with his own eyes the passing of the old man. Elijah tried to go off alone, and only by constant vigilance (in us, that daily awareness that is so hard) did Elisha succeed in being there with his eyes open when the miracle happened.

We may imagine the possible result had the blessing been given to Esau. As far as outer matters went, Esau was more than competent, indeed far more straightforward and physically brave than his brother; but the blessing, bringing the capacity to "see visions and dream dreams," would surely have brought personal as well as collective disaster. If the "red one" starts dabbling in matters of spirit, he becomes the prey of superstitious and dark imaginings and is soon caught in magical practices. Esau would probably have been running after sorcerers and witches, as Saul did when, having received the blessing, he was disobedient to it. As it was, Esau lived his life in the way that was valid for him. He became just as successful outwardly as Jacob, simply by remaining what he was — a hunter, a crude man, but true to his own nature. The blessing would have ruined him, turned him dark and evil. So with the "red one" in the unconscious. If we feed him the red pottage, his own food, let him be his own earthy self, he will not possess or destroy us. If we deny his nature, try to make him into something spiritual, and so push him out of sight, he will start practicing "magic," and we shall be under his spell, whether we recognize it or not. He must be up where we can see him and meet him, and accept or reject his influence in our lives.

In Jacob's case, we are at first given no clue to his capacity for carrying the blessing—except the hint about his perception of the brother's false values in the pottage incident. He is timid and reluctant when his mother proposes the deception of Isaac. Rebecca is a woman who consciously faces an enormous risk, takes on a great burden of guilt, for the sake of an absolutely vital issue, and so exposes herself to the certainty of losing all she personally holds most dear. The future of the people of God is at stake. She is vividly aware of the necessity that the blessing be carried by Jacob, the sensitive, highly intelligent, intuitive son, rather than by the sensual, earthbound Esau. Of course there must also have been the purely personal desire that her favorite son should have the power—what woman does not feel that?

Nevertheless, we may believe that Rebecca served consciously the greater purpose. "On me be the curse," she says, in the full and lonely acceptance of the guilt that must fall on her because Isaac was blind. For this blindness surely has a symbolic quality. He was blind because he, too, really knew that Esau could not carry the blessing, but he lacked the courage to disinherit him. Perhaps this was, as we hinted earlier, a result of his own complete separation since childhood from his brother, Ishmael. Never having faced his own conflict, Isaac could not now make the hard sacrifice involved in disinheriting his elder son. It is obvious from the story that he could very easily have let himself know that he was being deceived. He persuaded himself to disregard the recognized voice of Jacob. Also he could not have failed to know, when he ate Jacob's meat, that he was eating kid, the meat of the tents, and not venison, the hunter's meat that he had asked Esau to provide. He just lay on his bed and let Rebecca take on all the pain and guilt of deception. It is notable, too, that he made very little fuss afterwards, did not even seem angry, as though he really agreed in his heart.

We come here to the curious but constantly repeated theme that the blessing is bestowed not on the "good," dutiful man but on the sinner—on Jacob, on David, on the Prodigal Son, on Paul, to name a few. This does not, of course, mean that a sinner who remains possessed by his or her sins can ever carry the blessing, but it does assuredly mean that one must be *able* to break loose from all conventional codes when it is a question of an essential value—provided he is willing to accept the guilt on one level (which remains guilt whatever the motive) and the payment and suffering it involves.

In the story of the Prodigal Son, the sinner is preferred because he has had the courage to break away from the safe family pattern, even though he has for a time succumbed completely to the "red one." The necessary suffering and repentance are experienced before the blessing is given. In the primitive story the blessing comes first, but the long years of payment are implicit in it. Only those are blessed who consciously, or unconsciously at first, have consented to this payment. This is an entirely different thing from the dangerous assumption that the end justifies the means. Those who embrace this attitude are precisely those who refuse the payment. They feel no guilt in the breaking of the law because they complacently delude themselves that their motives excuse them. They are among the cursed to whom Christ referred in his apocryphal saying about the breaking of laws: "If thou knowest what thou art doing, then thou art blest, but if thou knowest not what thou are doing then art thou cursed." It is exceedingly difficult truly to know what one is doing, and for most of us it is a matter of falling through our weakness under the power of the "red one" and waking up afterward.

The question, then, is not whether Jacob was a "good" man and had earned the blessing, but whether he had the capacity to hear the voice of God, and the courage and devotion to risk everything—reputation, safety, even relative goodness—in order to follow in obedience. We shall see that however unattractive we may find Jacob's character, he undoubtedly had this devotion. As it was for Jacob, so it is for ourselves.

So Rebecca and Jacob sinned, the blessing was given and received, and their sin was no less because it was a necessity of the spirit. Now they must pay. Rebecca paid immediately and all her life long in the loss of Jacob, for she never saw him again. This is the typically feminine payment — a willing separation from the beloved son. Jacob paid, as we shall see, in the many experiences of his long life.

The first consequence for Jacob was that he was forced to break away from his mother, to stand on his own feet. Hitherto he had lived under her influence, protected by her and therefore subject to her. The whole scheme for obtaining the blessing had been hers; he had done nothing but reluctantly agree. But though his fear had forced her to say "on me be the curse" (Genesis 27:13), he *had* agreed, and therefore accepted all that must follow. Isaac had uttered no curse, but the inevitable retribution could not be evaded.

Rebecca, knowing that Esau's fury could easily lead to murder, immediately sends Jacob away, hoping it would only be for a time. She knows that Esau's emotions are violent but shortlived and easily forgotten. She persuades herself on the surface, as we so often do, that the price will not be very heavy, though in her heart she must have known otherwise. She invents a polite fiction for Isaac, who could not stand, it seems, even that much truth, and tells him that Jacob must go and seek a wife among her own people (they disapproved of Esau's heathen wives). It was a fiction superficially (since her real reason was Jacob's safety) and yet profoundly true, for a man, having wrested the leadership from his shadow, his regressive other side, must now go on a long journey in search of his *anima* and his true feeling nature.

Jacob sets out alone. For the first time he must act and choose without his mother. One may imagine his loneliness and doubt as he journeyed, wondering, surely, if his deception of his father would invalidate the blessing, if he would be rejected by God. Thus everyone of good will, after a big step to freedom, involving perhaps a great hurt to a much-loved parent or friend, will look back in fear, wondering whether he or she had been merely self-willed to no purpose. Jacob lies down for the night with his head on a stone — as though, perhaps, he would say, "Whatever I have done is hard fact; I will accept, lay my head on this hard reality." Then the heavens open and he sees the angels of God ascending and descending, and God speaks to him. The blessing is confirmed. He sees the going up and the coming down and knows intuitively the constant exchange between earth and heaven. Then, waking, he swears to build one day a house of God upon this spot. This is his acceptance of the responsibility of the blessing, the full commitment of his life to obedience to the voice of God.

He continues his journey with new strength and sureness and comes at last to the well at the entrance to his uncle's village, and to his meeting with Rachel, the love of his life. It is a beautiful image, this meeting with the beloved beside a well. Her first action is to draw water for her love-to-be. So also did Rebecca herself, though it is noteworthy that in the earlier story Isaac did not go himself to find Rebecca; his father Abraham sent a trusted servant to seek her out for his son, and he found her beside the well. Isaac throughout seems entirely contained in the collective pattern and does nothing individually; hence, surely, his blindness later.

Jacob comes to the well and looks upon Rachel as she draws water for the sheep, and he loves her. The woman, the *anima*, is performing her vital function of drawing up the water of the unconscious that the man and his flocks, his instincts, may drink. A man depends always either on the woman outwardly or on his *anima* inwardly to bring him this life-giving water, without which his masculinity is sterile, his intellect dry, and his feeling dominantly emotion. So, in the first opening of his love, Jacob comes to his uncle Laban's house and enters at once on the next phase of his payment for the blessing.

Laban, one feels, was an older, more seemingly civilized version of the crude Esau. Materialistic, cunning, superstitious, he recognizes Jacob's value to him and immediately exploits his nephew's love for Rachel by demanding seven years' work for her. Jacob willingly agrees. Here we notice the difference of character between him and Esau. He will wait and work, subjecting himself consciously to the earthy Laban, and suffer cheerfully for the great value of his true love. His instinctual urge can wait — it demands no "red pottage" on the instant. The seven years pass and he asks for his reward, and now comes almost literal retribution for his earlier deception; the deceiver is deceived in circumstances that are a repetition in reverse of the original event. Whereas before there were two brothers, the red one and the white, now there are two sisters, the red and sensual Leah, the white and sensitive Rachel. The father sends Leah in to Jacob in the dark. Jacob does not recognize her and is bound to her for life. Ironically, Laban's answer to Jacob's reproaches is to point out the unbreakable custom that the elder daughter must be married before the younger. The poetic justice is complete.

Jacob has been altogether too naive. He must have thought, "Now that I have paid my price, I can unite with my beloved and we can go off and be free of this crude 'red thing' forever." This is the mistake into which we all fall at one time or another. After each emergence from a period of darkness and struggle we imagine that *now* we can go forward without the "other," the ugly one. Perhaps Jacob, like Isaac, *could* have known; perhaps he half-consciously recognized the inevitable rightness of this thing. A man cannot without great peril idealize or spiritualize his *anima*; he cannot live only with this aspect of her, or the other side of her will turn evil. Jacob, however, is forced willy-nilly to take both aspects, and so the earthbound Leah becomes the fertile mother to many of his sons.

Rachel, who nourishes his inner vision, must wait long and suffer the agony of seeming sterility before finally she brings to birth the bearer of the blessing, Joseph, the beloved son. Jacob still has a long apprenticeship to serve before he can give life to this son. He is allowed to marry Rachel seven days from the time of his taking of Leah, but he is bound to Laban for seven more years of service. Only after the "true son" is born, after, we may say, he has come by long patience and work to the birth of the new possibility of objective vision, which will carry the light into the future beyond his own personal life, is he set free for the next journey.

We are given a vivid picture of Rachel's sufferings during this period, of the jealousy between the two sisters, of her sense of her own unworthiness and the projection of her own resentment even onto her beloved Jacob. How well we know these reactions! She is even driven to send her maid Bilhah to Jacob's bed so that Bilhah may bear a son on Rachel's knees (a recognized custom), and she enters in imagination into the pangs of labor and birth in order to assuage her humiliation at her barrenness. This "make-believe" was not futile. It was all part of her inner preparation for the true birth. Maybe we could compare it to the active imagination we can enter into, which is truly like the labor of childbirth inwardly when we are up against a terrible rigidity of consciousness.

Jacob has now served his twice seven years. He has fathered new life both on this earth through Leah and in the world of the spirit through Rachel, and it is time for him to return to his own country to take up the mature tasks of later years. First, however, he carries out another "deceit." He persuades Laban to promise him all the spotted and ringstraked goats and sheep in his flocks, including those that shall be born during the year. He then practices some sympathetic magic on the ewes. Every time they conceive he sets up striped stakes for them to look at, and in due course their offspring are spotty! We may think this is a dirty trick, but all modern advertising is based on the same "magic." Show people the name of the product often enough and they will begin automatically to think it the best brand when they go shopping. Jacob was simply a good businessman as well as a visionary! Laban came out the loser because he had no imagination; there was really no actual deceit involved.

With his wives and his sons and his flocks Jacob sets off in secret from Laban's house, for he is afraid that his uncle will hold him by force, and he journeys for three days, not knowing that Rachel has stolen her father's household gods—the little images that protected the homes of those who were ignorant of the one God. This is an interesting episode. It looks on the surface like a somewhat childish, mean trick, but it perhaps symbolizes a deeply significant moment in Rachel's development. It is the moment of her final breaking with her father, and, as so often in myth, we meet the motif of theft. All conscious growth is in one sense "stolen" from the point of view of nature and of the unconscious. Prometheus had to steal the fire from heaven. In stealing the household gods Rachel is breaking the *spell* of the father image. It is a theme in modern dreams, this stealing of something that has given power to the spell of the hitherto all-powerful unconscious conflict. In the story it has precisely this effect, for it cannot be mere chance that *after* the stealing, Laban has a dream in which the true God of Jacob orders him to be friendly to Jacob, to make peace with him no matter how angry he may be. He follows Jacob, and, in spite of his resentment about the theft, makes a covenant with him in which they set up a clear boundary line. In Jacob there is now discrimination and conscious acceptance of all that Laban represents. Rachel does not confess or give back the images. She just sits on them while Laban searches, and his spell is broken. It seems that woman is always the one to practice guile!

The journey continues, and the moment approaches when Jacob must again meet his brother Esau. At first he is overcome by his usual timidity; Esau's resentment may still be fierce, he is a man of war who will easily overthrow the peace-loving Jacob. So Jacob takes human precautions and divides his possessions and servants into two bands, hoping to save at least half of them, but it is clear that he knows all this to be superficial. He must meet with his brother as with his own soul, face to face, alone and unarmed. At the brook called Jabbok he sends all his company ahead, including Rachel and her son. Alone he will spend the night in wrestling with himself, with his fear, with his inner shadow brother. This time there will be no trick about it; he must find the deeper blessing. "And there wrestled a man with him until the breaking of the day" (Genesis 32:24). There is no overt mention of an angel in the biblical account. Brief but intensely vivid, what an extraordinarily moving account it is of a man's struggle with the unknown in himself! It expresses his absolute determination to know this stranger, to prevail, to find its "name." He realizes that the seeming enemy is the one who can bless him, this time individually and from within, not ritually and from without, as in his early, unconscious days. He is wounded in the thigh, exhausted from long hours of effort and says, "I will not let thee go except thou bless me" (Genesis 32:26). So must we all hold on with the last ounce of strength, through all the ups and downs of our interior struggles until the blessing comes. The moment of transformation for Jacob is the speaking of a new name. Jacob becomes Israel, "For as a prince thou has power with God and with men and hast prevailed" (Genesis 32:28). When Jacob finally dares to ask the ultimate question, "Tell me, I pray thee, thy name" (Genesis 32:29), the blessing is fully given. The hidden name cannot be humanly spoken, but, as in other myths, the issue hangs on the asking of the right question at the right time, though the answer may not be given. Jacob now knows that in this long struggle of love he has "seen God face to face" and his life is preserved. It should not be inferred from this that the "stranger" was God himself, but rather that the new blessing revealed for a moment the face of God.

Jacob does not come from the struggle unscathed, for the stranger has touched him in the hollow of his thigh, and he will be lame from this time forth. We are human and must so remain. If we dare to wrestle as Jacob did, we may be in some way crippled in ordinary collective living. Without this we would not be able to stand it. We would rise out of the weakness of our humanity into the *hubris* of fancied equality with the gods. After a new insight there are two dangers; either an inflation of the ego may possess us, or we may fall into discouragement, imagining that the insight means that we *ought* now to be free of all our old inadequacies. The "lameness," accepted, cures both these delusions. Indeed we may feel even more inadequate than before on certain levels.

Jacob is now ready to meet his human brother. No more is said of his fear. He sends gifts ahead as proof of his friendliness, and when he meets Esau he finds no rancor in him—indeed, Esau is almost embarrassingly affectionate. There is an indication in the text of how deeply Jacob's struggle at the brook was connected with his brother, inner and outer, when he repeats at the meeting with Esau almost the exact words he had used after the stranger blessed him. "I have seen thy face," he says to Esau, "as though I had seen the face of God" (Genesis 33:10). He has not confused the levels of experience—this is evident in the words "as though"—but it seems that his vision of the night before has made possible this seeing of the divine behind the face of his opposite, the long-estranged red brother.

The next pitfall into which Jacob could have fallen now opens before him. Esau, the simple, exuberant fellow, is sure that, all quarrels forgotten, they can settle down to live side by side and have a fine time together! But Jacob's discrimination does not fail. He replies vaguely that he will come later (still wary of crossing his impulsive brother too abruptly), and each goes his separate way in peace. This pitfall is very familiar when we have fought through to freedom from an unconscious dependence or entanglement. We are all too ready to think that now it will be easy to enter into close contact with the people onto whom we used to project our problems. This is usually possible only when the other person involved has also grown toward consciousness to some degree. When a person gives him or herself to the search for individuation, those who are close to that person will either catch the spark, welcome it, and begin to change too, or they will feel threatened by the new freedom and will attack it, consciously or unconsciously. This is an inevitable risk. Except where there is plain human obligation, physical separation is the wiser thing, even for the one who feels himself deserted. Esau would have suffered just as much from Jacob's proximity as vice versa.

Jacob has now a new name; he is a prince inwardly, and in the world wealth and honor lie ahead of him, but nevertheless the new blessing bestowed on him at the brook is the prelude to far greater suffering than any he has yet endured. We persist in imagining that blessing means prosperity. How often we hear people exclaim that they have been greatly blessed, meaning that they have been healthy, happy, with plenty of money in the bank, and how rare it is to hear the recognition of blessing after a catastrophe! Outer events, one way or the other, have little to say about it, but those who carry the blessing will inevitably meet great suffering inwardly.

Jacob now has to suffer in the place where it most hurts, in his sensitive, feeling nature. He was his mother's specially loved son, and the mainspring of his life lay in his intense personal loves. These one by one he must lose.

Rachel is pregnant again, but although Jacob must have known she was delicate and should not travel, he has been told by the voice of God that he must now return to Bethel and build the altar he had promised long ago, and he does not hesitate in his obedience. On the return road, near Bethlehem, Rachel's labor comes upon her, and giving birth to Benjamin, the last and twelfth of his sons, she dies.

All Jacob's love now centers on Rachel's son Joseph, whom he singles out and favors until the jealousy of all the brothers is aroused. Joseph, alone of his sons, Jacob knows, has inherited the inner ear, the capacity to accept the blessing. "Behold this dreamer cometh" (Genesis 37:19), say the contemptuous brothers, and they sell him into Egypt. Now Jacob is alone. The years pass, and the old man's grief for Joseph is still alive in his heart when the brothers bring the extraordinary news of his survival in Egypt. Human feelings do not sublimate themselves with the breakthrough to deeper consciousness. Indeed, the capacity for personal love is thereby increased, and with it the capacity for suffering. Detachment does not mean freedom from love and suffering on the personal level—it means the full opening of the heart to their power and the experience of them, not as an insignificant personal emotion, but as a part of the whole meaning of creation. Detachment is the cessation of personal demand, not the deadening of feeling.

So Jacob journeys to Egypt and is reunited with his son. The time of his death is near, his sons are gathered round his bed, and we read that beautiful chapter in which he sums up the characteristics of each son, each future tribe of Israel. It is sheer poetry, and, most fittingly, the story ends, as it begins, with a blessing. We will quote first the blessing of Jacob himself, as it was understood by Isaac with his limited consciousness. "God give thee of the dew of heaven and the fatness of the earth, and plenty of corn and wine; let people serve thee and nations bow down to thee; be lord over thy brethren, and let thy mother's sons bow down to thee; cursed be everyone that curseth thee, and blessed be he that blesseth thee" (Genesis 28:28-29). Finally, here are the profound and lovely words of Jacob's blessing of Joseph, which seem to sum up the distilled wisdom of his whole life, the blessing, we could say, which may fall on everyone who is willing to be "separate," to stand alone before God.

> . . . the Almighty who shall bless thee with blessings of heaven above, blessings of the deep that lieth under, blessings of the breasts and of the womb; the blessings of thy father have prevailed . . . unto the utmost bound of the everlasting hills; they shall be on the head of Joseph, and on the crown of the head of him that was separate from his brethren (Genesis 49:25-26).

Chapter Twenty-Seven

The Story of the Exodus

IT IS POSSIBLE to read the story of the exodus from Egypt as the inner life history of three kinds of people. Moses is the hero, the man of great capabilities, of imagination and vision, born to be a leader, whose integrity of will remains unshaken by success or adversity. Pharaoh is equally a man born to lead, but his will is corrupted by power and luxury so that he is incapable, in the end, even in the face of conclusive evidence, of recognizing the truth of any fact that threatens his pride or his comfort. The children of Israel in their slavery to Pharaoh, in their response to Moses, in their long endurance in the wilderness, in their alternating faith and grumbling disobedience, in their courage and their cowardice, are ordinary people; they stumble along with many falls and backslidings, but they retain the fundamental good will that keeps them journeying in spite of everything toward the promised land. Each individual enduring in the wilderness carries within himself or herself the Moses image and the Pharaoh image—the hero and the renegade (in its sense of one who denies or betrays his inherited commitment)—and only at the journey's end will the struggle between these be resolved.

PHARAOH

There are actually two Pharaohs in the story; the son succeeded the father during Moses' exile, but for our purpose we may take them as one symbolic figure. Pharaoh was born to the purple, to riches and power, but one does not have to be a king to have such an inheritance. One may be born with other kinds of inherited wealth—money, social position, riches of intellect, artistic ability, or bodily strength, all of which means that one is in a position to exercise power without having done much to earn it. One may do this harmlessly for a while, as did Pharaoh, but the test will surely come that will either shock a person into the beginnings of detachment from this power or will plunge him or her into a course of ever-increasing identification with it.

Pharaoh's test is clearly stated. He suddenly became aware that the people of Israel, who had been his predecessor's friends and respected allies, were rapidly increasing in numbers and were becoming rich and prosperous, and he felt himself threatened because he was both jealous and afraid. Jealousy and fear—these are the insidious enemies that in all of us may start a landslide; but they are also Lucifer in his role as light-bringer. A violent, negative emotion of some kind is about the only thing which has power enough to jerk us out of complacency and give us the chance to recognize that we are evading our own shadow side. Pharaoh had a choice thrust upon him. He could have looked at his jealousy and fear and recognized them as signs of unconscious weakness and insecurity hiding under his conscious sense of power and security. Then the strength of the Israelites would have been spent in Egypt's service, and his personality would have acquired depth and wisdom. Instead he gave rein to his fears, decided to enslave and *use* for personal ends this increasing power in the land, this potentiality in his soul. In order to protect himself, he chose to maintain his conscious, one-sided view "lest they multiply; and it comes to pass that, when there falleth any war, they join unto our enemies and fight against us" (Exodus 1:10).

How right he is! If we do not recognize the seemingly alien thing in the unconscious, it will certainly fight against us—against our assumptions of power and invulnerability. We very often do as Pharaoh did—repress the growing power of this alien thing, appoint "overseers" to keep it within bounds, and thus we steal the energy (which would have been freely available to us in creative form if we would allow these repressed instincts to speak *their* truth) and make it work for us to increase our sense of importance and power. "And they built for Pharaoh treasure cities" (Exodus 1:11). We need not look far for examples of this. A man obsessed with making money has almost always phenomenal amounts of energy and capacity for work. He will swallow up competitor after competitor with growing ruthlessness and skill, not because he needs more money, but because to stop driving ahead would mean that the enslaved Israelites within him, whose energy he steals, would immediately revolt; his image of himself would be threatened. So also with any drive for power, no matter how dressed up as good work, which becomes for a man or woman a *necessity*. A woman who must dominate through emotional ties or through compulsive work for others, a scholar who must defeat his colleagues in argument, an actor who must hold the center of the stage at the expense of the play and of his colleagues, an unsuccessful person who must always be a victim, often displaying real ruthlessness in establishing this—all are enslaving the strong, free energy of the alien in the soul that threatens the dominance of the ego's demands.

The pressure from below does not, however, decrease. On the contrary, it increases. The Israelites continue to multiply and Pharaoh resorts to new stratagems. He tries to persuade the midwives of the Israelites cruelly to destroy the male children as they are born, but the midwives "feared God" and would not obey. This perhaps may be seen as the first indication that on his feminine side, Pharaoh has some repressed strength and integrity, and we may find in this the reason why he is given so many chances for awakening. There is no record of his ever having shown cruelty toward women. Now he makes no attempt to coerce or punish the midwives. His true, though deeply buried, feeling, symbolized by the midwives, will not commit the murder of the children. The conscious Pharaoh, however, will not listen to this and sends his own *men* to kill the male children, though he does charge them to save the girls—an interesting point, since most ancient civilizations tended to care little for the death of a female child.

The next incident makes this saving grace in Pharaoh even more clear. His daughter (his personal feeling side) actually saves and adopts the Israelite baby who is to become his greatest enemy but who is potentially his savior, the one who will offer him chance after chance for redemption. Pharaoh's feelings are still working for him, raising up in his own family, in his personal unconscious, a strong saving shadow figure whom Pharaoh will eventually be forced to confront in full consciousness. It is a case of the shadow carrying the positive values, as is always the case when a man lives out the dark side of his personality. Through the years, the rejected shadow, whether positive or negative, grows always stronger until it is finally accepted or rejected with the ultimate "yes" or "no."

Pharaoh becomes aware of Moses as a force to be reckoned with when the latter, grown to manhood, is aroused to pity for his people and kills one of the overseers. The boy he has allowed to grow up in his house, who has served him well as a soldier, and whom he never thought to fear, suddenly becomes a threat. Moses is driven out into exile for many years. It is as though Pharaoh represses violently a twinge of conscience, and so again his evil will gains added strength. But the repressed shadow in his banishment is also gathering strength, making contact with the deeply buried divine nature, with God himself, whom the conscious Pharaoh denies. When the time is ripe, the shadow, filled now with numinous power, returns, and Pharaoh can no longer evade the confrontation with himself.

Pharaoh is first asked by Moses with respect and courtesy to grant the Hebrews three days of freedom in the wilderness so that they may offer sacrifice there to God. So we may be asked to give up in some very small matter the thing upon which we base our security—a woman, to let her child be free to make a mistake; a rich man, to risk giving money where he will get no return, not even a sense of virtue; an actor, to refuse the limelight so that another may be recognized; an analyst, to refuse patients when he is already too busy to give any time to his wife and to his inner life. A small and temporary thing, it seems, and yet, of course, we sense, as did Pharaoh, that to give way in this matter would mean to set foot on the way to total loss of the sense of importance and power we have built by enslaving our inner Hebrews. We cannot let them worship the true God, or we might be forced to recognize his validity ourselves, to change the whole direction of our lives. We protest that we have no use for the new value offered to us, but nevertheless there is an uneasy doubt in us, a fear that perhaps this new thing comes from a power greater than ourselves and our gods of possessiveness—and we look for "signs." We are given them in full measure.

In the exodus story the rod becomes a serpent when Aaron throws it down, and it turns back into a rod when he picks it up. Could that perhaps mean for Pharaoh that he is shown in an image that to let go of the rod of his authority means to let loose a serpent, indeed, to free a threatening unconscious content, but that if he faces it, seizes it again, he will not lose his true authority? That is easy, he replies, my magicians can do that. In other words, I can do this kind of thing on *my* terms, make sure the generous gesture doesn't really cost me anything, and pick up the rod quickly on the same old terms, changing nothing.

Pharaoh dismisses Moses and Aaron with mockery and increases his cruelty to the Hebrews. The first chance is refused and his evil will grows stronger. But the repressed content also grows stronger and is filled with ever more numinous power. When the inner voice has been refused and rejected, the series of plagues begins. The river turns to blood, frogs invade the land, then gnats, then flies, followed by disease, boils, hail, locusts, blinding sandstorms. Having refused the opportunity of free choice, Pharaoh is now given chance after chance through *fear* to come to his awakening, to arrest his descent into hell. Most of us have experienced this. Very few make the vital turn without a severe jolt — terrifying dreams, a loss, an accident, an illness, a disabling neurosis — "the gifts of God," as Jung says. We are shocked into awareness as was Pharaoh. But often, too, we follow Pharaoh's pattern of going back on our recognition of the truth. After each plague was removed, he forgot his fear and began to rationalize. We say, "It was only a dream," or "These things were simply bad luck without any meaning. It won't happen again. I can go on as before. The stock market has recovered; I can ease my loss with distractions; I can take care not to have another accident; my neurotic symptoms can be cured with pills." And so on.

We may compare the plagues with warnings coming from different layers of the unconscious. The first is the turning of the water of the river into blood. When there is a moment of choice, such as Moses offered Pharaoh by courteously asking for the release of the Israelites, and the new way is refused, then the unconscious turns hostile. We dream of running in panic from some threat or murderer, an animal, an earthquake, an invasion, and so on. The waters of the Nile no longer nourish the fields of Egypt but spread corruption and breed the next plague of loathsome frogs that invade the land.

So the waters of the unconscious, when rejected, will cease to fertilize our lives and will breed images and other happenings to plague us. Nevertheless, it is clear in this story, as in all human life, that there is purpose behind all this. The plagues, we may say, begin with things that Pharaoh in his palace could no doubt keep at a distance, but the pressure grows greater after each refusal, as though the devil is forcing the individual to the extremity in which he or she may find redemption.

The frogs are the first thing to emerge from the corrupted water, and in all legends and fairy stories they are the symbol of that which appears ugly and loathsome to a human being, but if accepted, or eaten and digested, will work a great transformation. The frog bride or bridegroom can become princess or prince only if wholly accepted in the hideous form of the toad. Nietzsche refused to swallow the repellent creature in his vision, though he knew that he should do so, and it was this refusal that turned him finally on the way that led to his madness. He was afterwards committed to his identification with the superman. So also Pharaoh.

After the frogs come flying insects, gnats, and then flies—the symbol of the fragmentation of the unconscious. In a fragmented state the mind and the emotions have no center, no root in reality and love. Every little thing is an irritation; our nerves go to pieces. We are frantic and promise ourselves that we will work now on our basic attitudes, that we will face these things, set free the imprisoned energy. For a week, perhaps, we work on our dreams; the gnats and flies decrease; we are relieved. But the effort to focus our attention each day soon ceases. The interval of peace is short and this time the rejected value strikes deeper. The next plagues are diseases and boils. The body is affected and Pharaoh can no longer retreat into his palace. We may know the physical symptoms are psychosomatic, and again we are afraid and promise, as Pharaoh did, to say "yes" to the inner demand, only to fall back as soon as we have the comforting thought that it was "nothing but" a temporary physical illness. Locusts follow, devouring every growing thing, every blade of grass, leaving behind a complete aridity of soul. Again we promise; again we deny. Even the terror of the blinding sandstorm choking all vision, blotting out the sun, hiding man from man, crippling all activity, does not succeed for more than a little while. The wind of the spirit blowing over the aridity of the psyche brings complete blindness and isolation from humanity, instead of the freshness of inspiration and the spark of vision and creative work.

One last disaster is left whereby Pharaoh may be shaken out of his blindness. All the plagues so far can be rationalized away as temporary bad luck. Not so the loss of the greatest value, the most precious thing, his first-born son, his heir, the one he seems to have loved most genuinely. Almost all of us have to come to this last-ditch situation in one form or another, and if we do not embrace it willingly and consciously, sacrificing, letting go of our first-born, our greatest value, our seemingly best, most cherished accomplishment, then, by the grace of God, the experience will come to us outwardly in the form of loss or failure. The last-ditch situation is constantly appearing in the vital dreams of our lives, and in all legend, all real storytelling, it is this kind of situation that carries the power and meaning of the tale.

The death of the son is Pharaoh's last and supreme chance of redemption. He does not take it. He collapses, gives in, cannot get rid of the Israelites quickly enough, and for a moment, it seems that he will really face himself and the suffering of a change of heart.

At this point Pharaoh could have accepted the death of his son and his own responsibility for it and allowed true repentance to enter his heart. Then death would have become a sacrifice and the transformation of his will would have begun. But he could not face it. His disintegration, checked for a moment, took hold again, fed this time by bitter, blinding hatred. He pursued the children of Israel with all his chariots and horsemen and men of war, thinking to trap them between sea and mountain. But the sea of the unconscious opened before Moses, as it opens for all who will set forth on the inner journey with integrity, and it closed over the strength of Pharaoh, just as it swallows all those who make what Dante called "the great refusal."

MOSES

Now we turn to the story of the life of the man who hears the inner voice and who is willing to pay, step by step, the great price which is asked of one who will be obedient to it.

The story of Moses' birth under the threat of murder by Pharaoh, of his mother's hiding him in the little ark among the rushes in the river, and of his finding and adoption by Pharaoh's daughter, is the archetypal theme of the hero's birth and of the hatred generated in the collective mind by the appearance of the promise of individual consciousness. The hero's life is threatened as soon as he is born. He can only be saved at the outset if he is entrusted to the water, to the arms of the great maternal unconsciousness from which he must be reborn if he is to survive. Christ was saved from the slaughter of the Innocents by the *descent* into Egypt, a symbol of these depths.

The great value in each of us must be twice born. A new insight may be spontaneously, naturally born in any of us, but if we immediately expose it to the world and try to preach it or to live it outwardly in its infant stage, we will inevitably become identified with it, become personally inflated, and then be destroyed by the greed and envy of the collective shadow, the Pharaoh within. Many writers have spoken of the absolute need to keep secret a new idea for a play or a book, for if it is exposed too soon, the inspiration will die. The revivalist preacher, filling vast auditoriums with hysterical followers, is another example of the man who has identified with a genuine insight and has destroyed it by declaring it to the world in its raw, unassimilated stage. The destruction may come about in any of these ways. The power goes out of the vision, or else we are delivered over to possession by the negative side of it. If it is to live, the new value must be given back to the unconscious at what seems like the risk of losing it. It must be constantly remembered. But it must be left alone to mature and grow until the time is ripe and it has transformed us from within so that we are strong enough to carry it in full consciousness before the world and to face the suffering it involves.

Moses had two mothers—three, really—his natural mother, Pharaoh's daughter, and the water of the river from which he was "drawn out." (The name *Moses* means "drawn out of the water.") Like the mothers of most men who come to greatness, Moses' mother was surely a remarkable woman; both his personal mothers seem to have had unusual qualities. His natural mother had the courage and intelligence to contrive her scheme to save him and to trust him to the water, whereupon he was given back to her to feed and nurse, but not to possess. If we will commit the inner child to the water, keep him hidden, let him go, then he is given back to us to nourish in secrecy but never to possess personally. Pharaoh's daughter in this context would be an image of the Self, the royal woman in the psyche of Moses' mother. Moses, thought of as the inner child of his mother, is nurtured both by his natural instinctive ties and by the great value of that which unites all opposites.

To return now to the young Moses himself, we may imagine him growing up in the luxury of Pharaoh's court but protected from it by his loyalty to his origins and by the nourishment that true feeling in the mother gives to the son. It is surely clear that both Pharaoh's daughter and his own mother loved him without possessiveness, that shadow side of a woman's feeling that kills all the true warmth of the heart. As we have seen, his natural mother had let him go, trusted him to the waters, and Pharaoh's daughter had the greatness of heart not to separate him from his roots, from his own people. How easy it would have been for her to bring him up in ignorance of who he was and whence he came, even in hatred of his own blood, since that must have been the acceptable attitude! There are many instances of this today—people bringing up their children to reject all that is dark and despised in themselves. We may imagine that Pharaoh's mother was both possessive and cold, spoiling him one moment, failing to discipline him the next, and encouraging an overwhelming sense of his own greatness.

Moses at first followed the conventional pattern for young men in his position, fighting with the army and proving himself as a man. He had probably always felt sorrow and pity for his people's plight, but it had not yet penetrated to his heart and made action imperative. It probably never occurred to him to become really involved until the day he killed the unjust overseer in a fit of furious anger. It was an impulsive, pointless killing, arousing hostility among the Hebrews themselves. Yet the chance of awakening comes almost always with a breakthrough of violent emotion, usually negative.

Moses must have seen at once that to meet crime with crime was no answer. In contrast with Pharaoh's reaction to such tests, he accepted responsibility for his shadow and the consequences of his act. He went into exile into Midian, there to spend long years in the search for discrimination, wisdom, and selflessness. As so often happens to all of us, it is the impulsive giving in to an emotional reaction, and the acceptance of full responsibility for it, which marks the beginning of reflection. Moses' fury sprang from the generous emotion of pity, but his action was merely a destructive release of his own painful feelings without objectivity or real compassion. Yet because of his integrity and willingness to pay the price, it must have marked for him the beginning of self-knowledge.

For Moses, as for all men, the conscious confrontation with the shadow was followed by the meeting with the *anima*, the finding of his individual feeling, his emotional freedom from the personal mother. As so often happens in the beautiful symbolism of the Old Testament, his *anima*, his future wife, comes to meet him at the well on the threshold of his new life in Midian. Surely in every true marriage the man meets the woman at the well, and she draws up water from the earth for him to drink. So also, inwardly, the *anima* in man draws water for him from the unconscious depths.

The seven daughters of Jethro, priest of the Midianites, are drawing water from the well, and Moses protects them from some rough shepherds who are interfering, thus rightly fulfilling his man's role as the women fulfill theirs. He is welcomed by Jethro into his house, marries his daughter, Zipporah, and settles down to the quiet life of a shepherd in the service of his father-in-law. At this point Moses probably envisaged his whole life as being spent in this uneventful, prosperous way. How very hard it must have been for this young man, an aristocrat by upbringing, a soldier who had dreamed of heroic exploits, no doubt, and whose warm heart and vivid imagination would keep alive in him the memory of his people's suffering! A hint of this is found in his cry when his son is born: "I am a stranger in a strange land" (Exodus 2:22). Yet he accepted without complaint the necessity of the long years of discipline.

With Moses, as with all of us, the turns of what seems like chance bring us to the exact situation in which we have the opportunity, if we will, to find the buried sides of our personality without which we can never live our true meaning as individuals; and usually the opportunity comes as a direct result of some major sin or failure of our earlier life. Moses' solitary life as a shepherd, the days and nights alone in the desert with his dog and his sheep, the gentle patience and skill so alien to his passionate nature (which he had to learn at lambing time), all these things nurtured the hitherto unlived potentialities of his psyche. Thus the door opened to the inner world; his ear opened to the voice of God in his heart; his eye opened to the vision of the divine. Imperceptibly, through the discipline of the daily simplicities, his shadow side was confronted, his sensitive individual feeling was discovered, and he came finally to so deep an awareness of the *mysterium tremendum* that God spoke to him face to face.

The manner of the first vision, the breakthrough of the new consciousness in Moses that had been maturing for so long, is of great symbolic meaning. Moses' sin had arisen from a destructive feeling impulse that had possessed and blinded him. His vision of the burning bush was of a fire that burned but did not consume, out of which came the voice of God and the realization of his unique task as an individual. This is the moment of transformation. The intensity of the fire of natural instinct, never repressed or rejected, is transmuted through discipline and acceptance into the fire of creativity, which does not destroy but liberates. In Moses' case, this fire was powerful enough to liberate a whole nation from its slavery. The objectivity of real enthusiasm (which means "being filled with God") had taken the place of subjective anger.

We should not, however, make the common mistake of supposing that such an experience immediately rids the human personality of all its weaknesses and hesitations and that such a man has only to go forward in a state of detachment and certainty, freed once and for all from doubt and fear and anger. On the contrary, he has probably to carry a far greater burden of doubt and a more constant temptation from the shadow side than ever before. This was certainly so for Moses until the end of his life, and he remained altogether human in strength and weakness through all the great events of which he was the instrument.

Almost always when such a moment comes to a man, he is faced with the necessity of doing the very thing for which he is sure he has no natural gift, the thing he most fears. Moses had always been a man of action, but now he is told that he must go to Pharaoh and use *words*—that is, he must work through his inferior function, which, as Carl Jung says, is always the way of redemption. There are two ways in which we may evade this voice which commands us to enter the new way. We may become inflated with the power that now fills us, or we may take refuge in false humility. Moses is in danger of the latter. "Who am *I* that I should go unto Pharaoh?" he asks. "I am not eloquent; I am slow of speech, of a slow tongue; they will not believe me" (Exodus 3:11). But God rebukes Moses and tells him that Aaron, his brother, will go with him. (The necessary support from the "brother" without and within will be at hand.) God tells Moses to say that *I Am* has sent him. With the realization of the name of God, Moses cannot cling for long to his inferiority complex, which is the underside of inflation. Only true humility can bring the knowledge of this name. So Moses accepts his way and sets off on his journey back to Egypt.

Moses now carries out his task in the face of the grumbling disbelief of Israel. For Moses it is a time of preparation for leadership, for *doing the next thing* in obedience to the voice of God, without thought of risk and without discouragement. This is a stage we all know. We fail and fail and fail in our struggle with ourselves and must go on to the *next thing* until suddenly the moment of liberation comes. A transformation releases us from our conflict and we must make ready for the new journey. We must eat the Passover, the symbol of the crossing over into a new way of life. We must eat it standing, as did the Israelites, in complete readiness to seize the moment. In the exhilaration of freedom, we probably imagine that the land of milk and honey is just around the corner but, if so, we are soon disillusioned. There is a desert to be crossed—a long, austere journey through the dark and empty times that come to us after the old attitudes have been left behind and the new vision has been glimpsed but remains a hope unrealized.

Soon after the departure comes the moment of great danger. The pursuit by Pharaoh is the revenge of our old attitudes. They try to return and we have the feeling that we are shut in between mountain and sea. We can go neither forward nor back, and we are certain that we shall be destroyed by the irresistible force of past habit and the overwhelming strength of collective reactions. It is a repetition of the theme of the newborn child threatened with extinction. Nothing we can humanly do or consciously decide will help us now. This is the moment at which only one kind of realization can save us; personal success or achievement, even in the realm of the spirit, must be seen as irrelevant. All that matters is that we have done our best; we have made the choice and eaten the Passover. Reason and will can do no more, and we entrust the "new child" to the water again. Moses knows this. He does not panic, for he has heard the name of God, and behold, the wind of the spirit begins to blow over the sea. There is a meeting of wind and water, of spirit and instinct, a mighty, creative moment. The water is blown back, a clear path ahead is opened for Moses and his people, and when they have passed over, the same wind and water swallow up and destroy the power of the old attitudes. We are set free to grow if we will. The children of Israel can move on to Sinai, to the holy mountain where Moses again meets God, face to face, and brings down to the people the covenant and the law.

A beautiful incident worth recounting happens before Moses and his people reach Sinai. Jethro, Moses' father-in-law, comes from

Midian to meet Moses. We feel the love between them and the wisdom of the old man. Moses has been making the usual mistake of the man of good will who takes on a tremendous responsibility. He is trying to carry the burden on the *wrong level*. Every day he sits from morning to evening hearing the problems of the people, settling individual disputes, until he is weary to the point of collapse. With wise common sense, Jethro tells Moses that he must appoint elders for this task; Moses himself must deal only with questions of vital importance. If he continues to wear himself out in this way, he will have no energy left for maintaining the contact with God, the vital spark in the hearts of the people that alone can bring them to their goal. Only so can he carry the weight of his vocation. Moses accepts Jethro's insights immediately and with humility.

Moses now ascends the mountain and once more meets God face to face. He hides his face before the glory of this vision. He cannot bear more than a glimpse, but the glimpse has transformed him. When he comes down from the mountain, his face is shining with so great a light that he must wear a veil over it, for there are things that cannot be borne by unconscious people, which must be hidden for their sake. T.S. Eliot wrote that human beings cannot stand very much reality. Moses has spent forty days and forty nights alone upon Horeb. During tt wrote that human beings cannot stand very much reality. Moses has spent forty days and forty nights alone upon Horeb. During this time he has not only come to his great inner vision, but he has also understood many things of an entirely practical nature. The truly great mystic, contrary to popular belief, is not someone floating on a cloud, detached from outer reality; on the contrary, the mystic has a far better grasp of the essentials in human affairs than the busy man or woman of action.

Moses now knows the necessity for laws whereby a society must be held together, the essential disciplines that the unconscious individual must accept from without if he is ever to grow to self-discipline. He also brings down from the mountain plans for the building of the Ark, for he understands the immense importance of ritual, of the symbols essential to maintaining contact with the inner meaning of one's life. If Moses needed confirmation of this importance, he found it when he returned to his people from the mountain. During his long absence, they had been unable to retain the sense of meaning that he personally embodied and carried for them. They had made a golden calf and projected all their unconscious needs onto this idol.

When Moses discovers his people's golden calf, he furiously hurls to the ground the tables of stone on which the law was written, breaking them to pieces. Yahweh is equally angry, but Moses recollects his humility and stands between his people and the wrath of God, the revenge of the unconscious forces. Yahweh's anger is turned away and the tables of the law are restored.

Later on, when the children of Israel have refused their first chance to enter Canaan and Yahweh has said to Moses, "I will disinherit them and make *thee* a greater nation" (Numbers 14:12), Moses does not falter. He does not abandon his people, who, while depending on him, constantly abused him and cursed him for bringing them away from the fleshpots of Egypt. It is often a very great temptation for a man or woman of great understanding to say, "Why bother anymore with these people who are so blind? God is doing great things in *me*; these others are hopeless."

The Psalmist wrote of the children of Israel, "He [Yahweh] would have destroyed them, had not Moses, his chosen, stood before him in the gap to turn away his wrathful indignation" (Psalms 106:23). In every age there are people like Moses who "stand in the gap" — poets, artists, men and women of vision, who bridge the widening split between conscious and unconscious, between darkness and light — mediators without whom the opposites would fly apart to the ultimate destruction of humanity.

Moses refused personal glorification; he refused to identify his ego with his vision of God, to become a *Fuehrer*, a *Duce*. He retained the essential humility of the true leader and guide. The incident of Joshua's protest when he found two men "prophesying" in the camp shows this beautiful quality in Moses. He replied to Joshua's anger at the thought that anyone other than Moses should presume to prophesy: "Enviest thou for my sake? Would God that *all* the Lord's people were prophets and that the Lord would put his spirit upon them" (Numbers 11:29)

Moses also knew how to accept help. In battle he needed two men to hold up his arms because he was so weary. In moments of danger we are arrogant indeed if we will not recognize our need for those who will "hold up our arms."

Moses' weaknesses are never glossed over. They are seen clearly, even as an essential ingredient of human greatness. He had moments of great despondency in those forty years of unremitting labor. At one of these times God appointed seventy elders to help him. "They shall bear the burden of these people with thee" (Numbers 11:17). Help came at all these times.

There was, however, one moment when Moses fell seriously into possession by his old angry shadow, in spite of all his wisdom and humility. The children of Israel were grumbling and complaining because there was no water. As usual, they blamed it on Moses, forgetting all the proofs of God's protection that had been given to them. God told Moses to "speak to the rock" and ask it to give forth water, but Moses was less patient than Yahweh this time. He lost his temper, just as he had lost it so many years ago in his youth when he killed the overseer. "Hear now ye rebels," he said, "must we fetch you water out of that rock?" (Numbers 20:10) And he struck the rock in anger and the water gushed out. He was guilty of a major sin—discourtesy to God, to man, and to matter. In *hubris* he identified with God. "Must *we* fetch you water . . .?" He spoke to his fellow Israelites with contempt, a very different thing from healthy anger, and he struck the rock with violence instead of with respect.

For this sin God forbade Moses himself to go into the promised land. Power that is not relinquished at the right moment can be a very great danger, not only for the one who wields it, but for his or her followers also. If Moses had gone into the new land with his people, the projection upon him would have been so great that it would have been almost impossible for Moses to resist identifying with the personal love of power that was a characteristic of his shadow. The danger from the shadow becomes greater, not less, for such a man, and by the deepest paradox, he is saved at the high point of achievement by the shadow itself. If Moses had not fallen into the sin of striking the rock, he would never have realized that the moment had come for him to renounce his leadership, and a subtle corruption would have begun.

In *The Lord of the Rings* it is Gollum who saves Frodo at his supreme moment, when he falls under the power of the Ring on the very brink of success. If Frodo himself had thrown the ring into the fire, he would almost certainly have identified with his heroic role. He might have lost his humanity and have begun another reign of power in the world. So always must a person's salvation come in the supreme moment, after the long purging, from beyond the ego.

If Moses had gone into Canaan with the children of Israel, they would have continued in a state of childish dependency and refusal of adult responsibility. Moses, accepting his sin, his humanity, darkness and light, was now freed from the final danger and the "promised land" was no longer a goal, but a fact of the spirit. He went up onto the mountain, looked on the new world he had opened for his people, and died in the fullness of wisdom.

THE CHILDREN OF ISRAEL

Moses and Pharaoh are the images of the hero and the renegade, but the story of the children of Israel is the story of the ordinary person who inwardly carries both these images, responding first to one and then to the other. This ordinary person instinctively knows that beyond the opposites of hero and renegade there is harmony and an answer to all questionings, and so he or she continues to stumble along toward the promised land.

The Hebrews were enslaved in Egypt just as we all are enslaved in different ways — by our blindness, our identification with collective attitudes, our clinging to one kind of safety or another. Sooner or later this darkness is suddenly broken by a glimpse of freedom, usually coming to us, as it did to the children of Israel, through contact with a free person, a Moses. Such a person fires a spark in us, by the light of which we know for a moment the potential Moses in ourselves, the possibility of becoming a free and aware person. The glimpse, the momentary enthusiasm, brings with it almost at once a resistance, for we know instinctively what it is going to cost us if we consent to recognize the Moses within. The Pharaoh in us is increased in strength by the threat to his "domination," so we begin to make excuses. The children of Israel, rejoicing at Moses' first message, turned against him again as soon as they felt Pharaoh's increased oppression. Great as their sufferings were, they had at first an even greater fear of the unknown. When we do finally consent to face the unknown and confront Pharaoh, our shadow side, it appears incomprehensible that for so long we preferred to stay in "Egypt," tormented by the meaningless horrors of neurotic suffering, rather than to endure the truth about ourselves. But at first we cling desperately to our neurosis as to a lifeline. To let it go feels like letting go of one's identity because it means an end to identification with our particular cherished image of ourselves.

Suffering of the Hebrews had grown so great, however, that when Moses bade them be ready on the Passover night, one and all were obedient, and the greater journey began. The Pharaoh within is defeated for the moment—and this is the crucial moment for the children of Israel, just as there always comes a crucial choice for an individual. It is the crisis at which a "no" is fatal, but a "yes" means a fundamental choice of direction. The weaknesses that lead to all the ups and downs and regressions of daily living do not, except in cases of real, conscious betrayal, alter this direction, though they increase the length of the journey.

The Egyptians have loaded the Israelites with presents to speed their going. In addition, the Israelites have taken all the gold and precious things they can lay hands on, for the Egyptians are too terrified to resist. The first effort toward freedom is usually accompanied by a kind of greed, the nature of freedom being very dimly understood. At this point it is merely a promise of relief from old kinds of suffering. "Immediate" wealth is demanded and, for a brief time, experienced.

No sooner, however, have the Israelites set out than Moses reveals to them the price they must pay. The angel of death, which killed the firstborn, has passed them over because they have heard the voice of God and are willing to face the unknown wilderness. But that which happens disastrously and meaninglessly to people who refuse consciousness must also be experienced by the "chosen" freely and willingly. Every man of the Hebrews must dedicate his firstborn son to the service of God. Here is the symbol that carries the meaning of true freedom. Only that person who is free can willingly and gladly submit to another kind of bond. The firstborn, the heir, is the greatest value, that which carries the essential meaning of our personality and its creativity. To dedicate this to God means to let go of all our possessiveness, our stake in our achievements, our sense of personal "rights," our conscious assumptions that we are owed a return for effort. Only when we have learned through our forty years in the wilderness to *choose necessity* with absolutely no reservation do we come to the truth that makes us free.

What a shock to the children of Israel, congratulating themselves on their chosen state, rejoicing in their plunder and their escape from bondage! Probably, however, few of them realized at this point that the "sacrifice of the son" represented more than a special kind of life for their eldest boy, or recognized it as a hint of the long and agonizing process of purging hidden from them, as it is mercifully hidden from us when we begin the journey.

At the first major setback between the mountains and the Red Sea, the Hebrews are rudely awakened from their dream of a quick triumphal procession to the land of milk and honey. Pharaoh is not to be thrown off so easily. We find that the old habits of bondage are immensely strong. The first upsurge of enthusiasm recedes and the chariots and horses of the old way of life, the old easy attitudes, come galloping after us. There is no escape. The unconscious is silent; conscious resolutions to change are of no avail. We begin to grumble, to accuse the "Moses" within, and also our friends (upon whom he is projected) for having brought us to this impasse. Maybe we have made some big change in our outer life, expecting a new and satisfying experience, and all it has brought us is a feeling of a dead end. We don't even have the old sense of safety in bondage; will we listen to Moses or go down under Pharaoh? Maybe it is in this moment that we fully realize that "Moses" has offered us "blood, toil, sweat, and tears," not a quick, easy way to marvelous inner experiences. We know for a moment a full acceptance of this way. This is indeed the crucial moment. If we say "yes" to it, the wind of God blows back the waters so that we may make that essential crossing over from the old to the new way, and Pharaoh and his might are swallowed up behind us. We have made the fundamental choice of direction, which frees us, not from the long journey with its many backslidings, but from the danger of complete regression through a weak discouragement, which can kill us at this point. It is a far worse danger than it was before the Passover because the new way has been glimpsed and we have actually set foot upon it. If we hold firm and cross over to the other side out of Egypt, the end is no longer in doubt, however long delayed, unless we deliberately, and with full consciousness of what we are doing, betray and deny our original choice. (This is the Church's definition of mortal sin.)

The sea is crossed and the journey proper begins. There is now a visible guiding symbol—the pillar of cloud and of fire. In the daytime, in the light of extraerted life, it is a cloudy, indistinct thing, but it is nevertheless unquestionably real. At night in dreams, in introversion, it burns with a clear light. The multitude, weighted down with all their possessions, travels slowly and soon runs out of food. For the first time the so often repeated cry is heard: "Why did you bring us out of Egypt? At least we had enough to eat there." The answer, not because they *deserved* it, but because the "Moses" within them did not lose faith and courage, was the manna that fed them unfailingly through the coming forty years.

The manna is a small, round, colorless thing lying on our door-step, so to speak, to be had for the picking up. Its peculiarity is that we cannot hoard it; it is food for one day only. Each day, if we are to have strength to continue the journey, it must be picked up. This much effort only is required. There is no *kick* to this basic nourish-ment. It has little taste or savor. Perhaps these qualities symbolize the day-to-day picking up of the most ordinary colorless tasks that every human being must face and "eat" — that is, *accept*. The manna is the essential food for the journey. The Host in the Mass, the bread from heaven, is an ordinary, tasteless fragment of daily bread trans-formed by its conscious "lifting up" into the body of Christ — the essential incarnate essence of truth, of the Self. So the Hebrews, by simply picking up and eating what was there in abundance all around them, unearned, unsought for, were fed and nourished on the journey.

Fairly soon, however, the Hebrews got bored with this daily, tasteless food which did not leave them with lovely feelings or titillate their appetites. They demanded flesh to eat. And because they were weak and could not get along without some external "kicks," God sent them quails. The Psalmist says, "Lust came upon them in the wilderness and they tempted God in the desert. And he gave them their desire and sent leanness withal into their soul" (Psalms 106:14-15). We always get what we really want, though we may seldom recognize it as the thing we think we want. It is most certain that every demand for personal power or satisfaction is immediately counterbalanced by a leanness of soul. That is not to say that the good things of the flesh are not to be enjoyed to the full. It is no long-faced puritanical denial of instinct and the beauty of good food and wine and so on. It is a matter of the *demand* for such things at the expense of or to the exclusion of greater values. Still more, it is a symbol of the lust for spiritual power, the clinging to lofty feelings, which is much more intoxicating than wine. These demands make us fat and comfortable in one sense and induce an exactly corresponding leanness and starvation in the innermost places of the soul.

After they have arrived at the holy mountain, the Hebrews are in for a long delay. It seems at this stage of the journey that "Moses," the spark that leads, is no longer visible. We know in our heads that he has only receded out of our awareness and is gathering strength in the depths—or on the heights of the mountain—to lead us farther, but gradually we forget and lose faith and end in a panic, looking for other gods—gods we can see and touch, or easier concepts of an all-powerful anthropomorphic deity who will make us feel safe and answer our immediate prayers. Even Aaron (the "priest" in us, who is closest to Moses and is his brother) breaks faith and serves the collective panic. They make a god out of the gold, the values they have brought from Egypt, a golden calf, a bull, the symbol of un-bridled instinct.

After such a fall we must be ruthless with ourselves. Moses causes the ringleaders to be killed; we may have to cut out of our lives many things, even relationships, which have hitherto seemed natural and pleasant but have lost their meaning. This letting go of things would, however, be pointless asceticism if, at the same time, we did not pour the energy released from the "golden calf" into new channels of creation. Moses immediately set the Israelites to work on the build-ing of the tabernacle. In their repentance and new humility they made free gifts of the treasures they had brought from Egypt for the creation of the most beautiful symbol of their deepest faith—the Ark of the Covenant. The actual building of the Ark was carried out by those who had proved themselves "wise hearted." So if we listen and pay the price, the wisdom of the inner world will create for us the symbols whereby we may hold to the meaning of our journey.

After only two or three years in the wilderness, the Israelites come to the borders of the promised land, and Moses sends out scouts into Canaan. When they return with their reports, all but two are fright-ened and urge the people not to risk entering the country. Only Joshua and Caleb are for the bold course, but the children of Israel will not listen to them and fall into an ugly panic, abusing Moses as usual and demanding another leader to take them back to Egypt. It is a major refusal and must be bitterly paid for.

It must be remembered that at this stage of the journey a refusal is a very different thing from the weak backslidings of the beginning. This conscious turning back is a betrayal of their quest, and in rage Yahweh condemns them to wander long years in the wilderness. Their children will enter the promised land; they will not. Only Joshua and Caleb are excepted. The people now repent under this threat and insist upon going out and fighting a battle with the Canaanites in spite of Moses' warning. "The Lord is not among you," he says, for they are acting out of fear, not faith. They are defeated and the years of wandering begin. It seems a harsh punishment, but there are indeed moments in the life of an individual when a refusal such as this is irreversible without long years of suffering, perhaps even for the rest of this mortal life, in which case it will mean that the children must pick up the burden of the unlived lives of their fathers or mothers, and to them also in due time will come the moment of the great choice on the threshold of the holy land.

Chapter Twenty-Eight

The Story of Saul

SAUL'S LIFE HAD all the elements of great tragedy. He was a man broken by his fate, a noble failure, who disobeyed the divine vocation laid upon him and thereafter was utterly rejected by Yahweh until his death. Yet Saul emerges with a kind of greatness and power to move us that David, with all his heroic qualities, cannot surpass. His story has particular relevance in these days when so many are broken by the same kind of possession by the unconscious that overthrew Saul.

Rivkah Schärf, in her paper "King Saul and the Spirit of God" (Guild of Pastoral Psychology), has pointed out the essential differences in the accounts of the two elections to kingship—Saul's and David's. Whereas David was anointed "in the midst of his brethren" and the Spirit of the Lord immediately came upon him in direct association with his vocation as king, Saul was anointed in secret by Samuel, who told him that he had now been chosen as king but that the Spirit of the Lord would not come upon him until later, when he would meet a band of prophets on the way and would receive the spirit of prophecy. In other words, the "spirit" was not directly connected with his outer task as king, but was a gift to his inner life.

The word "prophecy" has come to mean a foretelling of the future, but in those days a prophet was a person capable of ecstasy, of being filled with the Spirit. The prophet was the "seer," or, as we would now say, one in whom the deep unconscious has been activated and to whom is given the choice between meeting and relating to the powers thus released or succumbing to possession by them. In the former case a true "prophet" or seer is born—a person burning with the strength and beauty of an inner vision, a channel for the wisdom of God, but one who nevertheless remains human, related to this gift of the spirit and never identified with it. But, one who allows ecstasy to remain on the emotional level, who loses his or her ordinary humanity or is incapable of the kind of obedience that the inner voice demands, will be split and destroyed by this "gift of the spirit" and will end up in the clutches of the demonic side of it, as did Saul.

It seems that Yahweh made an abortive attempt in Saul. Israel had hitherto had no king. It had been a theocracy, and Yahweh was angry that the people now demanded a king; he even accused them of idolatry. Nevertheless, he saw that a king was a necessity if his people were to survive in the struggle with the heathen, so he told Samuel to give in and anoint a king. There seems to be considerable ambivalence in God's attitude at this point (ambivalence in the God-image of Israel). Yahweh's choice of Saul was perhaps an attempt to resolve that ambivalence by anointing a man to be king who had also the capacity for ecstatic inner vision. Saul was therefore called to be a great military leader, a ruler of power and great possessions. At the same time, however, he was called to be a man of the spirit, following the inner way, which has always involved for the seer separation from the world, from outer possessions and power. It was an almost impossible demand, and Saul was split in half and destroyed by it. Yahweh appears to have been trying to bring to birth overnight, so to speak, the totality—a union of opposites in one man who would be both king and prophet in Israel. We could say that the soul of Israel was trying to have it both ways—to become a strong, rich nation in this world and at the same time to retain its peculiar spiritual vocation as God's chosen people. It is indeed a conflict that emerges in every individual soul, but Israel attempted in Saul an impossible collective solution, and the personal Saul was broken by his fate. Perhaps that is why a later legend speaks of the people's "debt" to Saul.

It is said that God "repented" of his choice. Next time he knew that he could not ask so much of his kings, just as he had never asked so much of his prophets. David was given the blessing as king, not as prophet, and in the light of this it makes sense that, although his sins were much more frequent and seemingly more serious than Saul's, nevertheless he was never deserted by the Spirit of God, never rejected. To Saul, God had given his greatest inner gift, and therefore one disobedience at a vital point could wreck the whole. It was as though the failure of Saul made it finally clear that no man could carry this double burden and that kingship could only be reconciled with prophecy in the inner world of the individual. Therefore it was of peculiar significance that Jesus was born of the royal line of David—that the Messiah is also the King, but that his kingdom is "not of this world." This was the rock on which the Jews stumbled when Christ made his claim. They still could not conceive of a king who had no outer power and was not a great leader of his people in the world. They had not learned the lesson of Saul. The Priest-King remains in legend, but only in legend (Prester John), expressing an inner truth.

There are three separate accounts of the election of Saul. The first account is of his secret anointing, followed by his first experience of the Spirit when he met the prophets. When Samuel tells him of his destiny, Saul is already frightened of it—"Wherefore speakest thou so to me?" (1 Samuel 9:21) The second account tells how Samuel called the people together to cast lots and the lot fell upon Saul. The story tells how Saul, knowing his weakness, had hidden himself as though wishing still to evade his fate. Even after this he seems to have gone quietly home, and some of the people still did not accept him, until the city of Jabesh-Gilead was besieged and sent out a cry for help. Then the Spirit of Yahweh came again to Saul in the form of great courage and anger against the heathen, and he rose up and entered into his kingly task and freed the city. Then the people fully acclaimed their king.

There followed a series of wars against the heathen. Then came a command from Yahweh through Samuel, and Saul was told to go out and destroy the Amalekites and not to spare any one of the people nor any part of their possessions or flocks. Saul now showed that he had allowed power and wealth to weaken disastrously his obedience to the inner voice. Victorious, he spared both Agag, the enemy king, and all the best flocks, though he slew the citizens and the poor flocks and told Samuel he had fulfilled the will of God. We might be tempted to ascribe to Saul the motives of a noble rebellion against this barbarous demand for slaughter, but this would be an anachronism. For the primitive, possessions were a part of the owner's personality and the meaning of Yahweh's command was simply that no part of the evil attached to the "heathen" should be allowed to survive.

Saul's motive in sparing the flocks was plainly that he could not bear to give up such riches. The temptation of power was too strong for him; he had begun to covet possessions. Worst of all, when

Samuel rebuked him, Saul made excuses. Had he admitted his fault and repented, the sequel might indeed have been different, but instead he justified himself by a lie. "The people spared the best of the sheep and of the oxen to sacrifice unto the Lord" (1 Samuel 15:15). He blames others and invents a noble motive for the disobedience. Then comes the terrible retribution. "And Samuel said, 'Hath the Lord as great delight in burnt offerings and sacrifices as in obeying the voice of the Lord? Behold to obey is better than sacrifice and to hearken than the fat of rams. For rebellion is as the sin of witchcraft. . . . Because thou has rejected the word of the Lord he hath also rejected thee from being King" (1 Samuel 15:22-23). One feels that Samuel is speaking here as one seer to another. For the man who can inwardly hear the voice of God, the primary sin is disobedience to that voice and the inevitable result is "witchcraft." The Spirit remains but turns demonic. For the ordinary man's disobedience there would be retribution, but not that kind.

Saul admits his sin, but immediately makes another excuse. He says he is afraid of the people. This again is an impossible excuse in the seer, though forgivable in another. Then, as Samuel turns to leave him forever, Saul catches hold of his robe and it tears in his hand—the symbol surely of the split that now begins in Saul—the separation from his brother prophet, Samuel, the part of himself that has been truly given to God. Thus, Saul shows again, in his grief at the now inevitable loss, how far his corruption has already gone. He begs Samuel to delay his going in order to maintain his, Saul's, prestige before the people. He is full of remorse, but will not pay the price of humiliation and repentance. He has chosen worldly power and betrayed the inner voice. The great love between Saul and Samuel comes through these few verses with the force of tragedy: "And Samuel came no more to see Saul until the day of his death: nevertheless Samuel mourned for Saul" (1 Samuel 15:35). God himself, as it were, admits that he has asked too much of the man he chose: "The Lord repented that he had made Saul king over Israel" (1 Samuel 15:11).

From now on the disintegration of Saul proceeds. "The Spirit of the Lord departed from Saul and an evil spirit from the Lord troubled him" (1 Samuel 16:14). Notice that the Spirit was still "from the Lord." This shocks our modern rationality, but in truth it was the same spirit as before though now it had become an emotional state of possession. The gift of the Spirit is a *capacity* for vision. It can carry us to wholeness if we accept the price, or it can consume and destroy our humanity. The story of Saul makes utterly clear the turning point. If we *use* this capacity to acquire any kind of power, prestige, or personal possession, however seemingly harmless or even "good" our superficial motives may be, then we open ourselves to possession by the dark side of this power. This is the theme of Tolkien's *The Lord of the Rings* from beginning to end. This is why Saul's tragedy can make so great an impact in this age of reaction from nineteenth century materialism, when we are surrounded by attempts to reconnect with the numinous in so many forms—drugs, astrology, tongue-speaking, depth psychology. We yearn for the gift of the *Ruah Yahweh*, the Spirit of God, and we are thereby exposed to the dangers of Saul in extreme form, because for the most part we seek the experience without the commitment, and so confuse the end with the means. To refuse the kind of obedience that is the price of vision is to abrogate our humanity, and then indeed, as Samuel said, "Rebellion is as the sin of witchcraft." A breakthrough of "vision" is very frequently followed by dreams that insist on the importance of the ordinary day-to-day human values and disciplines, so great is our danger of floating off into some kind of inflation, or "mission," or spiritual possessiveness, whereby we fall prey to witchcraft in the unconscious, as Samuel predicted for Saul.

In our moments of choice how do we *know* that we are obeying the voice of truth? We can only do our best to discriminate our motives, free ourselves from conventional opinions, watch our dreams, use our intelligence, together with our intuition, weigh the values involved and the effects on other people, and then act wholeheartedly from the deepest level we know. If our choice proves to be a mistake, it will be a creative mistake—a mistake leading to consciousness. If it is a question of a big change in our lives, something almost always comes from without to meet the urge from within, and we have a chance to *recognize* our way—either by resisting a temptation or by accepting a new attitude. If our commitment to our "fate," to the will of God, includes the willingness to pay the full price, we will not go astray—we will relate to the Spirit within, not succumb to possession by it. There is no rule to tell us whether this or that is the right attitude, the right way to behave in all circumstances.

Recurrent fits of melancholia now fell upon the king. David appeared at court, having slain his giant, and Saul surely recognized, unconsciously, in the newly anointed one his own refused vocation, and inevitably in his split condition he both loved and hated him. Already, however, we sense the nobility and the enduring love in Saul, which no failure or disaster can ultimately tarnish. It is this that accounts for David's lifelong devotion to him. Perhaps at this point if Saul had stood up and fought his "evil spirit," he would have been saved from the evil to come, but he seeks only soothing music, a panacea, from David, the symbol of new life, new opportunity. He clings more and more frantically to his old attitude toward power until, when he hears the people exalting David's achievements above his own, he succumbs to his envy and fear, and hatred turns to murder. He is sucked into the abyss and kills, or tries to kill, all those whom he most loves. He attacks David with the javelin, then drives him from court (unconsciously intending, we may feel, to save him for the future). Later he throws the javelin at his own beloved son, Jonathan. The horrible crime of the murder of the priests of Nob, who have innocently helped David in his flight, is the measure of his blind and bitter rejection of his own call to holiness. Saul the tenderhearted, Saul the seer, has come to this.

Only for one moment after David leaves does the veil lift, and we see that the old Saul lives. After David has spared his life, when Saul lies asleep and at his mercy, the two speak across the gulf—the space between their armies—and Saul says: "Is this thy voice, my son David?" And Saul lifted up his voice and wept. And he said to David: "Thou art more righteous than I; for thou hast rewarded me good, whereas I have rewarded thee evil. And thou hast shewed this day how that thou hast dealt well with me . . . wherefore the Lord reward thee good for that thou has done unto me this day. And now behold I know well that thou shalt surely be king and that the kingdom of Israel shalt be established in thy hand" (1 Samuel 24:17-20). Saul's true heart is not dead, only submerged. As always with us all, chance after chance is offered. Had he stripped himself then and there and gone into the wilderness, the final horror would have been avoided. Jonathan, his son, his flesh and blood, might have survived to stand beside David the king, with his gentleness and his wisdom. But Saul is not capable of *action*, though his heart's generosity still lives, and this is what lifts the story to the level of high tragedy.

The end comes with the final betrayal of the seer within. All sense of contact with God is gone. Saul is rudderless, unable even to decide when to fight the Philistines and when to refrain, and he descends finally to seeking guidance from the ghost of Samuel, his dead inner wisdom, through a witch—he, the king who forbade all practice of witchcraft in the kingdom when he was strong in spirit. Samuel's prophecy about witchcraft is fulfilled. The witch of Endor raises Samuel's ghost, but the dead thing can promise only death: "Tomorrow thou and thy sons shall be with me." So Saul, finally accepting his fate, goes out to fight and his three sons with him, and, after he is wounded, he falls on his sword and his three sons are killed with him, as though there can be nothing left behind of his failure.

Nothing is left—and yet the immediate sequel to his death begins to establish the *meaning*, the strange, dark beauty in this story of unendurable conflict and defeat. The men of Jabesh-Gilead, who have felt personal love and devotion to Saul all through the years since his rescue of their city, rise up and, at great risk to themselves, go and cut down his body from the walls of the Philistine city where it hangs dishonored and take it home with them to give it honorable burial. It has been said that a man can only be judged by his effect on others, and we become aware as we read that the dominant reaction to Saul of almost everyone with whom he came into close contact was one of love. Samuel loved him, David loved him, Jonathan loved him; one senses the loyalty and love of Abner, the captain of his host, of the servant and his soldiers, watching him in his dark moods and bearing with him; even the witch of Endor shows him a kind of maternal tenderness after his encounter with Samuel's ghost. Only a man who is himself full of love can inspire this kind of devotion. Saul betrayed or murdered or tried to murder everyone he loved best, but it is clear that the darkening of his consciousness, the surrender to demonic possession, or to the destructive split in his personality, as we should say, could not finally extinguish the validity of his real love, the nobility of his essential nature. So we have a tragedy, with all its cathartic power, instead of a meaningless story of a diseased mind and a jealous tyrant. David's lamentation over Saul and Jonathan sweeps away the cruelty and the failure and lifts the image of Saul into beauty: "Saul and Jonathan were lovely and pleasant in their lives and in their death they were not divided; they were swifter than eagles, they were stronger than lions. Ye daughters of Israel weep over Saul. . . . How are the mighty fallen!" (2 Samuel 1:23)

Finally a Jewish legend pays the highest tribute of all to the memory of Saul—God himself gives proof of his love and ultimate acceptance of his servant. The legend tells that there was famine in Israel, and David, the king, sought to find the reason for God's anger. Finally God spoke to him and said that it was because of Saul—because due honor had not been given to him since his death. So David sent to Jabesh-Gilead and Saul's body was dug up and found to be uncorrupt, and David ordered that the coffin should be carried into every part of Israel, to every village, so that the people might pay homage to the body. So it was done and Saul was buried in his home: "And when the Lord saw that the people had paid due honor to their king, he became compassionate and sent rain upon the land" (2 Samuel 21:14).

A record of facts and deeds tells one kind of truth about a great man, but a legend tells truth of another kind, in another dimension, projecting us for a moment beyond the opposites to an intuitive vision of the whole.

Chapter Twenty-Nine

The Little Prince

TWO FAMOUS BOOKS have been written in the twentieth century about the "eternal boy," as different from each other as they can be, except in their essential theme of the boy who refuses to grow up. James Barrie's *Peter Pan*, written in 1902, is an entrancing fairy-play for children, a fantasy of pirates, fairies, Indians, a loving mother, adventurous children who learn to fly, and the hero boy who can face death as "a great adventure" but who refuses to live in the human adult world. *The Little Prince*, by Antoine de Saint-Exupéry,[1] written almost forty years later, is not really addressed to children at all, in spite of the words of the dedication, but is a book about the child in adults, an infinitely sad story of the sterility of the world and the lost wisdom and beauty of childhood. It is the tragedy of those people of our times, of whom Saint-Exupéry was one, whose eyes are open to the inner world of dream and image, who know the child's wisdom of innocence and folly and the emptiness of collective values, but who fail to bridge the gap between their inner vision and the harshness of outer reality. These people are split apart to the point of suicide, sometimes actual physical suicide, conscious or unconscious, but certainly to the suicide of one value or the other.

From the beginning it is plain that the book is not concerned with the experience of an actual child. A little boy is not separated from humanity in this way, living in a remote and empty place with three volcanoes and sadly watching the beauty of the sunsets. Already the feeling of the tragic end is there. Childhood is sunrise, not sunset, whether we speak of the human child or of the archetypal child in the unconscious of an adult. The child who appears in our dreams speaks of new beginnings, or hints at the wholeness of the end, when sun and moon shine together. Compare the atmosphere of the Little Prince's planet with the Never-Never Land of Peter Pan and the lost boys. (If anyone knows Peter Pan only through Walt Disney's cartoon, let him banish that travesty of the story from his mind.) The

Never-Never Land is also remote from the everyday world but vig-
orously alive with the sparkling fantasy of the child. The boys fly in
the air, they live underground, they fight the evil pirates among
whom, delightfully, is the "lovable" Smee, they have Indians and
fairies for friends, they vanquish wolves, and Peter is rescued from
the rising water of the blue lagoon by a bird. When Wendy comes
among them the boys turn her at once into a mother, and through her
they are finally brought back into the real world, and all, except Peter
himself, accept the necessity of growing up, of meeting the dreary
world of school and work and responsibility. There is sadness, for
most will lose, one knows, their contact with the bright world of
childhood and its wisdom, but only so can there be any hope of final
wholeness. In Peter there is a hint of the archetype—living in the
trees alone but visited each year by Wendy. It is all in a light vein,
with touches of sentimentality, but nevertheless we may see in
Wendy a hint of the function of the *anima*, connecting the conscious
with the unconscious world of fantasy.

It is interesting to compare with this the symbol of the feminine in
The Little Prince. In the human boy it is love and care of the mother
that connects him (if she is a true mother) with the world and pushes
him out of the nest when the right time comes. The *arrested* child in a
man may be awakened from his disconnected state by the dawning of
an uneasy perception that all is not well with his own feeling life,
however "beautiful," and so he is driven to attempt to connect with
the world of men. The Little Prince's single rose (his potential
relatedness) shows herself as vain and not altogether truthful, so the
boy rejects her and starts on the journey that leads to the earth.

His first experiences are not encouraging. He comes to several
other tiny, isolated planets, on each of which a man as lonely as
himself lives in his private world, pursuing his empty goal of power
or wealth or knowledge or pleasure. On the last one he meets the
lamplighter, with whom he feels some kinship—the ordinary man,
not imprisoned by an obsession with his own importance, but nevertheless still alone, bound by his daily task and never looking beyond
it, lighting and extinguishing his lamp with the setting and rising of
the sun every few minutes on his tiny, tiny world, with no time for
rest, no eyes for beauty. In his first glimpses of mankind the Little
Prince has seen only the polar opposite of the simplicity of the
child—that is, the obsession with goals.

The Little Prince now finally reaches the earth itself. He is still alone in the desert, but being on earth he is confronted immediately with the life of instinct. He comes upon the snake, the most earthbound of all, the furthest from human consciousness, who warns him that the world of men and women will prove just as lonely as his planet and reminds him that the bite of the snake can bring death and release. He will not bite the child now, for snakes do not harm the completely innocent; only when the Little Prince wishes to return to his planet and comes back to this place will the snake bite him and so release him from the earth. There is an undertone of the cynicism of the devil in this. The snake has no belief in the success of the child's attempt to meet the grown-up world. At the very outset the Little Prince assures himself of a line of retreat from his venture. How unchildlike! He is fatally uncommitted, one feels. He has an insurance policy.

Now the Little Prince crosses the desert looking for men and grows more and more unhappy, until he comes one day to a garden of roses. For the first time he knows that *his* rose on *his* planet is not unique in the universe, and he lies down and cries. His rose for the moment becomes a "nothing but"—that well-known state of mind, the polar opposite of possessive pride. It is at the moment of the breakdown that he meets the fox.

The fox is a kind of Mercurius or Hermes symbol in the inner world. He is cunning and wise, the trickster and the guide—an image carrying, even today, the numinous intuition of the tie between the hunter and the hunted. *The Running Foxes*, by Joyce Stranger, is a very beautiful and true story on this theme. It seems proven that an old fox will even invite the hunt to pursue him. It is this animal, the ruthless hunter, the constantly hunted, who teaches the Little Prince what it means to have a friend and what the real nature of uniqueness is.

The fox asks the Prince to *tame* him, and in answer to the boy's questioning he says that to tame and be tamed means "to establish ties"—in other words, to have relationship and responsibility. He teaches the Little Prince that to be unique does not consist of possessing the only rose in all the world—uniqueness comes when love is awakened between oneself and another, whether the other is a fox or a rose or a person. It is, as we all know, an immensely powerful delusion of the ego, this identification of our personal worthiness with the possession of some special ability or virtue or achievement. The fox reveals the profound paradox that each person's uniqueness is born solely through his capacity to "establish ties," conscious ties between self and "other" (whether that other be an outer or an inner reality), and through a willingness to sacrifice the unconscious ties of possession.

The fox now instructs the Little Prince how to tame another. He tells him that with infinite patience he must sit near to him without words and move a little closer every day. It is also good to observe "the proper rites," which, he explains, means always coming at the same time every day, thus infusing the simple act with the power of ritual—a very sound piece of advice, particularly when it is a question of "taming" our inner images.

Then the fox comes to the heart of his message—the strange paradox that is an essential element in the establishing of a tie is the acceptance of parting—even of final parting. The uniqueness of the tie is not lost; indeed, it finds its greatest fulfillment in the inevitable separation, for out of the pain of this experience accepted (accepted daily, not only in the moments of outer loss), meaning is born where before there was no meaning. The gold of the wheat fields, hitherto unnoticed and meaningless to the fox, is now forever alive with beauty because of the gold of his friend's hair. Every wheat field is now unique because of the uniqueness of the Little Prince. The mark of a love that is purged of possessiveness and has become a tie between two who consent to be *separate* is that it does not exclude (so that everything outside of it becomes merged in a dreary mass). On the contrary, it begets an intuition of the uniqueness and meaning of every person, every experience that we encounter. All of this does not mean that the grief of parting is any less. "I shall cry," said the fox.

The fox's last message is this: "What is essential is invisible to the eye. . . . It is the time you have *wasted* for your rose that makes the rose so important. . . . You have become responsible, forever, for what you have tamed" (p. 87). That the Little Prince, deeply as he has understood the fox's lesson, has still missed the essential point becomes clear at once. Here is the passage that reveals this misunderstanding, which was indeed that of Saint-Exupéry himself. He is looking at the bed of hundreds of roses and he says:

You are not at all like my rose. As yet you are nothing. No one has tamed you, and you have tamed no one. You are like my fox when I first knew him. He was only a fox like a hundred thousand other foxes. But I have made him my friend and now he is unique in all the world.

   You are beautiful, but you are empty. One could not die for you. To be sure, an ordinary passer-by would think that my rose looked just like you — the rose that belongs to me. But in herself alone she is more important than all the hundreds of you other roses: because it is she that I have watered; because it is she that I have put under the glass globe; because it is she that I have sheltered behind the screen; because it is for her that I have killed the caterpillars (except the two or three that we saved to become butterflies); because it is she that I have listened to, when she grumbled, or boasted, or even sometimes when she said nothing. Because she is *my* rose. (pp.86-87)

It is true, but it is not the whole truth. He realizes his responsibility for the rose he has tamed on his planet, accepts its imperfections, and begins to know love. But he does not see that, just as his responsibility to the fox involved accepting his own and the fox's sadness when the moment of parting came, so his responsibility to the rose meant also the acceptance of parting so that the beauty of the rose could live *in* the world, not only on his private planet. So he looks at the hundred roses not with the joy of recognizing the image of the beloved in each one of them, as the fox looked at the wheat fields, but with an almost contemptuous pity.

   He passes on to meet the world of men — sees crowds going aimlessly to and fro in trains, talks to a merchant who has invented pills to quench thirst in order to save people from wasting time looking for water. (How very apt an image of our predicament today!) One could imagine that at this point the little fox might have said, "Look beyond what the eye sees and the ear hears and see the human being behind that false mask and take the trouble to tame him. The red glow of his cheeks, even the red paint on the railway engine, could remind you of your rose and give these people and things beauty and meaning. It is thus that you must carry the responsibility to your rose." But the Little Prince misses the point, misses his chance — he thinks only of the beauty of *his* rose, her need of him, and so he makes the final refusal to involve himself in life on this earth, and in clinging to his rose he most tragically betrays her. He starts on his regressive journey to the snake who will give him death—not the death that is acceptance of life and of fate, but the death which is refusal of life and of responsibility. Jung has said that the "threat of the snake" points to the danger of newly acquired consciousness being swallowed again by the instinctive psyche. This is precisely what happens to the Little Prince.

Before the final tragedy he meets the airman mending his crashed plane and asks him for a sheep to take back with him to his planet. The drawings the airman makes are rejected. The sheep is too old, or too sickly; finally the drawing of a box is accepted, in which the sheep lies unseen and can be imagined by the Little Prince in any form he pleases. This would be a delight in a little boy, but not in a man identified with the child. Surely it is again a dangerous misunderstanding of the fox's words, "What is essential is not visible to the eye," which certainly does not mean that you may turn a real sheep into a private image of what you would like it to be, but that behind the outer appearance of the sheep, be it sickly or old, there is an essential uniqueness that may be found if you will "tame" it. This is the fatal misunderstanding of the infantile personality, whereby the imagination, the intuition of ultimate truths, may be used to distort present reality instead of to fill it with meaning.

The man, led by the boy, finds a well in the desert. They do not just imagine it—they know that the water of life is there under the arid surface, for the beauty of the desert lies in the fact of the well. Here the man learns deep wisdom from the eternal child, but, instead of taking that wisdom to the meeting and taming of life itself, he will not risk it among men and thinks to preserve it remote and alone in the sky, so that he must spend his life with his eyes on the stars and in a continual torment as to whether or not it still lives. For the Little Prince had taken something back with him from the earth—the sheep that may eat the rose. The man had forgotten to add a strap to the muzzle he had drawn to control the sheep; the unconscious had seen to that, for we cannot ever ensure the safety of anything. The child, by coming to earth, had experienced the opposites; he could not return unscathed to his infantile paradise. He wanted to preserve only what he wished from his journey, but willy-nilly he took with him that unconscious instinctual urge that could eat the weeds on his planet but could equally well devour his rose and leave him more horribly alone than before. So the man who has refused to hear the *whole* message of the fox, and who tries to preserve the beauty of his inner life isolated from and untarnished by the world, must live with a gnawing doubt forever in his heart. Has the sheep destroyed the rose? It is a doubt that haunts us all whenever we turn even briefly from the fox's message.

So the book ends with the same image with which it began. The actual child's drawing of the boa constrictor with the elephant inside of it is full of imagination and promise that the dull adult cannot see, but the image has passed through the separation of the opposites to the opportunity of consciousness, only to end in a regression in which one opposite may be swallowed again in the belly of the other — the tender uniqueness of the rose devoured by the sheeplike collectivity from which the Little Prince sought to fly. The man lives now with his eyes on the stars, seeing their beauty and filled with an insatiable longing, for he has known and loved the child within. But the earth under his feet he has rejected with contempt, and wholeness must forever elude him in this life. It is a moving and beautifully told story, with the impact of a tragic truth, but a feeling of sadness and hopelessness pervades the whole book.

Thus it was in the life of Saint-Exupéry himself — a man of potential genius who never broke his identification with the eternal child. Someone who knew him well wrote of him that he had in equal degree "real and profound mysticism, great appetite for pleasures of the senses and total irresponsibility in daily life." Also, it was said that he was "an extremist in all things. He could not bear contradiction." These are the marks of this identification. It is interesting that some psychologists have said that a large proportion of airmen are of this kind, particularly, perhaps, the dare-devil pilots — fighter pilots of the war, test pilots.

Saint-Exupéry was rarely happy except when flying. It was an essential need of his nature — almost as though he were constantly trying to reach his Little Prince, alone and sad on his planet. In the air he felt free of all the deadening smallness and meanness of the ordinary man, of whom he writes with such withering contempt. Even his greatest admirers admit this contemptuous attitude in him. He was a pilot of great skill but caused everyone the greatest anxiety by what was known as his "absent-mindedness." He would forget to let down his undercarriage; lost in his inner dream, he would fly off course and suddenly return to reality to find himself in danger, and so on. There is an unconscious courting of death in such men—a yearning for the bite of the snake that can restore them to the lost child. Finally he did meet death in the air, living out the symbol. His plane was lost over France on the last mission permitted to him in the war. No trace of it was ever found. It just disappeared as the Little Prince's body had disappeared.

He had been, as usual in the case of such personalities, his mother's special favorite, and he adored her all his life. Barrie, too, had this devotion to his mother. In *Peter Pan* the father, Mr. Darling, is shown as stupid, even pettily cruel. Saint-Exupéry's marriage was a stormy, irresponsible affair, as one would expect, of violent quarrels, separations, and equally passionate reconciliations. When separated from his wife he would write movingly of his responsibility for his "poor Consuelo." He genuinely felt it, but he could not live it. He could never live responsibly because he had rejected one-half of the fox's wisdom, and so his delicate perception of real values remained "in the air," constantly threatened by the "sheep." The sheep, double-sided like all archetypal images, is the symbol of both innocence and of the collective stupidity that he so bitterly despised.

The images of his unconscious—the King, the Wise Man, the Practical Worker, the Lover of Play, the Servant—remained forever on their lonely planets, possessive and meaningless to the end. For the child, who could have brought them all to earth, if he had heeded the message of the fox, had chosen to return to his planet. Thus the man could not grow to that true meeting of opposites in which the inner child remains vividly alive but "tamed," related to outer reality. Saint-Exupéry had genius, and he did *not* evade his responsibility to express it. But inevitably his genius did not mature. Perhaps only in *The Little Prince* did it truly come to earth, for in it he describes his own tragedy with power and truth. Many have acclaimed *The Wisdom of the Sands* as his greatest book. He thought so himself. Beautiful as so many of the sayings in it are, it remains somehow remote from humanity and therefore tinged with unreality and sentimentality. In it the king of a desert kingdom speaks all his thoughts about life and its meaning. It is significant that near the beginning of the book the king goes up onto a high tower and *looking down* on men he pities them and resolves to heal them. He then claims to have "embellished the soul of my people." The king is concerned with "people," not individuals. He is alone with his rose to the end. The book's French title is *La Citadelle*—the tower, the fortress, the safe place from which the king looks down on the world.

One such boy-man came for analysis many years ago. His quickness of understanding, his intuitive awareness of the unconscious and eager enthusiasm were full of promise. But he was not seventeen; he was near thirty and had no notion of what it means to accept the responsibility of manhood. Such men often have very great charm, carrying as they do the image of the eternal promise of youth. Older women will forgive them again and again their enormities! This man was continually in and out of jobs, and it was his wife, older than himself, who earned their basic living. As with Saint-Exupéry, partings and reconciliations succeeded each other with bewildering speed. He was not a flier but courted death through reckless driving of cars. When his license was revoked, it never occurred to him to stop driving—the risk just made it a bigger thrill! The taking of wild risks in the outer world is a compensation for the inner refusal to risk the infantile psyche in a meeting with the responsibilities of a man. He made endless good resolutions, with complete sincerity, but they broke down at the touch of reality and the necessity for discipline. Yet how much he knew of a wisdom closed to the dull and respectable! He died violently in an accident. He had returned to his snake, refused to leave his infantile paradise and expose his rose to this world.

The *puer aeternus* personality is rarely met in such extreme form. But for every one of us there is a warning in the images of Saint-Exupéry's story. We need to become conscious of the partial ways in which we identify with and so banish to a lonely planet our inner child. For whatever we identify with is lost to us as a reality. If we will hold to the child's value of innocence and folly while at the same time fully accepting the realities of space and time, and if we will endure the separations through which possessiveness and the demand to be "special" are dissolved, then our feet will be firmly planted on the earth while we watch the stars in their courses. Only then, having emerged from the easy paradise of unconscious childishness, we may "tame" and "be tamed" by the Child within, who brings true uniqueness and ultimate wholeness. This lovely image comes to us in our dreams, grave and gay, wise and innocent, the promise of the beginning and the fullness of the end. "Unless ye become as little children ["become as," not "identify with"] ye shall not enter the Kingdom of Heaven" (Matthew 18:3).

As Jung has written:

> The child is the beginning and the end. . . . The child symbolizes the pre-conscious and the post-conscious nature of man—his wholeness. . . . The child is all that is abandoned and exposed and at the same time divinely powerful; the insignificant, dubious beginning and the triumphant end. The "eternal child" in man is an indescribable experience—an imponderable that determines the ultimate worth or worthlessness of a personality.[2]

NOTES

1. Antoine de Saint-Exupéry, *The Little Prince*, Katherine Woods, tr. (New York: Harcourt, Brace and World, 1943).
2. C.G. Jung, and C. Kerenyi, *Essays on a Science of Mythology* (New York: Harper Torchbooks, 1963), p. 96.

Chapter Thirty

The Novels
of Charles Williams

IN HIS ESSAY "On Stories" published in *Essays Presented to Charles Williams* (Oxford University Press, 1947), C.S. Lewis speaks of the neglect of Story in the modern world, and defines it as a form of literature in which "everything is there for the sake of the story." The novels of Charles Williams are of this kind. The stories they tell are largely concerned with the relationships of men and women to the archetypal powers behind human life, and, like all real stories, they are about individual choices and the interaction of those choices with the operation of fate.

The fascinating thing about a story, in this sense, is that, whereas the characters may not be felt as "real" people, the effect of it on an individual hearer who listens with his whole attention may be so truly real as to sow the seeds of major changes in his way of life— something that surely does not often happen through the novels of so-called realism.

All Williams' novels celebrate the holiness of the flesh, the beauty of matter, and the essential values of feeling. Moreover, like Jung, he leaves us in no doubt of the reality of evil and of the part that it must play in the process of redemption, or individuation, and he points clearly and repeatedly to the *coincidentia oppositorum* in the image of God. His work is a great contribution to the continuing creation of the Christian myth.

Marie-Louise von Franz in *C.G. Jung: His Myth in Our Time* wrote of Jung's life and work:

> Little by little there was being prepared, in the alchemical tradition, a
> fundamental transformation of outlook which is in fact nothing more
> nor less than a new image of God and man, an image which brings the
> official Christian image of God and man into a new fullness and

greater completeness. This transformation is a process in the collective psyche which is a preparation for the new aeon, the Age of Aquarius.

Charles Williams was another creator in this process of transformation, bearing witness to the truth that the new age is to be built not on the destruction of Christianity but on the birth of "a new fullness and completeness" in the Christian myth itself. There are signs that now, almost fifty years after his death, the voice of Charles Williams, heard at first by very few, is being recognized by growing numbers of seekers. Everywhere Christians are becoming conscious individually of the great renewal to which Jung mapped the way, and to many of them Williams may open the door to the vital transformation described by von Franz.

The first five novels—*Shadows of Ecstasy, War in Heaven, Many Dimensions, The Place of the Lion*, and *The Greater Trumps*—were all written between 1929 and 1932; each of them is primarily concerned with the nature and use of power. At the end of his life Williams wrote a final novel, *All Hallows Eve*, in which he returns to the theme of power in the full maturity of his genius. These novels are deeply relevant to the problems of our time, for powers have been given to man in this century—powers over matter and over the psyche which increase yearly and which may very easily destroy him unless he can achieve in time a wholly new attitude to their meaning and use. Moreover, the dangers from the manipulation of the psyche, about which Williams wrote, are even greater than the perils of technology. The novels of Charles Williams, if we will listen inwardly, and not simply enjoy them as wild fantasies, bring us face to face with these horrors, and point to the only way in which they can be met and transformed—through the integrity and humility of single men and women.

SHADOWS OF ECSTASY

The confrontation with the urge to power was obviously of major importance to Charles Williams, as it is for us all, however unconscious of it we may be. It was not by chance that Williams' contemporary and friend, J.R.R. Tolkien in his great story, *The Lord of the Rings*, was also deeply concerned with man's relationship to power. It is indeed the vital question of our age. Shall we use power or sacrifice and transform it? *Shadows of Ecstasy*, the first and least successful of the novels, opens for us this theme.

It is interesting that the mode of power which Williams writes about in this book is the same as that which is the subject of his last novel, *All Hallows Eve*. In both books the world is threatened by a single man who has acquired immense supernatural power through centuries of intense self-discipline and exploration of the "other world" — of the unconscious, as Jung would say — which is the source of all power. Considine in *Shadows of Ecstasy* and Simon in *All Hallows Eve* have suspended the laws of mortality, and, living on and on, they seek the ultimate conquest of death. Contemptuous of every living soul, Considine sincerely and Simon hypocritically, proclaim that if the world can be brought under their personal domination it will be for the good of all and will produce peace on earth; moreover both men dream of extending their dominion over souls in the world beyond death. They have reached this high degree of psychic power by denying, it is true, all the smaller greeds and demands of the ego, but at the same time, in their unbounded *hubris* they have fed the ego's overmastering demand to possess the Omnipotence. Both characters share the same delusion, but there is a great difference between Nigel Considine and Simon the Clerk. It is probably a measure of the change which took place in Williams himself. He had made a deep study of the occult in those early years, and it is clear that in *Shadows of Ecstasy* he has not yet discovered that the use of psychic power in the service of "good" must lead inevitably to its opposite.

Considine is shown as a man of immense charismatic charm and of real wisdom, and he retains this aura right up to and beyond the moment of his death by treachery. Roger Ingram, who, like Williams himself, is a lover of poetry, longs to become Considine's disciple. Roger's aim is not personal power but the ecstasy from which all poetry springs, and Considine can open the door for him to this. At the end of Williams' life he exposes in the character of Simon the horror at the root of all *hubris*, of all power-seeking.

The fascination emanating from Considine is easily credible to any reader with even a small awareness of the numinosity of the unconscious, and the description of Roger's plunge into the "ocean" must surely describe Williams' personal experience of ecstasy. The great danger to which Roger and all like him are exposed is that of failure to see until too late the evil underlying the experience of ecstasy when it is *used* to exert any kind of influence over people and things, and also when it is sought as an end in itself (as, for instance, when induced by drugs). In *All Hallows Eve* all such "glamour" has been outgrown.

Considine has trained and organized the black masses of Africa to take over the civilized world using the weapon of mass panic against which people collectively have no defense. He demands capitulation under the threat of complete destruction; perhaps at the time of its writing this might have seemed like crude sensationalism, but the history of the last sixty years makes it almost commonplace. Hitler had not been heard of in 1929, but ten years later he was to demonstrate to the world the almost inconceivable evils which follow when power is delivered into the hands of one man possessed by the unconscious. How much more devastating that power would be if wielded, not by an unconscious fanatic, but by a cultured, highly educated "old wise man"! Gandalf in *The Lord of the Rings*, when Frodo offered him the Ring of Power with the words, "You are wise and powerful. Will you not take the Ring?" replied, "No! With that power I should have power too great and terrible. And over me the Ring would gain a power still greater and more deadly. . . . Do not tempt me!" Considine is a corrupted Gandalf.

Moreover the power of the long-repressed and despised instinctive forces in our world—the black masses—once harnessed to a highly developed conscious mind using the resources of modern science and technology may indeed destroy us all. The number of thrillers which are written nowadays around this theme of one man's bid to take over absolute power is highly significant. "Magical" technology takes the place of the Ring of Power, but, whatever the means, power itself operates through an individual's manipulation of the unconscious forces in his fellow men. A society in which spiritual values are degraded to a search for "good" through social welfare or group activities inevitably feeds the power drive in men. The refusal of the conscious way of individuation means the rise of individualism in a few leaders and the regression of the majority to sheep-like imitation. (There is growing, however, in these later years of our century a wonderful revival in the midst of the darkening of values, in some of the popular science fiction programs. For instance, *Star Trek: The Next Generation*, in incident after incident, stresses the triumph of the values of true human feeling, compassion, and respect for all life. So hope and wonder are restored and technology is seen as a means and not an end.)

The emphasis in Charles Williams' books is always, as has been said, not on the collective happenings themselves, but on the response of each man's psyche to the images of power. The characters in this first novel foreshadow many of these varied individual responses to the threat or temptation of power which Williams develops with such depth of insight in the later stories. Most of the people concerned are ordinary men and women without any special degree of virtue or vice. They are saved or destroyed by what one might call the balance of their choices — their marginal willingness to use or to forego power.

Sir Bernard, the retired surgeon in the book, is an agnostic, a person of great intellectual integrity, who quite consciously refuses to involve himself with any irrational forces that defy reason, but who will not condemn those who differ from him. He is thinking to himself, on hearing Roger commit himself to support Considine's bid for power, "A man had come out into the open from behind the fronds and leaves and it was Roger. A trumpet had answered the horns and drums that were crying to the world from the jungle of man's being, and the trumpet was Roger's voice. Was Africa then within?" (p. 114)

Here is the explicit affirmation of that truth which alone can change the world. "A man had come out into the open . . ." The voice of one man was the "trumpet" answering the forces of the unconscious with his individual choice. So we are faced, if we will hear, with the measure of our responsibility and at the same time with an intuition of the profound dignity of what it means to be a man with freedom to choose.

We are made to feel that Roger, who is a university lecturer on poetry, has chosen rightly for himself. He is blind to the evil core of Considine's will to power but in his choice he has been true to the deepest of his inner voices at that time, and through it he is released from the dangers of the superficial intellect and affirms his allegiance to the reality of *meaning* in the poetry he loves. The "trumpet" of the voice which has responded to the darkness within will sound out into the world when he has emerged transformed from his dangerous journey, and he will carry to his hearers the word of meaning instead of the mere wordiness of arid intellectual criticism.

Sir Bernard knew that the intellect could not encompass ultimate truth, but he gave also his full devotion to that aspect of truth which he loved and served. It is his "prayer" that is the vital thing, wherever our devotion may lead us in this world. Whether our selfless love is given to poetry, to scholarship, to relationship, to psychology or religion, to the work of our hands or minds or hearts, the prayer is the same—that the object of our love may "turn the light of its awful integrity upon us and preserve us from self-deception and greediness and infidelity and fear." (p. 121) As long as we are aware, as Sir Bernard was, that a dedication of this kind is not the whole truth, our devotion is saved from the danger of exclusiveness, which is the mark of "possession" by the unconscious.

It was Considine's failure to make that prayer that brought him into his treacherous self-deception. He sought to transcend the Christ by rejecting the death on the cross, by denying the necessity of defeat as essential to victory. He had indeed succumbed, though he denied it, to the third temptation of Christ. Satan had "showed him all the kingdoms of the world and the glory of them" and had said to him, "these things will I give thee if thou wilt fall down and worship me." Considine worshipped the collective "good" and denied the "awful integrity" of every least individual's right to choose, and so was lost. Roger's longing at the end that, beyond all hope, Considine would return from the dead is a hint of the journey to self-knowledge that still lies ahead for Roger himself. The resurrection and rebirth of the whole man within him will come to him only when he has accepted defeat and death.

Among the lesser characters in the novel, Ian Caithness is an Anglican priest who truly lives by his creed and is prepared to make any sacrifice for it. Nevertheless his inability to "encounter darkness" makes him half-consciously condone a murder. He lives by an outer creed that he does not dare fully to explore within, and so is betrayed into that deadly thing, the encouragement of an evil thing for the benefit of a cause.

Rosamund is a young woman who is moved only by her greed and her infantile desires. She shrinks even from love when it seeks any real response from her; she hates and fears Considine and the Zulu king Inkamasi, while at the same time she is unconsciously attracted and swallowed by her dark impulses. Williams gives us an image of her when she was a child, greedily gobbling a whole box of chocolates in secret. As she grew she covered her greediness with a facade, but she could not fight nor evade her unacknowledged greed — so she both hated and longed for the instinctive response. "Power was in her and she was terrified of it."

The Zulu king Inkamasi reveals for us the nobility and tragedy of a man who is identified with a great role and who is incapable of finding the image within himself. He will die rather than live without the power of his royalty. The ritual death to which Considine forces the king's will is a fascinating exposure of Considine's own much more fatal error. He has dominated the mind of the king so that he may be brought to this sacrificial death. He is entirely blind to the fact that by putting Inkamasi to death he is demonstrating his own refusal to accept the sacrifice of personal power.

Isabel, Roger's wife, is the first of Williams' mature women, who recur in most of the novels. Channels for the Power and the Glory, wells of the "wise water" of the unconscious, they have finally transcended the possessiveness of feminine love, which for women is the instrument of power *par excellence*. Isabel manipulates no one, least of all her husband, and so the power in her is transformed into love. She was constantly provoked by the selfishness of her sister, by what was, to her, the obvious blindness in her husband, by natural fear of the threat to her own and Roger's lives; but worst of all she must have known a temptation to jealousy of an exceedingly painful kind, when Considine's hold on Roger took him away from her not only physically but emotionally. Yet, in spite of all this provocation, she never fell, as most women would have fallen, into protest or any kind of assertion of opinion through her animus. This function had become in her the true masculine discriminating spirit, disciplining but never stifling her heart. She spoke her mind quietly, as when she suggested to Considine that his elimination of the value of defeat was a fallacy, but she never imposed her opinion or even expressed it at the wrong moments (as the animus is so prone to do). She knew that Roger whom she loved must follow his own way, must find for himself the way to greater consciousness. She urged him to follow his passionate urge to be with Considine, because she loved him, not for what he could give her, but for himself. She was in truth a woman, one-in-herself.

WAR IN HEAVEN

"And there was war in heaven: Michael and his angels fought against the dragon; and the dragon fought and his angels, and prevailed not." (Revelation 12:7-8) The dragon and his angels were thereupon cast out of heaven into the earth. But to the earth also there had come down out of heaven "the kingdom of our God and the power of his Christ;" so that men overcame the dragon "by the blood of the Lamb and by the word of their testimony; and they loved not their lives unto the death." (Revelation 12:10-11)

The theme of Williams' second novel *War in Heaven* is as its title proclaims, but again the author sees the great cosmic battle as it is fought in the lives of a few individuals on earth. Indeed the writer of Revelation himself, no doubt unconsciously, hints that only on this battlefield within the human soul is the war resolved. The battle in Heaven had resulted in the expulsion of the dragon, but with him the son of God also descended out of Heaven. Official Christianity interpreted the overcoming of the dragon on earth as an even greater rejection, whereby it was hoped that he could be eliminated altogether; the conflict, far from being resolved, was thereby greatly accentuated.

In the work of both C.G. Jung and of Charles Williams, we are brought face to face with the reality of evil, and are made aware of the true nature of the fight with the dragon on earth in which a man, through blood and the word, may heal the split in creation by confronting but refusing to repress and reject evil. When a single man or woman is ready to give his life "unto the death" in the service of the "word of his testimony," his own consciousness of truth, then the "word is made flesh" within him and he makes his lonely contribution to the resolving of the conflict here and in the beyond.

In this second novel, the two protagonists are symbolic of this battlefield; the "power of his Christ" lives in the Archdeacon, and the power of Lucifer in Gregory Persimmons. Both men have followed their chosen Lords for many years before the story opens, and both have reached a high degree of selfless devotion to that which they worship. This sounds an odd thing to say about Gregory Persimmons, who uses every person and thing to get what he wants, even when it involves murder and the destruction of the soul of a child. But the word "selfless" here has quite a different meaning from the term "unselfish." The Archdeacon was selfless because there were no hidden motives of greed left in him, and he had reached an awareness of the Christ, which precluded all use of power to manipulate life. Persimmons was equally selfless in his devotion to the Lord of Destruction, the dark brother of Christ; but at the very heart of that devotion is the search for power to destroy all that opposes the desired ends. Devotion to the Christ is inclusive—it embraces the validity of the dark and the right of every man to make his own choices; devotion to Satan is exclusive, seeking always to swallow the light and to eliminate choice.

Both Persimmons and the Archdeacon seek union with that which is beyond themselves, the source of power, but the Archdeacon never uses any artificial means to come to that union; he simply attends moment by moment to the giving of his conscious consent to the movement of the Omnipotence within him and without. In contrast, Gregory's whole concern is to contrive a deepening of his mystical experience by one use of power after another. For this he seeks the magical ointment, for this he steals the Grail and plots the offering of a child's soul to his Lord. Yet in Gregory's soul, too, at the very end, there is a dawning of the inclusive vision; for all the evil that he has wrought is at bottom an offering, however misdirected. At the moment of his utter defeat, he learns that no man can sacrifice anything but himself, and live. He gives himself up to the police, confessing to the murder he has committed, and for this he will hang, and so has the chance to pay with the offering of his own life.

The figure of Prester John in this book is an image of the *psycho-pompos*, the union of opposites, the Great Man within. He is Priest and King, having power in both inner and outer worlds, a power which becomes manifest in and through the individual's choices.

In the last analysis all men seek what Jung called the Self and unconsciously strive for wholeness and a return to the lost Paradise. It has been said that the religious instinct, which is the longing for wholeness, is perhaps a deeper and more universal urge even than hunger. But there is no way back through an infantile longing for the unconscious paradise. That way leads inevitably to the exclusive affirmation of the destructive aspect of the Self. The way to conscious return lies through blood and the word, through sacrifice and rebirth.

The story involves the finding of the Holy Grail (Williams spells it "Graal") in the Archdeacon's ancient parish church of Fardles. The legendary cup of the Last Supper is a living symbol. It is the container of the mystery of sacrifice, of death and resurrection, and as such it has become, as the Archdeacon recognizes, a material center of power, as do all objects onto which have been projected the love of generations of men. The attitude of the seekers after wholeness towards it reveals at every stage in the story the great gulf between the two kinds of devotion. For Gregory wholeness means the destruction of the light by the dark power; for the Archdeacon it is the unity of the light and the dark, known through sacrifice and the lifelong quest for consciousness. The distorted Christian attitude which tries to eliminate the evil thing by repression, and by the use of power for "good" ends, is in fact a kind of inverted Satan worship, rendering more powerful the evil it would deny.

Gregory is determined to possess the Grail in order, through his inner concentration and the magical rituals of Satanism, to reach its center of power and to use it to gain control of the soul of the child, Adrian, and offer it to his Lord. This is a symbol of the universal truth that only when we become as little children can we enter the "kingdom." Gregory and those like him, refusing the sacrifice of the ego's power, seek to fulfill this inner need through vicarious sacrifice, and that which the Satanists practice deliberately is present to some degree in all the unconscious projections whereby we evade responsibility.

Gregory first tries to trick the Archdeacon into selling the cup; then he steals it, physically injuring the priest. The Grail is passive, responding to the human will that seeks it, as Prester John affirms, until at the end Gregory and his fellows (who have gone much further than he on the way of destruction) set it on the breast of the bound Archdeacon and attempt through its power to bind the psyche of a murdered man to the psyche of the priest, so that his individual identity will be destroyed. This is the ultimate evil, the deliberate attempt to destroy the individual, and because of this their will touches the center of the Grail's power, as it rests over the heart of the true lover of wholeness. The cup blazes into life and the evil destroys itself and those who, beyond all human emotion, were wholly abandoned to it. They have sought destruction, and the Grail, which gives every man his fundamental desire, gives them

destruction. But Gregory who was still capable of devotion, however distorted, is awakened and choice is restored to him.

The Archdeacon's attitudes and actions may easily be glossed over
in the excitement of the story and of the descriptions of magical
practices; but if we meditate on them at leisure they may shed
penetrating light on our daily choices.

We meet him first in the Persimmons publishing office. He has
written a book; and, while he shows normal interest and pleasure in
the possibility of its publication, it is at once clear that here is a man
who does not seek power or prestige for his ego. "Whether you
publish it or not, whether anyone publishes it or not, doesn't matter
much. I think it might matter if I made no attempt to get it published,
for I honestly think the ideas are sound. But with that very small
necessary activity my responsibility ends." (p. 32) These two sentences may seem simple, but implicit in them is the fundamental
attitude to life of a man committed to the quest of the Self—the
inclusive devotion. *Results* are of no importance for such a man
except in so far as they may contribute to his self-knowledge (in both
senses of the word); the thing that intensely matters is his responsibility for the necessary action of the moment. The point is clear; an
attribution of importance to the results of our actions is at bottom a
demand for power, and therefore a deviation from the Way.

Such an attitude requires a very high degree of attention and
accurate discrimination. It is in no way, as many may think, a woolly
tolerance or an indifference to what is going on in the environment.
The Archdeacon's thoughts and comments about people and ideas
are extremely pungent, and in situation after situation we may note
his accuracy and decisiveness, his enormous charity combined with
clear-sighted judgment and his assertion of authority whenever the
inner and outer "necessity" are one.

Before leaving this novel, it is interesting to look at Charles Williams' Christianity and his relationship with the Church. Obviously,
as has been said, his Christian faith was the foundation of his life and
work, but it is a Christianity very different from that of the majority
of churchmen. He would have said that Christian dogma was the
most accurate of all formulations of the truths of being, but he
excluded none of the other ways to God. He loved the Anglican
Church and knew it to be his way—but he always also said, with the
Hindu sages, "This also is Thou—neither is this Thou."

Christianity for Williams lay in the essence of a human life. T.S. Eliot wrote in his introduction to *All Hallows Eve*:

> No one was less confined to conventional morality, in judging good and bad behavior, than Williams: his morality is that of the Gospels. He sees the struggle between Good and Evil as carried on, more or less blindly, by men and women who are often only the instruments of higher or lower powers, but who always have the freedom to choose to which powers they will submit themselves. (p. xvi)

It therefore need not surprise us that the intense and profound Christianity that informs all the novels is rarely defined in the usual Christian language.

Prester John, speaking at the end of *War in Heaven* of church-going, said, "It is a means, one of the means. But perhaps the best for most, and for some almost the only one. I do not say that it matters greatly, but the means cannot both be and not be. If you do not use it, it is a pity to bother about it; if you do, it is a pity not to use it." (p. 249) The church was for Williams a great and numinous symbol of the co-inherence of all men with each other and with the center of all. But he surely never conceived of the Body of Christ as *confined* to any institution whatsoever.

MANY DIMENSIONS

In this novel following *War in Heaven*, the image carrying the same meaning as the Grail is a stone. In Wolfram von Eschenbach's poem *Parzifal*, the Grail itself is called a stone; in *Many Dimensions* the stone is a small half-inch cube, appearing whitish with hints of gold and dark markings which are the four letters of the Tetragrammaton, the Hebrew name of God. The four letters are not marked on the outer surfaces, they are an integral part of the stone itself. This stone is set in a gold circlet said to have been the Crown of Solomon, and it has been guarded in its long seclusion from the world by a noble Moslem family, dedicated from generation to generation, sworn to the utmost secrecy and forbidden ever to use it.

This is the *lapis* of alchemy in which all opposites are one; it is at once the *prima materia* of creation and the final unity for which all men yearn. Like the Grail it therefore brings strife and, ultimately, death and destruction to those who seek to possess and to use it, while to those who refuse all such temptation it is the light and the Way; and if anyone is able to give him or herself to it in a total surrender of will and desire, it is a door through darkness and the experience of a crucifixion to the Unity. It is called by Hajji Ibrahim in the book "the End of Desire."

We have met these themes already in *War in Heaven*, but in *Many Dimensions* there is a difference of emphasis. In the earlier book our attention is largely focussed on the two protagonists, Persimmons and the Archdeacon, both of whom are aware of the nature of the power which the one seeks to use and the other guards. The lesser characters are a supporting cast. But in *Many Dimensions*, though indeed the world is in danger of destruction through Sir Giles Tumulty and is saved through Chloe Burnett and Lord Arglay, our interest is held by a large number of characters in the book, ordinary men and women, sincere and devious, greedy and generous, through all of whom the power of the stone spreads outward into the world. Even Sir Giles and Chloe are nearer to our own states of consciousness than such experienced adepts as Persimmons and the Archdeacon.

Superficially read, *Many Dimensions* may seem loaded with "magical" happenings, but it contains a great deal of practical wisdom for us all, exposing for us, if we have ears to hear, the terror and ugliness, the beauty and joy of the forces underlying our daily choices, and revealing the profound implications of so many of our casual assumptions and demands. The seeming "magic" wrought by the stone merely dramatizes and makes real to us through imagination the working of the unconscious in our lives.

It is significant that in both *Many Dimensions* and *War in Heaven*, the mystery is brought out of seclusion and let loose upon the world through the agency of the same character, Sir Giles Tumulty (who plays a minor role in the previous novel). He has bought the stone from a corrupt member of the Moslem family purely in order to experiment with it, and he is the epitome of the scientific spirit of our age, so admirable in its objectivity, and so deadly when divorced from feeling. We cannot, however, blame our predicament on science or technology or on the apostles of "progress." Always it is the individual who is responsible for his own choices, and individuals who create the spirit of the age. The scientific attitude can bring to each of us either objective vision or cold inhumanity.

Sir Giles' devotion is given to scientific enquiry to the exclusion of any other value whatsoever, and to the extent that it remains a selfless dedication, however horrible the cruelties that are its side-effects, it must, Williams says, command a measure of respect. But the human emotions ruthlessly repressed by such a man build up slowly in the unconscious until they suddenly burst out and possess him. Thus he is immediately exposed to the destructive power of that which is the end of all desire. Tumulty is a traitor to his own scientific coldness in his overwhelming hatred of Lord Arglay and of Chloe, and, trying to use the stone to destroy them, his gaze is drawn at last to the deep center of that mystery where, instead of knowing the unity, he is torn in pieces, divided "nerve from nerve, sinew from sinew, bone from bone." "When they found him he was lying on the floor . . . twisted in every limb, and pierced and burnt all over as if by innumerable needle-points of fire." Similarly, in our own time, the penetration by scientists to the secrets of the atom (which is indeed a symbol of the *prima materia*) has disastrously brought repression of the heart in innumerable individuals, and has therefore produced the threat of total destruction. Laurens van der Post points out that Jung's penetration to the essence of the psychic "atom" at the same period of time is a complete parallel in the inner world: the way is opened through the growth of consciousness and the affirmation of human feeling values to the end of the split between the two worlds of matter and spirit.

The image in *Many Dimensions* is exact. The mystery of the Stone, of the "First Matter," has been evoked and is being *used* with power motives in the outer world and with complete disregard of its potential meaning within. The revenge of the repressed emotions today is everywhere apparent—the violence in our cities, the ever-growing incidence of psychoses, the mass-produced "magic" solutions to every kind of problem, and the underlying fear that a violent emotion might one day move some politician to press the button releasing atomic war.

All these things are implicit in *Many Dimensions*, but out of the darkness shines the way of salvation. Through individuals the mystery, as Jung also affirmed, is returned to its place at the center of creation from which it has been wrenched by the greed of those who seek power.

Lord Arglay, Chief Justice of England, and Chloe Burnett, a young, ordinary, middle-class girl who is his secretary, are the two who, through their individual integrity and through the love and respect which grows between them, become the conscious way of salvation for the world on the edge of disaster. For though it is true, as Williams and Eliot say, that each man is free to choose whether he will submit himself to this or that power, it is also true that vast numbers of men are as yet so unconscious as to be the "little ones" of Christ's warning. "It is impossible but that offenses will come, but woe unto him through whom they come. It were better for him that a millstone were hanged about his neck, and he cast into the sea, than that he should offend one of these little ones." (Luke 17: 2) The little ones are not only children; they are the unconscious victims of the conscious and half-conscious manipulators—not in the sense that any man's individual identity can be ultimately destroyed by any person or collective force without his own consent, but certainly victims in that they are exposed through the unconscious to forces beyond their strength and so to untold sufferings in this world.

These sufferings, and the mistakes, desires, betrayals and loyalties of the little ones are a major element in this book, and Williams defines again with extraordinary penetration the essential difference between the way in which the users of power, "good" as well as "bad," work on the unconscious of others, and the way in which the saviors among men affect it.

The effects of Sir Giles' ruthless experiments spread in widening circles. He will never involve himself in any real risk, and so he first plays on the avarice of his nephew Montague, whose sole interest in the Stone is to make money out of it. Through Montague he proves that the Stone can transport a man through space in a few moments to wherever he wishes to be, and he also discovers that it can be divided and redivided and that each chip becomes a complete cube, identical in every respect with the original without changing the original at all. Each "new" stone is a replica of the first and contains all the same powers. Like the Atman in India, like the Self and the Christ image, it is one and many—a symbol of that which is at the same time the whole and unique in every individual.

Montague secretly sells a Stone to an American millionaire, who owns an airline, and who wants it, not knowing of its divisibility, to ensure the safety of the ordinary means of transport, and also as a toy for his spoiled and shallow wife. All he knows about it is its ability to move people in space. Thus the spreading of the danger begins. By a series of "accidents" it is lost and comes into the hands of a bedridden old woman, who happens to express her longing to walk again — and she rises up and walks. The news spreads like wildfire through the village. The only thing these people know about the Stone is that it heals; so all the sick now clamor to obtain it.

Simultaneously a transport trades union official has got wind of it, and, realizing that, if multiplied, it constitutes a threat to the livelihood of hundreds of thousands of workers, appeals to the government to suppress it. The politicians are at their wits' end. The Americans have reestablished their ownership of the Stone that began the healings, but the Mayor of the village concerned is calling for its release in the name of the sick and the suffering. The politicians cleverly play off the transport official against the Mayor, making clear that the good of the one is the destruction of the other's good; but at the same time they plot to keep the Stone in secret and use it in the power politics of the world. They are frustrated by Sir Giles who cares nothing for the sick, for the worker, or for world wars either. The Stone is his and he is going to continue to experiment with it, come what may.

All this defines exactly the forces at work in the pursuit of power, and the inevitability of discord, strife, and war so long as human beings seek either to use a truth or to suppress it. If we *demand* healing or any other supposed good for ourselves or for others we also constellate its opposite somewhere, however ignorant of this we may remain; if we seek security through deceit and evasion we invite an equal danger. The politicians in the novel even produce an imitation Stone and say the power of it has been exhausted, hoping secretly to steal the power for the so-called good of the State.

We may watch these things at work in our world. The apostles of healing, in all its forms, like the Mayor, so often seek to abolish suffering and conflict rather than to evoke wholeness, and succeed only in shifting a symptom from one place to another. A good doctor or teacher or a real priest is one who follows his calling because he loves it for its own sake — not because he has a mission to save people. The latter attitude is the root of all the horrors of religious wars and persecutions. Nowadays we are exhorted by every sort of propaganda to adopt innumerable panaceas which will solve our problems and make us happy, attempts to use the Stone to heal all human woes, and in each individual who succumbs to them they generate a darker shadow than before.

On the other hand, moved by greed and fear, men who resemble the millionaire and the transport official seek to hide and suppress new consciousness and the knowledge which may undermine their exercise of power or their sources of wealth, and in an individual this fear can prevent all growth in conscious awareness because he refuses to pay the price. Meanwhile the power of the ruling collective attitudes, symbolized by the politician and the egotist-scientist, increases to our downfall.

Only Chloe's absolute refusal to use the Stone for any conceivable purpose — even to save her life, even to save herself a bus fare — brings release from the growing danger. The latter is perhaps the more difficult and rarely achieved refusal.

Chloe Burnett from her first glimpse of the Stone has felt a growing love and wonder; she has recognized the essence of the beauty and wholeness it embodies. She is an ordinary young woman without any specific religious beliefs, but she intuitively knows the Power and the Glory when she sets eyes on its image, there in Lord Arglay's study. In her is made manifest the utmost purity of feminine devotion and willingness to suffer. But this by itself, we are made aware, would not avail to reach the center of the Stone. She could not possibly have made her offering without the clear masculine discrimination and the equal integrity of Lord Arglay's consciously accepted authority. From a psychological point of view we may think of Chloe as a symbol of Lord Arglay's projected anima, and Lord Arglay as a symbol of Chloe's animus, but we must beware of letting such analytical thought destroy the equal truth of the need for free exchange between two actual individuals, which is the beauty of this story. Chloe and Lord Arglay recognize and respect in each other their opposite strengths.

Lord Arglay is a character of the same kind as Sir Bernard in *Shadows of Ecstasy*, but more deeply seen and described. Not by chance is he the Chief Justice of England. He does not know if he believes in God; he does not yet affirm the Mercy, in Williams' phrase, though he is indeed a merciful man, but he is certain of what he calls Organic Law. In fact he is writing a book about it. An organism is a fundamental "whole having interdependent parts" (according to the *Oxford English Dictionary*), such as a living body. Organic Law is therefore something that springs out of the nature of life itself and may be given a structure by human consciousness, and it is distinct from inorganic laws, which are invented by man to preserve society or to serve some end.

The power manifest in the Stone was clearly of this organic nature, therefore Lord Arglay with his devotion to justice could never be persuaded to use it for himself or for a cause. "There is no case beyond law," the Chief Justice answered. "We may mistake in the ruling, we may be deceived by outward things and cunning talk, but there is no dispute between men which cannot be resolved in equity. And in its nature equity is from those between whom it exists: it is passion acting in lucidity." (p. 150) This kind of equity must remain forever unknown to those who, in adversity, protest, "It isn't fair!" It cannot exist until the will to use people and things is dead.

Though he would never use the stone for a purpose, nevertheless Lord Arglay will *act* within it out of his central passion for equity, directed by the lucidity of his conscious choice. But before he can do this he must decide, he knows, what to believe. Like the Archdeacon in *War in Heaven*, he insists that beliefs must be consciously decided upon. This probably means that in matters inaccessible to reason a man must affirm their validity by a detached conscious decision, not merely by emotional participation. Faced with the ultimate mysteries of life we recognize the incapacity of human consciousness ever to know the absolute nature of God; but we must at all costs remain free of blind belief, for in that blindness all lucidity is lost and passion becomes fanatical emotion. At the same time we must be equally free of that cold logic which despises belief in the indefinable, for then there can be no passion, and lucidity of the intellect becomes another kind of blindness.

Chloe left to herself can only know that she loves the Stone, for that is the mainspring of her nature; Lord Arglay by himself can only be true to his clarity of judgment, through which he sees that the whole thing is either romantic sentimentality or else something "extreme and terrible" behind which of necessity lies a truth beyond reason. He comes to his decision out of his passion for justice and his need to oppose by his own lucid action the treachery and cruelty and injustice of Giles Tumulty. But he cannot believe without Chloe, nor she without him. Her love must inform his justice, his clear authority must direct her love. Therefore he says to her that if she will believe in God, so also will he, and together they will stand against Sir Giles Tumulty and his evil works, for indifferent they cannot remain. Not yet admitted to the direct experience of that which is beyond the Stone, they decide to *believe* that God exists.

All this sounds strange to our ears, accustomed as we are to thinking that beliefs either arise spontaneously or else that they are delusions to which people cling for safety. We are, as Charles Williams repeatedly makes clear, inaccurate. Such unconscious beliefs are forces possessing us and lead always therefore to possessive desires for some kind of power. We can only safely believe in what we do not yet know by experience if we are at all times ready to discover that our beliefs may prove invalid.

There is a vital message here for those on the way of individuation. Seeking an always deeper awareness of the Self, of the Stone, through conscious confrontation with the unconscious and the experience of the opposites, and glimpsing the goal in their union, we may easily close our minds to that which may exist beyond all our experience in this life of the Self. Man cannot know what God is in Himself; he can only know his own inner experience of the Self and his own image of God; yet all truly wise and conscious men in every age have chosen to believe that beyond the battle between good and evil, beyond the logic of the opposites in the Stone, there is that which Charles Williams called "The Mercy," in the unfathomable mystery of the godhead. It is symbolized by the point of light, referred to in both these books and indeed in all religions, which blazes out for an instant when the central mystery of the opposites is touched. In this Light, beyond the marriage of dark and light we can "decide to believe," when once we are wholly committed to accept every fact of the universe as it is, not as we would have it to be.

Near the end of the book the "exchange" between Lord Arglay and Chloe deepens, culminating in her offering of herself under his direction to be a way for the Stone, so that it may reabsorb into itself all the types that are abroad in the world. Jung has spoken scathingly of that arrogant assumption of the ego, "where there's a will there's a way." To put the will of the ego first is deluded arrogance and precludes any finding of the way. Chloe having recognized the necessity of her way freely wills it. So the Stone returns to the center within, where individuals who have grown to wholeness may in

God's time unite with its power in safety, and the horrible danger, which arises when its numinous power is constellated in the unconscious of the masses, is averted. Immature as she was on the Way, Chloe was the chosen one because she chose, when her fate offered her the opportunity, to love instead of to use the Stone, and also, no less important, because she loved the authority of the Spirit, as incarnate in the Chief Justice, whom she also personally loved.

In the presence of the great supra-personal images Williams never allows us to forget this for a moment: Chloe and Christopher Arglay have found personal love; a future of very great human happiness might have come to them. Yet both of them, while affirming this love, know that they must let it go; at the same time it is abundantly clear that without it they could never have embraced the greater love.

Chloe's body is broken as she holds the Stone in her hand and it passes through her to its place. Matter as it is known in time cannot yet stand the impact of eternity. We cannot know how often the world is actually saved through just such an offering made by just such a single obscure person, who has refused to use power for the satisfaction of even the smallest desire; but we may be very sure that it is so, and give thanks in our hearts.

THE PLACE OF THE LION

The Place of the Lion is the story of how a young man, Anthony Durrant, comes to a moment in his life when he dares to affirm his authority as an individual in the face of the unleashed powers of the collective unconscious. It should be made clear at the outset that the word "authority" is not used here in the sense of an assertion of the ego's will, but rather as descriptive of a quality inherent in an individual. The word "author" means an originator, a creator, and when we say that a man is an authority in his particular field of knowledge, we mean that he has penetrated imaginatively to the heart of his subject, not that he simply has information about it. To have authority in this sense over oneself therefore means, not that a man is rigidly controlling himself according to a set of rules, but that he has achieved real self-knowledge, which includes conscious and unconscious areas of the psyche, and he has therefore become a creator: "He taught them as one that had authority, and not as the scribes." (Mark 1: 22)

At the beginning of *The Place of the Lion*, the great Powers which are the archetypes of being have escaped from their place in the order of the universe and are roaming the English countryside in their animal forms. Anthony Durrant says, " . . . perhaps the authority which is in me over me shall be in me over them." He is replying to Mr. Foster, who has affirmed that the whole world will be absorbed back into the powers behind Creation, and that each man will either be joined willingly to that power which he best serves and desires, or, if he runs away, will be hunted by it to his destruction. Foster adds that it is absolutely impossible for anyone to resist the imminent end of the world, now that the breach has been made between this world and that.

How has that breach been made? Once more Charles Williams points to the power-seeking of one man. We are told nothing of Berringer's character in this novel, but it is plain that, like Tumulty in *Many Dimensions* and Persimmons in *War in Heaven*, he must have sought to experience the inner world and experiment with its powers without accepting the discipline of self-knowledge and the purging of the will, symbolized by Dante's journey through Hell and Purgatory. Even though Berringer may not be a cold manipulator like Tumulty, nor a Satan-worshipper like Persimmons, it is certain that his will is not "free, upright and whole," because the great powers evoked by him are let loose, uncontrolled, into the outer world, or, as we should say, into the unconscious of those around him. We may guess that he is like so many well-meaning people who experiment with numinous phenomena, calling them experiences of the Spirit. Anthony and Quentin, watching at his gate, see him pacing to meet the manifest image of the Lion, and falling into a coma or trance, as the beast enters into him. This is another warning of the extreme danger of even seemingly sincere efforts to experience the archetypal world, before the will to power of the ego has been purged.

Lying in his house, Berringer becomes a gateway whereby the Angelic Orders of being may invade the natural order of matter and enter the sphere of man. All the animals and creatures, the material images of their archetypes, are now drawn to their originals and absorbed by them. We see, with Anthony and Quentin, the escaped lioness from the circus merge with the great Lion. With Mr. Tighe and Anthony we watch the huge and gloriously beautiful archetypal butterfly rising and falling over Berringer's garden, as thousands upon thousands of ordinary butterflies fly swiftly to meet it and disappear into their own specific image of the "End of Desire." But all this is merely the prelude to the invasion of man. Beginning with Berringer's immediate circle of students, men and women begin to see the beasts in their original forms, and each individual is overwhelmingly attracted to, or pursued by, that Power which has been, within him or her, the "End of Desire."

Foster, in whom aggression and anger have long held undisputed, if hidden, sway, chooses with fierce excitement to unite himself with the nature of the Lion; Miss Wilmot, the seemingly harmless little woman, is fascinated by the apparition of the Snake, and her long repressed, venomous jealousies and hatreds take possession of her until she almost becomes the Snake. Having delivered up their souls, the bodies of these two are hideously killed by the archetypes of their desires. They have chosen to be one with the subhuman, to give up the "good of intellect" in Dante's phrase; they have refused the agony of the individual way, and with this refusal they destroy the dignity and meaning of the human body itself, which in the language of myth is made in the image of God. Such people may in fact go on living on this earth, but their wills are in bondage to the powers of the unconscious and their bodies are empty shells inhabited by ghosts (as in Canto XXXIII of Dante's *Inferno*).

People at the other end of the moral scale are likewise irresistibly drawn to their desire. Mr. Tighe, the entomologist, true lover of butterflies, passes, after his vision of the return of the butterflies to their archetype, into a complete withdrawal from every outer concern with people or things; he is absorbed into his worship of Beauty itself as he saw it in the Butterfly, just as Foster was absorbed by the strength of ferocity he knew in the Lion, and Miss Wilmot by the subtlety and venom of the Snake. There is however a vital difference. Mr. Tighe, unlike the other two, is not seeking *power* over others in his worship. He is therefore received gently into his rapture, his body dying peacefully in his bed. But he too has surely refused wholeness, for he has been content to unite with a part, albeit glorious, of reality. He has abandoned all responsibility for exchange with other human beings. He even pushes his daughter away when she appeals to him in her fear. He is uncorrupted by power, but has rejected the authority which alone brings individuation.

It is possible that Williams is saying here that we only survive in the Beyond as *individuals* to the extent that we have taken up the responsibility which is expressed in the myth by the words, "and God gave man dominion over the beasts of the field and the fowls of the air." This is what it means to be human—neither angel nor beast, and it is very certain that no such "dominion" can ever be exercised by man except by the discipline of responsibility in community with other people, whereby we know ourselves and renounce personal power. Only so, emerging again into the innocence of the Earthly Paradise, is man crowned Lord over himself and over creation. Yet at every stage of our journey, if only we are true to the commitment we have made, we too may contribute in our small choices toward a healing of the breaches through which men are constantly exposed to psychic invasion in the present age; for the old rituals which were man's protection, and were a safe bridge to the experience of the numinous, have lost their validity for most, and man is thrust into his lonely quest for individual authority.

Even Richardson, preferring Nirvana to human responsibility, is *absorbed* by the Whole, rather than united to it as a complete individual. The breach between the worlds at Berringer's house has progressed from the release of the beasts to the release of the archetype of Fire. The house burns unquenchably and, like all fire, it may destroy or transform. Williams likens it to the fire which consumed the nest of the Phoenix, in which the mythical bird died and was reborn. Nevertheless, when Richardson enters the fire, symbol of his own longing for transformation, he is really forcing the immediate fulfillment of his desire for that Unity which is beyond all human concern, beyond every created thing. Therefore, though far more conscious, he is not essentially different from Mr. Tighe. He desires the dissolution of his ego and will receive that which he desires, but he will not know that state which is symbolically expressed in the image of the *hierosgamos*—the Earth, the life of flesh united to the eternal life of the Spirit. He has renounced power, but he has also refused authority and all concern with human relationships.

There are two characters in the story who reveal to us the fate of those who, through their weakness, childishness and fear, would be lost, were it not for the freely given love and concern of another person who has accepted responsibility. One is Anthony's friend, Quentin Sabot, and the other Damaris Tighe, the woman Anthony loves. Quentin is Anthony's equal in intellectual integrity and ability but, when put to the test, is revealed as a child in the emotional realm, and therefore he is at the mercy of panic when Foster, possessed by the Lion, pursues him with intent to rend and kill. For a man who is emotionally immature cannot confront the supreme majesty and masculine strength of the Lion within; he can know only its fierce aggressiveness and cruelty with which he either identifies like Foster or from which he runs in terror, blind to every concern but his own danger. Quentin is saved in the end precisely because somewhere in the midst of his panic a human loyalty to his friend Anthony still lives, and he is able for a brief instant to cry out a warning of danger to "Anthony's girl," in spite of the added peril, as he thinks, to himself.

Damaris Tighe, whom Anthony loves in spite of his clear perception of her infantile shadow, is a woman whose animus has taken possession of her emotions and distorted her mind. She is a considerable scholar and her chosen subject is the relationship of the Platonic ideas to the Angelic powers of great medieval thinkers such as Peter Abelard and St. Thomas Aquinas. She is writing a thesis about these profundities, and has no perception whatever that the ideas, of which she makes many charts, have anything to do with human life on this earth—that they are in fact overwhelming forces latent in every man. She even regards Heloise as a boring interlude in Abelard's life! Her constant concern is with her own work, with the prestige she so deeply covets, and with her success and recognition in the academic world. She has no time, no energy left, to think of Anthony as a person, or of her father's interests. So it always is, when the animus dominates a woman instead of guiding and serving.

Having derided and rejected all meaning outside her narrow intellectual ambitions, Damaris, when she is brought face to face with the great bird of wisdom and philosophy, sees it, inevitably, in its destructive aspect, as a hideous prehistoric bird of prey, emitting the nauseating smell of decay. Thus does the archetype pursue and threaten us when we, despising its reality, divorce it from our daily life with empty words. The soaring eagle has become for Damaris a foul smell, grasping claws and a huge destructive beak.

Nevertheless, underneath her intellectual arrogance and self-concern, as Anthony sees, there lies a frightened, rather than a malicious, child. Moreover, she has *worked* extremely hard with honesty and perseverance, even though the results are barren. Work is honest discipline, and her honesty forces her at the eleventh hour to recognize, in part, her debt to Anthony's love. Therefore in the midst of her terror she is able to cry out to him in the last extremity of danger, consenting at last to a knowledge of her utter powerlessness, her need for the strength of another.

The description of Damaris and her experiences is a hideous warning of the danger to which so many women who despise and reject their essential femininity are exposed. They are blessed if one day they are shocked by such a vision as hers into awareness of their power drives, and if there is one who loves them enough to awaken them. It might be well to say "we" instead of "they"; for although Damaris is an extreme, there is no woman today who, if she is truly seeking consciousness, does not have to face the Damaris shadow in herself.

Having in that dreadful moment accepted love, Damaris is now able to give it. Williams insists on this inner truth that if we cannot accept we cannot give. She remembers with horror her own disgusted and contemptuous rejection of the panic-stricken Quentin when he had tried to warn her of the Lion, and she goes out into the fields to seek and to help him at whatever risk. She does in fact save him, as Anthony saved her, and so the patterns of "exchange" begin to weave themselves into her new-found life.

We come now to Anthony himself. He is probably, we may guess, about thirty-three years old—the archetypal coming-of-age time. In all the novels we find wisdom concerning the journey of the individual toward wholeness and the various stages of the way, but the beauty and clarity with which Williams writes of Anthony Durrant's inner life is unsurpassed. Such whole people as the Archdeacon in *War in Heaven*, Sybil in *The Greater Trumps*, Peter Stanhope and the old woman, Margaret, in *Descent into Hell* have already arrived at maturity before we meet them. But in Anthony we are shown the process of realization—what one might almost call the anatomy of awareness—in a person whose love and reverence for all life leads him to reject no one of the four functions, no fact of the inner or outer worlds. He is a thinker by profession—a critic on a literary magazine—but his intellect, unlike that of Damaris, is balanced by true depth of feeling. His intuition and sensation are likewise balanced so that he is never withdrawn from the reality of the moment by his intuitive vision. This sounds as though he were a paragon of perfection, but somehow we have always a sense that he is a fallible human being, doing his best to make the immediate choice before him, and that his achievement is not something far beyond our reach, as we may feel about such characters as the Archdeacon.

There is a chapter near the beginning and another near the end in which we are given the meditations of Anthony on the nature of authority. Set between these, at the actual center of the book, is the great transforming vision which came to him unsought. His need to make small choices about the next thing to do continues unchanged after as before the vision, but there is a profound difference in their quality. Before the vision, before the crucial choice with which Anthony is faced within that vision, his decisions were thought out, using all the good sense and true feeling which were his; but after that great symbolic experience, he has merely to *listen* and his decisions are as sure and inevitable as the rhythms of nature. They spring out of that Authority which he no longer has to exercise over himself or anything else, but to which in free obedience he gives himself. It is not a passive state of waiting; he still must use all his conscious powers of reason, attention, memory and will; but there is no doubt any more, no self-conscious scrutiny of his actions. He is aware of necessity as it arises, aware of Damaris' need, for instance, though he is not within hearing distance when she calls his name in her extremity; and at the end he becomes a channel for the authority of the Great Man within. He calls the wandering powers by their hidden names, as did Adam in the myth, and leads them back to their place in the order of the whole. The threat to human consciousness of regression to chaos is averted.

Authority of this kind is born of a union between discrimination and feeling, and is that which enables man to *name* the powers within—and when we can name them we are no longer at their mercy; they are led by human consciousness, and function in unity instead of autonomously. There are many stories about the finding of the name as the alternative to disaster—the fairy story Rumpelstiltskin, for example. Either his name must be found or he will operate as destructive affect, stealing away the queen's child. Reason and effort alone are bound to fail; the name is finally "given," heard by what appears to be chance. Yet if the Queen had not spent that whole year searching, probing, using all her faculties to divine it, certainly the so-called chance would have been missed. The hidden name is a symbol of the true nature of a person or thing. Primitive man hid his name, believing that the knowledge of it would give power over him to an enemy. When we become aware of the true nature of our instinctual urges they can no longer possess us, for we can choose to follow or to lead, and they are transformed within us.

In the end, Anthony refuses identification with any one side of himself in order to touch his identity as a whole man; he refuses to seek safety either through escape or through abandonment, making himself a channel for the operation of the Self, which is man's true nature. He thus accepted the "unceasing and serpentine journey" (a phrase reminding us of kundalini imagery) to awareness.

In this supreme moment Anthony became aware of a great bird coming down from a far distance towards him—the Eagle, archetype of wisdom, bringing with it the image of perfect balance on the wings of God. As a drowning man is said before death to see his whole past life in a moment of time, so also did Anthony see himself, evading nothing of his past, looking objectively on all the evil and the good, the folly and the wisdom of all his actions—recognizing the thread of his passionate desire for intellectual and spiritual honesty which soared, like an eagle, even through the denials for which he now felt searing shame:

> His whole being grew one fiery shame, and while he endured to know even this because things were so and not otherwise, because to refuse to know himself as he was would have been a final outrage, a last attempt at flight from the Power that challenged him and in consequence an entire destruction by it—while he endured the fire fell away from him and he himself was mysteriously rushing over the abyss . . . existing by movement and balance among the dangers of that other world. He was poised in a vibration of peace, carried within some auguster passage. (p. 115)

He was indeed one with the Eagle, not by absorption but in unity, and was forever set free through his acceptance of authority from the temptations of power.

He saw now in his vision the Lion, the Serpent, and the Butterfly, and many other forms beyond his understanding and adored them; but he knew that the world beyond them was not yet open to him, that his service on earth was not yet accomplished. So he found himself again at the head of the stairs where he had been standing when the vision began, and heard the next word of the sentence which the doctor had been speaking at that moment.

Anthony went home and slept long and deeply, and woke in peace. All that he now did, down to the simplest action, came out of the certainty of this inner quiet. Something had been lost — "the little goblin of self-consciousness which always, deride it as he would, and derision in fact only nourished and magnified it . . . that goblin had faded and was gone."(pp. 119-20) From now to the end, momentous as are his choices, he moves in simplicity, clothed in an authority he does not need to think about, for it is his true nature revealed. In another image we might say he had found his "name."

The Place of the Lion ends, as did *Many Dimensions*, with the closing of the breach and the removal by one man's discovery of himself of the threat of invasion by the regressive powers of unconsciousness. In the earlier book, a woman offered her life in passive devotion, love, and endurance, whereas in this story a man dares to know in himself the ultimate meaning of authority. In both Chloe and Anthony, their final actions spring from wholeness. While in this world Chloe is a woman and her symbolic action is therefore an affirmation of the feminine way of endurance, yet her devotion and obedience are made effective only by her consciousness of the authority of the Spirit. Anthony is a man, and his crucial action is therefore an assertion of authority; yet power in a man can become authority only through his realization of obedience and devotion and the humble values of the earth.

THE GREATER TRUMPS

In this last of his early novels, Charles Williams returns yet again to the theme of the destructive powers in the unconscious, activated by man's attempt to use or possess them, then escaping from his control to threaten the world. Tumulty was completely ruthless and cared nothing for the havoc he caused; Berringer removed his consciousness from the whole outer situation; but Henry Lee in *The Greater Trumps* is simply a weak man who falls into the temptation to evoke magical power for his own personal ends. Using the Tarot cards he raises a great storm, hoping that the man who stands in the way of his desires will die in it, and thus evading the responsibility for what was virtually an attempt at murder. When he loses control of the storm he is terrified by what he has done and awakens to the enormity of his guilt. We know at the end that, through the love of a woman, he has a chance to face it and to find his way to self-knowledge. He is nearer to our own dangerous will to power than the others. Refusing to look at his shadow he seeks knowledge of the inner mysteries by a short-cut, without any thought of their relevance in his personal life.

Williams here stresses the fact that, not only the evil manipulators, not only the skilled adepts, are the originators of such invasions from the unconscious: any half-conscious man who gives way to his curiosity and longing for power, as did Henry, and justifies himself with talk of his valuable discoveries of the contrived and "magical" ways in which he seeks his ends, is as dangerous as those others. This has always been true, but it has become far more obvious today than it was when Charles Williams was writing; for the manipulation of the unconscious through psychological and so-called religious techniques by quite ordinary people, whose true motives remain unknown to themselves, is now a commonplace.

The imagery of this book is perhaps especially exciting to those who respond to the language of symbols; for Williams' imagination is fired by the images of the Tarot, and he brings to life those extraordinarily numinous pictures so vividly that we are brought to realize the impoverished way in which these things are usually expounded.

For most of us the images of the inner world and our daily life in this world remain in compartments—we attend to one, and then we attend to the other, and only after a long and painful journey do we begin to be aware of both as separate yet one in the same moment. For Williams, however, to quote T.S. Eliot from the introduction to *All Hallows Eve*:

> . . . there was no frontier between the material and the spiritual world. . . . To him the supernatural was perfectly natural and the natural was also supernatural. And this peculiarity gave him that profound insight into Good and Evil, into the heights of Heaven and the depths of Hell, which provides both the immediate thrill and the permanent message of his novels. . . . Williams is telling us about a

world of experience known to him: he does not merely persuade us to believe in something, he communicates this experience that he has had. (pp. xiii-xv)

Nevertheless, although there is no frontier there is no mixing; the two worlds are always distinct and simultaneous.

In *The Greater Trumps*, particularly, this "co-inherence" of the natural and supernatural, so called, is felt in the smallest incidents. The two levels of experience emerge as the warp and woof of daily life. When Henry sees the Emperor of the Tarots as they pass a London policeman in the rain with his white cape and helmet, we do not lose sight of the perfectly ordinary human policeman. Nancy, indeed, young as she is, is swept off momentarily into the world of images—a necessary stage on the way to the simultaneity, but it is Sybil, the middle-aged maiden aunt, who conveys to us the absolute balance, the ease in both worlds that was certainly Charles Williams' own.

In the story, Henry Lee, gypsy by descent, is shown an ancient pack of Tarot cards, a legacy left to Mr. Lothair Coningsby by a friend. Henry's grandfather, Aaron Lee, lives in a remote house on the Downs where he is guardian of an ancient heirloom of the gypsies—a table of gold upon which little golden figures, the images of the Tarot, move in a perpetual dance. He spends his life reading the future, trying to penetrate to the ultimate meaning of the dance which seems to have no coherent pattern. Henry recognizes the paintings of Mr. Coningsby's pack as corresponding exactly to the little figures and he shares with his grandfather the traditional belief that, if the original paintings are reunited to the golden images, all things will be known to him who holds them, and he will penetrate to the secret of the dance of Creation, as symbolized by the figures.

Henry is in love with Mr. Coningsby's daughter, Nancy. He hopes her father may be persuaded to part with the cards and give them to his daughter. But Mr. Coningsby, suspicious, possessive, and conventional, is obviously not about to part with them. Therefore Henry, scheming with his grandfather, invites him and Nancy and Mr. Coningsby's sister, Sybil, to spend Christmas with them at the house on the Downs.

Thus it is that he drives the four of them out of London on that winter night when Nancy and he see the policeman and the Emperor of Order and Law with his outstretched arm. It is later on this same journey that we become aware of Sybil's extraordinary quality, when the four travelers come on Henry's mad old gypsy great-aunt, Joanna, squatting in the middle of the road. As the car stops she calls out a string of curses on Henry, accusing him of hiding her child, her little one, and as all four of them stand in the road listening, it becomes clear that her delusion, springing from the actual loss of her baby in infancy, lies in the belief that she is the goddess Isis searching everywhere for her beloved son Horus.

Through their behavior in the face of the crazy old woman, the four characters in the car are clearly defined. Mr. Coningsby is outraged, shocked, and horrified, ready to condemn not only the old hag but Henry and all his relations to boot; Nancy, young but genuinely in love, with her feet already set on the first steps of the Way, and fresh from her first vision of the inner images, restrains her father and trusts her Aunt Sybil, though understanding little; Henry, versed in the myths and in the occult, with a great deal of intuitive insight but dangerously immature and in the grip of his power-seeking shadow, is furiously angry and contemptuous, fearing that his great-aunt's behavior will wreck his designs on Mr. Coningsby. Sybil alone immediately accepts and understands the old woman's delusion with compassionate recognition of its truth in the unconscious and of the validity of the myth.

Sybil's reaction is a wonderful picture of how a truly conscious individual really *meets* with the whole of herself every person and every thing in this world or the beyond. To quote T.S. Eliot again:

> I have always believed that he [Charles Williams] . . . would never have been surprised or disconcerted by the intrusion of any visitor from another world, whether kindly or malevolent; and that he would have shown exactly the same natural ease and courtesy [as he did with every sort of human being], with an exact awareness of how one should behave, to an angel, a demon, a human ghost, or an elemental. (p. xiii)

So between Sybil and the crazy woman there was a true meeting. Joanna was wholly possessed by the unconscious images, identified with them, and therefore insane; for Sybil they had equal power and truth, but she was *related* to them in full and serene consciousness. She was therefore able to respect and to love the truth which the old woman served in her madness, and she addressed the Divine Isis within, speaking with reverence of Joanna's search for the divine child, knowing it to be the universal longing of suffering humanity. There was recognition between them, and to the disgusted horror of Mr. Coningsby, his sister knelt in the road to receive the blessing of the goddess within. Joanna was quieted and went her way.

I am always delightedly reminded, when re-reading this passage, of Jung's attitude to the schizophrenics in the Burgholtzli, of his recognition of the beauty and truth behind their ravings, and of his astonishment when Freud said to him about his study of one patient, "How could you bear to spend so much time with such a repulsively ugly old woman?" It was not just his scientific curiosity at work, it was his penetration to the meaning of these so-called delusions and his respect for every single human personality, however seemingly lost or ugly.

For anyone to reach this degree of ease and *courtesy* in both worlds one thing is essential. The ego's demand for power here or in the Beyond must have been known and sacrificed. Sybil, of all Charles Williams' characters perhaps, most directly manifests this truth. Like Anthony at the end of *The Place of the Lion*, but with an even greater simple maturity and strength, her every action carries authority within it—the authority which, as I have said earlier, involves no hint of being imposed, or directed at commanding the actions of others, but is a thing in itself, demonstrating the essentials of what it means to be a true man. For there is no authority without love, and in Sybil the mystery of love is indeed incarnate as we read of her exquisite courtesy and humor—those two essential elements of love—which never fail her in any conceivable circumstance. Moreover her authority has an essentially feminine quality as we shall see, in contrast to Anthony's masculinity.

Arrived at Aaron Lee's house, where Mr. Coningsby is soothed by Aaron's urbanity, the visitors are taken to the room where the images of the Tarots dance on their golden table. Among all the incessantly moving figures there is one which is still. At the center of the table he stands—the image of the Fool of the Tarot trumps, of the card numbered 0, the most mysterious of all the major arcana of the pack.

The most puzzling question of all in the minds of the two students of the dance, Henry and Aaron, is why the Fool never moves; they point him out to the others. To their astonishment Sybil replies that indeed she sees the image they describe but that it *is* moving. She says, "It's moving so quickly I can hardly see it — there — ah, it's gone again. Surely that's it, dancing with the rest; it seems as if it were always arranging itself in some place which was empty for it." (p. 74)

Aaron and Henry are intensely excited for there is only an ancient tale to tell them that the Fool moves. Aaron can't understand why Sybil, whom he regards as commonplace, could see it when they, whose family has studied the images for generations, cannot. But Henry, far more conscious than his grandfather, says:

> I tell you she's a woman of great power. She possesses herself entirely; I've never seen anything dismay or distract her. She's like the Woman on the cards, but she doesn't know it — hierophantic, maid and matron at once. . . . this woman couldn't see it [the Fool] in the place where we all look for it. She saw it completing the measures, fulfilling the dance. . . . She's got some sort of a calm, some equanimity in her heart. She — the only eyes that can read the future exactly, and she doesn't want to know the future. Everything's complete for her in the moment. It's beautiful, it's terrific — and what do we do about it? (pp. 85-86)

It is now that Henry betrays his own insight, and worst of all, betrays his love for Nancy. He plots with his grandfather to use Nancy, by persuading her to "borrow" Mr. Coningsby's cards, and further to use her in his magical operations. It is the ultimate sin, the manipulation of the beloved — the more so as he is a man capable of recognizing the quality of Sybil. He consciously and coldly refuses to allow this recognition to affect his life, to awaken him to his rationalization of the greed which is leading him to attempted murder.

Henry's words about Sybil did not move his heart, but, if we will allow it, they certainly have the power to move ours. Yet we know she will never use her power. It will flow through her to complete the present moment in every situation, and through the rest of the book we watch it doing just that; for the Fool is moving in her and therefore in her he awakens authority in the sense in which I have used the word. Like the Zen master, sitting beside the stream and commanding it to flow, her acceptance of the present moment is not an act of resignation but of command — she creates the moment as it is, through the divine faculty of Imagination, and, because she is entirely free of any demand to change its nature, she has authority over it. It is perhaps the deepest of all the paradoxes of being—that the Fool, the wholly spontaneous and irrational Fool, is the only one who can give life to true authority in a man or woman. Every Zen koan is designed to awaken the response of the Fool in the seeker—a response which cannot come until we have passed through the long discipline which frees us from bondage to infantile desires. "She possesses herself entirely. . . ." Later Williams says of her:

> Such a state . . . had not been easily reached. That sovereign estate, the inalienable heritage of man, had been in her, as in all, falsely mortgaged to the intruding control of her own greedy desires. Even when the true law was discovered, when she knew that she had the right and the power to possess all things, on the one condition that she was herself possessed, even then her freedom to yield herself had been won by many conflicts. Days of pain and nights of prayer had passed while her lonely soul escaped. (p. 124)

The word "possess" or "possessed" applied to the psyche has usually a very negative meaning; it indicates subjection to the ego's greed or the state of unconscious possession by an archetype; but here it has of course another meaning, as when used by St. Paul in his phrase "as having nothing yet possessing all things." When a man is empty of ego demands he both possesses and is possessed by the whole.

To the unconscious observer Sybil's outer life must have seemed dull and insignificant indeed. A middle-aged spinster keeping house for an exceedingly tiresome self-centered brother, her niece and nephew already grown up—and yet she was, as Henry had seen, one-in-herself, a unique individual with far more impact on the world than those philanthropists, men of affairs, or paragons of good works, who act out of the need for ego achievement.

Henry raises the magical storm while Mr. Coningsby is out for a walk on Christmas day. Nancy, realizing what he is doing, tries to stop him—the cards slip from his hands, and nothing now, it seems, can stop the wild destructive force of the elements from laying waste the world. Sybil is simply moved by her love to go out into the storm to find her brother. Great shapes of men with clubs (the suit of Wands in the Tarot) loom through the snow, beating him and driving up the snow around him. She finds him, and helps him up and back to the house, typically letting him assume he is helping her. Few modern women understand this essential quality of feminine love. It looks like a shameful admission of woman's inferiority, but is in fact a perennially beautiful gift of woman to the immature male; for it is not a condescending thing—that would indeed be destructive; it springs from her recognition of the man's real inner strength, which he cannot yet make conscious, and of his need for reassurance.

At the same time Sybil finds a kitten in the snow and carries it with her, enduring without a word its terrified clawing at her, which she cannot prevent because of her brother's weight. She could no more abandon the kitten than her brother. In the house the storm is breaking down the doors; Aaron has sprained his ankle and is in pain; the maids are in danger of panic. Sybil quietly does whatever is possible; her authority brings the maid to a sense of her particular duty; her healing hands relieve Aaron; the door is closed for the moment by their joint efforts. Sybil simply does the next thing with the whole of her being in each moment.

Meanwhile upstairs in the room of the golden figures Henry is near to despair and to annihilation, overwhelmed by the powers he has tried to manipulate; Nancy, novice though she is, compared with Sybil, on the "serpentine journey," rises in the strength of her love for Henry to meet the danger. Her knowledge of his murderous intent has made no manner of difference to her love, for love is not love if it is shaken by the darkness in the beloved. She joins hands with him, and her hope receives and integrates his despair; together they confront the raging powers. She finds herself at last alone, as everyone with courage such as hers must ultimately be; and then suddenly she faces across the table the crazy hatred of the old woman Joanna.

Nancy has not yet come to the state of being in which Sybil lives; but she has dared to love, and in loyalty to human love a man or woman will not run away, though he or she is threatened by all the powers of hell. Nancy's effort to control the storm fails, but her courage and integrity bring her to her own essential confrontation with the devouring mother which is the turning point of the individuation process. Joanna, the outcast, has penetrated to the center of the chaos in the room of the images, accompanied by the kitten which has gone wild and has become the familiar of the witch. The rejected feminine always returns in the furious revenge of the witch and her cat in the unconscious.

It is now that Nancy is transformed from a girl in love, however true and courageous, into a woman essentially freed from unconscious possession by either the negative or positive mother, for she does not respond with hatred or with panic to the attack of Joanna and to the fury of instinct in the cat. She gives herself to the terrifying experience with a total effort towards compassion and acceptance — the immemorial response of the true woman. At this moment help comes from the most unlikely source, and Williams brings to us the sense of pattern, the synchronicity of life when its deepest springs are touched. Mr. Coningsby arrives on the scene uttering dire threats against Joanna, for he has realized that his daughter is in danger and this he will not tolerate. Magical happenings, witches and such things are nonsense to him, but he acts without hidden motives of greed out of the good as he knows it — and that action is as effective in its proper sphere as the far more profound responses of those who are aware of the powers within.

We realize the truth, apparent in every real Story, that while the final redeeming act comes through a single individual, as it comes here through Sybil, yet all the acts of the other characters who are true at their own levels to such consciousness and awareness of love as each may be capable of, are inherent in it. That most of us try to confront and to assimilate our darkness and fail, and fail again, is not important. The failures and evil actions in a story are all necessary to it, as Judas was necessary to Christ. Salvation is individual, but it has nothing to do with an isolated individualism. All things co-inhere in a whole action.

ALL HALLOWS EVE

For five years after the publication of *The Greater Trumps* Williams did not write any novels. Then in 1937 came *Descent into Hell* (see the chapter on "Exchange"), which is the only one of the stories not primarily concerned with the nature of power, a theme which he returned to in his final novel, *All Hallows Eve*, which was published early in 1945. He died in May of that year.

There is a somber strength in this book, a plumbing of the depths of both evil and good which goes beyond anything we have yet encountered in the other novels. Williams has imagined another superman who, as has been said, resembles in many ways the character of Nigel Considine in the first of the novels, *Shadows of Ecstasy*. Like Considine, Simon the Clerk has already lived for 200 years, having transcended the ordinary laws of mortality through long discipline and training in the mysteries of occult experience. Like Considine he dreams not only of achieving complete domination in this world, but also of extending his mastery into the life beyond death. Here the resemblance ends.

Considine, we feel, in spite of his fatal mistake about the means to be employed, has truly sought what he believed to be enlightenment for mankind; but in Simon the Clerk Williams uncovers the stark ugliness and cruelty that are always inherent in the will to power. On the positive side also there is a new note in *All Hallows Eve*. In each of the preceding novels we have seen how defeat of the destructive power has come through an extraordinary individual; but in this book the answer to the threat is less dramatic in one sense, and nearer to our own capacities. The Archdeacon in *War in Heaven*, Sybil in *The Greater Trumps*, and Anthony in *The Place of the Lion* are all highly conscious people; and Chloe in *Many Dimensions* is an ordinary girl at the beginning, but her last act is of a highly dramatic nature. Lester Furnival and Betty, however, are two simple human beings of good will—one newly dead and one living—who bring about Simon's defeat by a gradual process of complete honesty with themselves and with each other, without even understanding the issues involved. By this honesty and lucidity in the face of their inner and outer realities they are made free of the City of God which is also the City of Man, and that which Williams calls the Acts of the City flow through them in all the seeming "chances" of their movements in time and space, to the undoing of the one who had made himself almost invincible.

All the previous novels have made clear that power in itself belongs always to the Self. The ego is contained in and moved by that power, and with dawning consciousness comes the power of choice. In each of the stories there are images of the Self, of the totality—the Grail in *War in Heaven*, the Stone in *Many Dimensions*, the Fool in *The Greater Trumps*. All these images manifest their power through darkness and light, and work evil as well as good. Man became aware of these opposites in the myth of the Fall through the Serpent (which God had created), and the way of return to wholeness, which Williams called "the serpentine journey," lies through the experience of these opposites as two powers at enmity with each other, and through the choices which this experience makes inevitable. Perhaps we need another word to express the difference between the consciously willed evil of power-driven men such as Simon and the darkness of evil which is an essential part of the rhythm of the universe and of the psyche. The man who seeks individuation must even be able to *choose* evil when the truth of the moment — the Tao — demands it.

This kind of choice of evil, which may involve anything from a killing to a white lie, must be clearly distinguished from the pernicious doctrine of "the end justifies the means." Williams clearly conveys this difference, especially in *War in Heaven*. The springs of creative action lie in the necessity of the individual in obedience to his particular responsibility at a specific moment. Such an attitude demands a constant attention to that center "where action is created," and a freedom from conventional notions of good and evil. It involves however a far more difficult and exacting individual morality, and in no way implies that we are absolved from fighting evil.

Simon, and those like him, are on the same journey as every other seeker of the One; like the saint he faces the tension of the opposites, sacrificing all lesser goals for his great end — the finding of the "transcendent function," the mastery of spirit and matter, but he seeks it not by surrender of his ego to his emerging consciousness of the Self; but by identification of his ego with the Self in order to direct all things to his personal will. This is deliberate evil which excludes all freedom, kills any exchange of love, and ultimately reduces creation to meaninglessness.

Writing of Simon, Williams said, "Illusion to the magician, as to the saint, is a great danger. But the master in Goetia has always at the center of his heart a single tiny everlasting illusion; it may be long before that point infects him wholly, but sooner or later it is bound to do so." (p. 182)

The "tiny everlasting illusion" whereby Satan's kingdom is divided against itself and therefore can never ultimately stand is the belief that individuation, freedom from the opposites, can be achieved without the acceptance of defeat. Already in *Shadows of Ecstasy*, Isabel hinted at this fallacy when talking to Considine. In *All Hallows Eve* it is Simon's refusal to break off his effort to separate Betty's soul from her body that leads directly to his downfall. He

cannot accept even a temporary defeat; and Christ's absolute submission to total defeat which involved the sacrifice of His own
divinity as well as of His human soul and body seems to Simon and to
all of his kind mere contemptible folly. So also we may know that,
wherever we reject with fury, or resentment, or despairing misery,
our small defeats, we are aligning ourselves with the monstrous
Simon within us and are divided against ourselves, rejecting the
wholeness of creation.

The actual destruction of the seeker of power by this illusion is
plainly demonstrated in the lives of the greatest men of power in
world history: Alexander, Napoleon, Hitler, all were overthrown by
their growing assumption that nothing and no one could defeat
them—Alexander pressed on and on until his precarious empire
collapsed; Napoleon and Hitler both invaded Russia simply because
they could not curb the need for victory after victory whereby they
staved off any hint that there could be a limit to their power. So the
tiny illusion grew until they were lost within it.

The images of the final dissolution of Simon himself at the end of
the book seem far from our experience, but this too can illuminate
our ordinary lives. In order to accomplish his aim of world dominion, Simon had by a magical operation multiplied himself, creating
two replicas of his body which he sent out—one to Russia, one to
China—to speak with his voice and proclaim his doctrine of love and
healing and peace. It is in these terms that the Anti-Christ speaks,
aping the words of Christ, and his power to move the masses is
infinitely greater than that of Christ himself, precisely because he
lifts responsibility from the individual and promises the end of all
defeat. The price paid unconsciously by his followers is their inevitable regression to the state of mindless insects, as Jonathan in the
book intuitively painted in his picture of Simon preaching to a
crowd. The end of such insect-men is inherent in their abdication of
responsibility.

Simon had planned, once his power in the West was established,
to recall his two types to himself and, reabsorbing them, to take over
the power they had established in Russia and the East. It is plainly a
distorted image of the Trinity, an aping of the Omnipotence, but
there is in it no *equality*—and without equality of fundamental value
there can be no exchange between persons, no "lovely balance," and
in the final outcome no unity. The basic meaning of the Trinity image

is, not that there are three abstract qualities in the Godhead, nor two mere copies of God the Father, but three *Persons*, whole in themselves, separate, equal, and yet one. The Trinity is therefore the archetype of all free exchanges between individuals. It cannot however become incarnate without the earth, the feminine, the woman, and it was precisely his rejection of every feminine value that turned Simon demonic. His types were merely extensions of his ego consciousness, and he was in no way related to them. We may compare them with what happens to us when, instead of relating to those other "selves" within us (to whom, in Jung's language, we give such names as shadow, animus, and anima), we first project and then reject them, or identify with them, so that they become merely vehicles for our own insidious desires for power. The result of this process, if persevered in blindly to the end is indeed terrible. For the other two Simons were not reabsorbed by him at his command as he had intended, they were drawn back to him in his moment of unaccepted defeat. He now discovered exactly what he had done; those others had become so much "he" that "to unmake them he must unmake himself." He hated those other selves and, because they were "he," they hated him. The division against himself was complete. Such then is the result of hating our own shadow figures, for thus we bind ourselves irrevocably to them in the unconscious, annihilating the exquisite balance of true meetings within and without. So it happens indeed that, when we try to destroy that which we hate in ourselves, we succeed only in destroying ourselves.

At the moment of his final defeat a crimson rose was forming around the multiple Simons and the "rain of the Hallows" fell in crystal drops of every imaginable color upon him. The rose is a great symbol, as also is the rain from heaven, but to Simon that glorious crimson of love and sacrifice was the red blood of the one he had tried to kill, and the burning of destructive fire; for this was his chosen experience of the City. Absorbed by his hatred of his multiplied self, he rejected utterly the healing rain—that rain, which has been called by Laurens van der Post, "forever the image of love in action." He continued to hate and to strive—and "all he could do against them was only done to himself." Down and down he sank into the Center of that which is the City—"If I go down into hell, thou art there"—He had succeeded in his quest for the center of power, and, carried by his hatred of himself, he was swallowed into "the rose and the burning and the blood," an imbecile now, wholly dominated as he had sought wholly to dominate.

These are great archetypal images, but all through the book we also watch them operating in the simple choices of two young women who have been killed by a crashing aeroplane on Westminster Bridge and are now wandering in that region beyond death where they are still very close to the life of the flesh from which they have been cut off. In that world there is no such thing as a trivial word or action; everything said, everything desired and done in the past life as in the present, has an immediate and eternal validity. Each individual, if he so chooses, has the chance to look clear-eyed upon the facts of his life, to accept responsibility for them, to ask for forgiveness—which, whether in the giving or the taking, is precisely the sacrifice of all taint of demand for power and justification. It is Charles Williams' version of the choice between the state of purgatory and the state of hell; Lester Furnival chooses the former, Evelyn Mercer refuses it. The choice, however, is not a disembodied thing, separated though they are from their earthly flesh. Such a choice can only be made through exchange with another human being. We often imagine, in our moments of reflection, that we have truly accepted our shadow qualities, but most of us cannot know that we have done so until we are next tempted to an emotional reaction by our projection of them onto somebody else. The individuation process is a solitary thing; it cannot take place without the experience of that aloneness in which we meet ourselves, and in which we must separate ourselves even from those closest to us. But equally essential is the experience of communication and exchange without which the solitary way all too easily becomes a denial of human love and responsibility. Charles Williams suggests in both *All Hallows Eve* and *Descent into Hell* that after death the opportunities for individual choice through human exchanges continue. However this may be in literal fact—whether we incline to belief in reincarnation, or in a purgatorial life after death, or even if we reject individual survival altogether—the fundamental necessity remains: there is no growth in the psyche without the self-knowledge which is born of "meetings" with other human beings.

Lester finds herself with Evelyn in the twilight world on the other side of death, and Evelyn, whom she has despised in life and often made use of for her own convenience, clings to her now. Lester makes her first affirmation of objective love; she will stay with Evelyn in the clear acceptance of her own past betrayal of friendship, in the compassion which has nothing at all in common with weak good nature. To follow the inner experiences of this dead girl is to realize with a new clarity many values to which we are often blind.

The only things that are real to Lester at first in the streets of the empty city in which she walks are the visual images of *things*—in her case quite ordinary objects which she has loved for their own sake and not in order to possess them. Her love for her husband has been real love, but tainted by her own wayward and often arrogant demands—"Why have you kept me waiting?" That taint she sets herself to purge by an agony first of deliberate memory and then by acceptance of all facts—her true love *and* her many betrayals, the pain *and* the joy of her ultimate separation from Richard. It is given to her then to communicate with Richard in the flesh before she leaves him finally, and also with Betty, Lady Wallingford's daughter by Simon.

Betty has been begotten by Simon only in order that he might use her to gain power in the Beyond through his attempted possession of her soul. His one concession to instinctual sex was a cold and deliberately contrived action—the end justifying the means—a rape in the worst sense of the word. Contempt for the feminine values can go no further. Our contemporary experiments with artificial insemination for human beings are of this nature.

Lester, Evelyn, and Betty had been school fellows; Evelyn had persecuted Betty with her incessant, malicious talk; Lester had once or twice interfered, but without real commitment, for Betty bored her. It is an example of the so-called small evasion of responsibility, seen in its ugly reality when we look objectively into that other world of the unconscious. These things as well as the larger betrayals must be redeemed by conscious forgiveness asked and given, but this exchange must be clearly differentiated from those superficial requests for forgiveness which often trip off the tongue without meaning. They are very often an easy externalization enabling us to avoid a profound inner experience.

Evelyn refuses the honesty embraced by Lester; and not for one moment will she stop the constant talking which is her protection against any increase of consciousness, and most of all she wants to continue talking to Betty, who is frightened of her, because this feeds her mean and petty sense of power. Meanness and pettiness are surely more dangerous and corrupting than the so-called great sins. Williams writes of Evelyn, "There was indeed, even for her, a chance, could she have taken it. It lay precisely in her consenting not to talk, whether she succeeded or no." (p. 178) She did not so consent and thus became a puppet, subject wholly to Simon's will.

When we consent not to do something which our ego, possessed by hidden greed for power, desires to do more than anything else—when we consent with our whole being as far as we are aware of it, even if we fail, then the power of the City will support us, always, of course, provided that we do not fall back on easy justifications of the failure. If Evelyn had consented not to talk it would have been for her a crucifixion as painful to her in her degree, as the acceptance of total failure would have been for Simon.

To Lester the experience of crucifixion came when she hastened to protect Betty from Evelyn's malice, and found rather that it was she who needed Betty's forgiveness. Only after this knowledge of humility had come to her was she ready to give herself in the way that did save Betty. No longer was she "helping" Betty from the heights of a believed superiority, which is of course a power attitude. She simply stood beside Betty when asked, and offered her whole being to her for any purpose that might be needed. It was thus that the Clerk, standing at the foot of Betty's bed and directing all his great powers into the effort to send Betty permanently into the other world as his helpless agent, was defeated by he knew not what. For Lester, not even aware of what was intended, stood there and received the waves of "death-light" rising up from her feet to her loins, enduring a great agony which she could only sustain because she felt herself lying on a wooden bed that carried and supported her. At the last moment she in her turn was saved by the released Betty, who, aroused from her trance, called out "Lester."

Anyone with knowledge of yoga or of other mystical techniques has heard of the importance of the Word of Power. The mantra in the East is the chanting of the holy sound "Om": in the West the repetition of the rosary, and the Jesus prayer in the Orthodox faith, are mantras. In all places, in all religions, in myth and folklore and fairy tale, it is a sound, a word of power that opens closed doors when they have no known handle or key—whether these doors open onto the thieves' hoarded treasure (Ali Baba), onto the next stage of the journey (the doors of Moria in *The Lord of the Rings*), or onto the Center of the "City" itself. The center of the power that invokes the Unity is reached in Williams' imagery, drawn from mystical tradition, by the pronunciation of the secret Name of God, called in the Jewish tradition the Tetragrammaton—the four letters of Jahveh. Similarly the ultimate power of division is given to him who can pronounce the reversed Name. It was this for which Simon had trained himself over 200 years, and it was the backward-intoned Tetragrammaton that he used as he stood beside Betty's bed and sought to separate her soul from her body and bind it to his will.

We may easily pass unheeding over the implication of this. Apart from the prevalence of directed vibrations nowadays, the increasing separation of words from meaning, from facts, is one of the most terrifying things in our culture—an enormously powerful tool when wielded by those who seek to direct things as they choose. When words become substitutes for facts, instead of the expression of the essence of fact, we are indeed on the way to disintegration. The empty meaninglessness to which our language is so often reduced reaches us through all the mass media, and this is comparatively easy to recognize, but it is much harder to resist the unconscious invasion of cliches, ugly language which has become habit, long pompous circumlocutions and euphemistic names for simple things. Perhaps it may shake us out of our unconscious slovenly language habits when we realize that all such talking partakes of that final emptiness of the reversed Name of God which is Hell. By our contempt for accuracy of speech we are in fact, like Simon, separating soul from body and adding to the divisive powers which threaten mankind.

Williams now brings to our imagination his unique version of the simple human answer to that reversed Name. It is no great saint or wizard appearing in the nick of time to set the power of this hard-won intonation of the True Name against the reversal. Simon's power is broken when Betty speaks with her whole heart the ordinary Christian name of her friend. Nevertheless the ability to speak a name in this way is most hardly won. It is no easy thing to know the equality of human exchange to which Betty and Lester had come through unclouded honesty with themselves and with each other. Yet Williams is affirming here that this speaking is not dependent on a mystical striving to transcend all images; it is a power given to the pure in heart no matter how simple that heart may be. Each of these two young women has found her individual meaning through the plain acceptance of fact—all fact, and this is indeed a definition of purity of heart. Therefore, the sound of a friend's name on their lips has become an affirmation of *the* Name. It is a Word of Power because a person's true name carries the meaning of his or her identity in all the worlds. The giving of the human name in baptism "in the Name of the Father, the Son and the Holy Ghost" is a symbol of our uniqueness as individuals, capable of the conscious finding of the transcendent function beyond the opposites.

Lester said, "Betty, if you want me I'm here," and meant it without any evasion of meaning. "I am here—the whole of me whatever may come." That is the crux of the matter. We say such things very often but mean the words only in part. Any reservation, conscious or unconscious, in our meaning is a small reversal of the Name. Lester, having spoken a *true fact* received the attack of the reversed Name for her friend, and Betty in her turn, freed from her danger and sleeping naturally now, spoke out of her unconscious memory of their conscious love and exchange one word—her friend's name, "Lester."

So it was that the Clerk heard at the center of the syllables of the reversed Name another single note. "As the word left her [Betty's] lips, it was changed. It became—hardly the Name, but at least a tender mortal approximation to the Name . . . it hung in the air, singing itself, prolonging and repeating itself." Then it "became itself only, and at that rather a single note than sequent syllables, which joyously struck itself out again and again, precisely in the exact middle of every magical repetition, perfect and full and soft and low, as if . . . it held just an equal balance." (p. 162) Then it went from the room, singing out through the City; the Clerk's incantations were broken, the death-light receded, and Lester and Betty both were reborn into a new and heightened awareness of that which is called the City.

Such are the great mysteries of the transforming power that flows unsought from a free exchange between two people who have learned to love with objective "largeness of heart" and trust—a strength against which the machinations of all the seekers of power in the universe cannot prevail.

Christmas, 1962

"WHEN ALL THINGS were in quiet silence and night was in the midst of her swift course, thine almighty Word, O Lord, leaped down from heaven out of thy royal throne." (Introit for Sunday in the Octave of the Nativity, from *The English Missal*) This is surely one of the most lovely sentences in the Christmas liturgy, and its breathtaking beauty is born of the meeting, the union, in a flash of intense vision, of six great images—swiftness and quiet, silence and the word, darkness and light. Light is not specifically mentioned; there is no need for it, because, as we read, we have so vivid a sense of the pitch darkness of midnight into which the great leap is made, and we feel and see the light springing to birth out of that darkness. This is Christ, the Incarnate God, this is Jesus, born in the dark stable in the middle of the night.

Why have we, in our generation, so terribly lost touch with the sense of this birth, the wonder of the tiny spark kindled in the dark? It is most surely because we grow progressively more determined to banish all kinds of darkness with artificial light. We have installed neon lights in the stable. With noise and flashing electricity and mechanical carols we herald the coming of Christmas for weeks beforehand. This we all know, and its vulgarity is widely deplored, but few look for the deeper sense, which lies in the almost universal rejection of darkness and silence by the individual soul. To reject darkness is to be blind to the coming of light, and so the personality is maimed and the soul starves and sickens.

From the sickness of countless individuals there gathers the collective sickness. It is true that we may look back with gratitude and relief to the tremendous progress of the last hundred years, to the banishing of some kinds of misery and filth, of some kinds of ignorance and disease; but there is a major and vital factor in this "progress" which is almost always ignored. No dark thing, no sin, no misery, no ignorance, can ever be truly done away except through a

321

redemptive process in individual souls. For every social injustice overcome, for every advance in medicine, for every labor-saving gadget and all the increasing comforts of daily life, there must be an exact equivalent of true sacrifice in individuals, sacrifice on other levels of being through an acceptance of inner darkness and suffering, and of the agony of greater consciousness. This is the inexorable divine justice, the ultimate meaning of Judgment. There is, in truth, no such thing as a collective progress that does not spring from individual growth. Christian love is not vague and universal; it is specific and personal; and the health of society depends on the capacity for devotion in each one of us, on our willingness to suffer personal darkness and failure—whether we are of those called to bring to birth new knowledge, or of those who are enriched by it. When there is no price paid, when progress becomes an end in itself, then the darkness is merely covered over with synthetic light, and the unseen evil is thereby increased and gathers power, to burst forth in due time in a far greater horror. Where there is no growth in love, there is no redemption, and progress becomes a lie, a mere displacing of the evil from one sphere to another more dangerous hiding place. The sterility of the modern hospital, when it invades the inner world, brings death to the roots of growth; and our answer to the ever-increasing feeling of bankruptcy is more and more synthetic light, more and more status-seeking education. The churches are not the least offenders.

It has been said that when light is spread *over* darkness, this is the Anti-Christ, for his great power lies in the imitation of Goodness, which leads us to fall down and worship. The true light never hides the darkness but is born out of the very center of it, transforming and redeeming. So to the darkness we must return, each of us individually accepting his ignorance and loneliness, his sin and weakness, and, most difficult of all, consenting to wait in the dark and even to love the waiting, like the wise virgins who did not try to light their lamps too soon. Then indeed we may begin to glimpse that radiant and holy thing, and the spark will kindle and the Christ be born.

"And darkness was upon the face of the deep, and God said, Let there be light; and there was light." (Genesis) "As it was in the beginning, is now, and ever shall be."

Christmas 1991

AS WE TALKED of and prepared the truly beautiful decorations in the Round House this year—the web of life in tiny white lights— the wonderful delicacy of the spider's web spun from her body around which so many legends have grown, I thought often of the "co-inherence of all life" (Charles Williams' phrase). I felt this even more strongly as I walked in here and saw it for the first time, and through the wonderful reflection in the windows all around, it seemed that the web of shining lights spread all over the world beyond the Farm. Nevertheless, over the last week or two it kept recurring to my mind that as we honored the image of the spider, mother of the web, we must also honor another small and often despised creature—the fly whose life is given to nourish and give life to the spider and her web. Always in the great web we and every other living thing must eat and be eaten, as the sacrament of the Mass affirms daily.

Then I remembered a fourteenth century Venetian painting by Carlo Crivelli that I had loved for many years, and found that I had kept a copy of it after buying some Christmas cards which the Metropolitan Museum in New York published about five years ago. In it the Mother sits behind a low wall gently holding, or rather supporting, the Child as he sits on a small cushion on the wide top of the wall. The painting of her hands is exquisite. She is clothed in a magnificent robe with mandala patterns of gold and black, and on her head is a coronet of pearls with one red ruby in the center of her forehead, reminding one of the third eye. On each side of her head are branches bearing beautiful fruits as though offering themselves to her—peaches, a cucumber, apples—and behind her is a lovely Italian landscape. The Child is dressed in a plain tunic with bare arms and bare legs and holds to his chest with both hands a beautiful little red, black, and gold bird. But the central impact of the painting is in none of these things, because neither Mother nor Child are attending to any of them. Both of them are gazing with intense concentration at an ordinary little fly which is sitting on the wall beside the Child. The Child, like every baby, is obviously enchanted with a new discovery, and the Mother seems to me to have a look of deep acceptance, but also of sadness and of the compassion which is mature love. It is impossible to imagine either Mother or Child feeling contempt or wishing to destroy the useless, unattractive, usually irritating, and perhaps unclean scrap of life. The Mother, I imagine, is aware of it as a tiny foretaste of the darkness which must enter not only her Child's life but the lives of all of us in this split world of time and space, and which is essential in the great web of the unity of All.

It happened, too, that at this time I had been rereading the chapter on animals in R.H. Blyth's wonderful book, *Zen in English Literature and the Oriental Classics* (now alas! out of print). Blyth quotes here some Haiku poems by Issa who wrote a lot about flies, fleas and lice.

> Don't kill the fly.
> See how it wrings its hands,
> See how it wrings its feet!

And Blyth comments that this might seem affected or sentimental, but Issa knew these creatures intimately as daily companions in those days. He is saying, "Don't kill it: it's alive just like you and me." There is no affectation, no theory of the sacredness of all life (that is, no moral rule never to kill anything—we all have to do this to live, even vegetarians.) "The poems," says Blyth, "are full of humor (for humor is co-terminous with life) *but devoid of condescension*" [italics added]

> I'm sorry my house is so small
> But practise your jumping,
> Please, Mr. Flea.

"So far from pity being akin to love, they have no connection whatever. Love is union; pity implies separation . . ."

Blyth goes on to say that the love of all living creatures is natural in us all—only destroyed by our collective customs, self-centered love and teaching, and he then points out a very seldom remembered fact—the difference between true love and compassion and the temperamental likes and dislikes which don't simply disappear after our moments of true vision. To the Buddha, Blyth says, even after his total enlightenment, "sweet was still sweet and sour still sour." If we don't like dogs or cats, that won't change as we glimpse for a moment the unity. What does change after each moment of truth is the use of our hard hands or hard minds, because the ego has decreased in importance. And he ends the chapter with a sentence I find extremely moving, especially in the context of our Christmas image of the web — the spider and the fly. "What a strange emotion I feel when a man pats my dog on the head and says with a smile, 'I don't like dogs very much!'" This is love, not an emotional pretence. The man is giving the dog the response the dog needs from true kindness of heart but without denying his instinctive dislike.

So let us drink to the Farm this Christmas Eve in the kinship of all life.

Glossary

ANIMA and ANIMUS: Personifications of the unconscious femininity in the psyche of man and of the unconscious masculinity in the psyche of woman. In her negative form the anima will manifest herself in a man's irrational moods and emotions; the negative animus is made up of a woman's second-hand opinions, sweeping generalizations, and imperatives. Their positive natural function, once we relate to them, is to act as guides to the unconscious and to the creative images within.

ARCHETYPE: The archetypes themselves are the indefinable natural forces underlying human life in all ages and all places. They cannot be known directly, but archetypal themes appear all over the world in myth, in fairy tales, fantasies, dreams, etc. We can recognize these archetypal motifs by their fascination, their irrational power to move us. A few of the most frequent archetypal symbols are the hero, the wise old man, the nourishing and devouring mother, the water of life, and so on.

CONSCIOUSNESS and the UNCONSCIOUS: The conscious mind contains all that we know, and the ego is the carrier of this knowledge. The unconscious comprises all that we do not know in the inner world, from personal repressions to all the vast possibilities of the psyche, future, and past.

EGO: "The conscious thinking subject" *(Oxford English Dictionary)*.

EROS: The Greek god of love. Psychologically, Eros is the love that brings healing and balance to the split in the psyche, but may also, if so *used* by the soul, degenerate into lust.

EXTRAVERSION: A psychic attitude characterized by a concentration of interest in objects; easily susceptible to outer influences, it often brings denial of the reality of inner, irrational values.

327

HIEROSGAMOS: Sacred marriage, union of opposites.

HUBRIS: The Greek word for overweening pride which seeks to usurp the power of the gods. It led to *nemesis,* the vengeance of the gods.

INTROVERSION: A concentration on inner psychic processes, oriented to an inner evaluation of experience. If extreme, it may lead to an undervaluation of outer reality.

LOGOS: The creative word of God; conscious masculinity, the seed of life.

MANA: A Melanesian word for a supernatural power felt in a person, event, or object.

MANDALA: A "magic" circle, symbolizing psychic totality and expressing the pattern of life around the center. Mandalas are found all over the world. They were used especially in India as "yantras" — aids to contemplation. Their structure is usually based on the number four within the circle. Their forms are often variations on the flower, the cross, or the wheel. Traditional mandalas, whether Eastern or Christian, have the Deity at the center. Individuals nowadays often produce mandalas spontaneously from the unconscious, and the center is apt to be a point. They are not consciously contrived patterns.

METANOIA: Transformation of spirit.

NUMINOUS: An adjective which describes that wonder which is felt by an individual who is moved by or transformed by a symbol (see below); a mystery transcending rational thought or analysis.

PROJECTION: Everything of which we are unconscious is "projected" into the outer world, and we see it in events and people outside ourselves. Thus the less conscious we are of our own rejected and inferior qualities and of the realities of the inner world, the less objectivity we have in our judgments of people and things, for they are hidden behind our projections of our unknown selves.

PSYCHE: The psyche is defined in the dictionary as soul, spirit, mind. As used by Jung it includes all the non-physical realities of the human being.

SELF: Jung has used this term to express the idea of the center — the center which is also the circumference — the totality of the personality, embracing all, both consciousness and the unconscious. This center of being has a thousand names: the Atman in India, Christ in Christianity, the stone in alchemy, the diamond, the child, the flower, the circle, the square, the Tao in China. All these are but a few of the symbols through which men have experienced this central mystery of life.

SHADOW: The shadow (in dreams always of the same sex as the dreamer) personifies all the inferior and rejected sides of the personality. These shadow qualities are not all negative, but may also be potentialities for which the ego has not taken responsibility.

SYMBOL: The meeting point of conscious and unconscious meanings which awaken in us an awareness of something that cannot be expressed in rational terms.

Index

abduction, ritual. *See* Persephone
Abelard, Peter, 299
Abraham & Sarah, 198
achievement: pride in, 8; striving for, 18
Adam, 82, 139, 141, 301
"Ad-dressing of Cats, The" (Eliot), 105
adultery, condemnation of, 20, 76
aggressiveness, 15
aging, 130
alchemy, 73, 81; lapis of, 287
Alchemy of a Modern Woman (Grinnell), 41, 79
Alexander, Christopher, 133
All Hallows Eve (Williams), 124-25, 277-79, 287, 305, 311-320
American Heritage Dictionary, The, 123, 125, 142, 171, 195
androgyny, 14, 29, 69-70
Anglo-Catholicism, 2, 81; dogma, 286
anima (Jung), 18-20, 34, 68, 70-71, 90-91, 95, 109, 158, 229-31, 245, 267, 315, 327. *See also* animus; masculinity
animus (Jung), 14-15, 27, 33-35, 38, 40-41, 44, 48, 58, 68, 70, 80, 84, 95, 282, 315, 327. *See also* anima; femininity; women
Anti-Christ, 314, 322
Apple Farm Community: Christmas, 323-25; origin of, 2; pamphlets, 3
aqua permanens, 81, 88
Aquarius, Age of, 88, 277
Aquinas, Saint Thomas, 299
archetypes: in animal forms, 295-96; butterfly, 302; cat, 104-10; definition of, 327; of desire, 297; eagle, 65, 299, 302; Jungian, 73; lion, 296-300, 302; snake, 104, 270-71, 297, 302; threat from, 299, 309; world of, 207, 295
Arthur, King of Britain, 74
artificial insemination, 317
authority: defiance of, 96, 97; definition of, 295; nature of, 301; of Self, 303

awareness, anatomy of, 300
Baker, Dame Janet, 212
baptism, 319-20; of fire, 25
Barrie, James, 266
Bast (Cat Goddess), 106, 110
Baucis & Philemon, 199-203
beauty: in life, 9; physical, 46; price of, 71; of Psyche, 45-46, 72; of self, 45-46
betrayal, 53, 77, 90
Bible, books of: *Exodus,* 238, 246-47; *Genesis,* 224, 229, 233-36, 322; *Isaiah,* 98; *John,* 30, 104, 179; *Luke,* 290; *Mark,* 130, 295; *Matthew,* 23, 182, 184, 186, 274; *Numbers,* 250-51; *Psalms,* 114, 250, 255; *Revelation,* 283; *1 Samuel,* 260-61, 263-65
biblical stories: Abraham & Sarah, 198; Cain & Abel, 79, 224; the Fall, 75, 79, 81-82, 312; Jacob & Esau, 224-36; Moses, 104, 237-57; Noah, 32, 106, 108; Saul, 258-65
bigotry, 9, 31
biological differences, 13-14
birth, 30, 60, 82, 88
birth control: and Catholicism, 172-73; validity of, 173-74
Blake, William, 99, 184-85, 196
bliss, 67
Blyth, R.H., 137, 179, 324
Book of Privy Counselling, The, 134
Book of Wisdom, 129-30
Bors, 75, 85-88
Brimo/Brimos, 29
Brunhilde (Ring Cycle), 90-103
Buddha, 325; coming of, 46; flower sermon, 32
Burnett, Frances Hodgson, 117
Cain & Abel, 79, 224
Calvinism, doctrine of elect, 121
castration, 46
"Cat That Walked by Himself, The" (Kipling), 104

Set in Simoncini Garamond by
Sarabande Press

Design by James Sarfati

Production Manager: Natalie Baan

Proofreader: Sonia Sampson

Indexing: Doric Wilson